The Compulsory Competitive Tendering Guide

Second edition

Andrew Sparke LLB
Chief Executive and Town Clerk
Lincoln City Council

Butterworths
London, Dublin, Edinburgh
1996

United Kingdom	Butterworths, a Division of Reed Elsevier (UK) Ltd, Halsbury House, 35 Chancery Lane, LONDON WC2A 1EL and 4 Hill Street, EDINBURGH EH2 3JZ
Australia	Butterworths, SYDNEY, MELBOURNE, BRISBANE, ADELAIDE, PERTH, CANBERRA and HOBART
Canada	Butterworths Canada Ltd, TORONTO and VANCOUVER
Ireland	Butterworth (Ireland) Ltd, DUBLIN
Malaysia	Malayan Law Journal Sdn Bhd, KUALA LUMPUR
New Zealand	Butterworths of New Zealand Ltd, WELLINGTON and AUCKLAND
Singapore	Reed Elsevier (Singapore) Pte Ltd, SINGAPORE
South Africa	Butterworths Publishers (Pty) Ltd, DURBAN
USA	Michie, CHARLOTTESVILLE, Virginia

A CIP Catalogue record for this book is available from the British Library.

First edition 1993

ISBN 0 406 08159 X

Typeset by Phoenix Photosetting, Chatham, Kent
Printed and bound in Great Britain by
Redwood Books, Trowbridge, Wiltshire

The Compulsory Competitive Tendering Guide

PREFACE

Even without legislative enforcement, competitive tendering in local government, as in Whitehall and the National Health Service, was always bound to become entrenched as budgetary pressures demand ever-increasing value for money. Compulsory competition now applies to the broad range of professional support activities as well as to most services provided directly to the public; voluntary initiatives are common even in non-prescribed areas. Nevertheless the guidance available from the Department of the Environment, individual district auditors, the Audit Commission and such bodies as the Chartered Institute of Public Finance and Accountancy, is frequently conflicting, there is a paucity of reliable case-law from the judiciary and possible conflicts with European law further complicate matters. Hence the value of a practical guide for lawyers and service managers, inside and outside local government.

This book covers all the consequences arising from requiring local authorities to tender in-house services against competing agencies in the private sector in order to determine the most economical, efficient and effective manner of providing those services in future. To local authority employees, competitive tendering is a threat to their jobs; to managers, it tests quality and forces improvement in service provision and productivity; to external contractors, it offers new or expanding markets for their products and services. The potential conflicts between these vested interests are of vital importance to all parties, and particularly to lawyers, whether employed in local government, representing contractors or competing in their own right against internal council legal departments.

While this is not a work intended solely for a legal audience, nor one limiting itself to matters of law and legal interpretation, the scope of the relevant statute law must be understood before the practicalities of competitive tendering can be discussed. This is therefore the priority for the early chapters, which lead logically into practical guidance and related issues: the application of tendering law within local government necessarily involves occasional digressions into the structure and powers of local authorities as creations of statute rather than common law. Finally, the overall effect of competition on the future nature of local government in this country is considered.

The book is modelled around the legal provisions applicable to England, Wales and Scotland, including the relevant affects of European law. Much of the advice it contains, however, is readily applicable to the introduction of compulsory competitive tendering to Northern Ireland.

In writing the preface to the first edition of this work, one of the people I felt bound to thank was Kieron Walsh of INLOGOV for his initial encouragement to commit myself to print. His tragically early death in 1995 robbed us all of an impartial and authentative commentator on compulsory competitive tendering able and willing to force us to rise above at least some of our individual vested interests.

However, I continue to receive valuable feedback, encouragement and support from a broad spectrum of colleagues and friends within local government. I owe particular thanks to Liz Bennett, Ann-Marie Davidson, Peter MacMahon, Jim Eccles, David and Susan Wells, Karen Winnard and Julie Anders for their various efforts towards maintaining my sanity whilst preparing this text.

Andrew Sparke
February 1996

Addendum — Changes to Regime to December 1997

Numbers in margin cross-refer to pages in the main work

Introduction

This note reflects the changes made by the LGA 1988 (Competition) (England) (No 2) Regulations 1997 (SI 1997/2732), the LGA 1988 (Defined Activities) (Housing Management and Security Work) (Exemptions) (England) (Amendment) Order 1997 (SI 1997/2733), the LGA 1988 (Defined Activities) (Exemptions) (Amendment) Order 1997 (SI 1997/2746), the Local Government (Direct Labour Organisations) (Competition) (Amendment) Regulations 1997 (SI 1997/2756) and the LGA 1988 (Defined Activities) (Exemptions) (Schools) Order 1997 (SI 1997/2748).

3 **De Minimis Levels**

The general de minimis level under the LGA 1988 has risen from £100,000 to £150,000.

6, 161 **Work for Schools**

All work for schools maintained by the local authority is exempt from CCT.

120 **Construction and Property Services**

The de minimis level is now £450,000 against a percentage competition requirement of 55%.

139 **Financial Services**

The percentage competition requirement is now 40%.

145 **Personnel Services**

The percentage competition requirement is now 40% against a reduced de minimis level of £300,000 (formerly £400,000).

149 **Information Technology Services**

The percentage competition requirement will fall from 70% to 40%.

155 **Housing Management**

The de minimis level is 4,000 properties.

112-114 **Competition Requirement and Credits**

The new Regulations simplify the calculation of the competition requirement and the credits which can be offset against it. The so-called T calculation starts with the cost of the defined activity (remembering that the cost of staff working less than 50% on a defined activity is excluded) and from this two credits are deducted as follows:

Credit A for work which has been indirectly contracted out (that is where defined activity work is being performed by an external provider on behalf of the defined authority);

Credit B for goods and services bought in externally (which would otherwise form part of the cost of the defined activity).

After deductions of Credits A and B, the competition free percentage (Credit C) is deducted from the total cost (ie for legal services where the competition requirement is 45% the competition free percentage to be deducted is 55% or the de minimis level of £300,000 can be deducted if this is larger).

Five other credits can now be deducted from the competition requirement. These are as follows:

Credit D: Work awarded in-house under voluntary competitive tendering before 1st April 1994 or after 12th December 1997.

Credit E: Work which has been exposed to CCT already.

Credit F: Work previously carried out by the local authority which has been tendered without receiving a bid from a defined authority.

Credit G: Work funded from a schools delegated budget multiplied by the relevant competition free percentage.

Credit H: Support work for housing management pending the completion of housing management CCT but only until 30th September 2000.

Statements of Support Service Cost (SSSC)

The requirement to produce SSSCs has been repealed.

Implementation Timetable

The CCT timetable is further amended by the regulations quoted above.

Erratum

Security services

The defined activity for CCT purposes is set out in the LGA 1988 (Competition) (Defined Activities) Order 1994 (SI 1994/2884) and applies to the security controls and patrols for any land in which an authority has an interest with the exception of any library, museum, art gallery or police establishment and any dwelling or dwellings, residential establishments (the last being exempt only as far as security controls are concerned not security patrols). Council employees working mainly in controlled places, as defined by the LGA 1988 (Security Work) (Exemptions) (England) Order 1995 (SI 1995/2074) are exempt from CCT if their work involves exercising statutory council functions. Residential caretakers are also exempt from CCT.

CONTENTS

ABBREVIATIONS

ACTO	Association of Chief Technical Officers
ADC	Association of District Councils
AMA	Association of Metropolitan Authorities
BS	British Standard
CCT	Compulsory Competitive Tendering
CFA	Competition-Free Allowance
CIPFA	Chartered Institute of Public Finance and Accountancy
CRE	Commission for Racial Equality
DES	Department of Education and Science
DFE	Department for Education
DLO	Direct Labour Organisation
DoE	Department of the Environment
DSO	Direct Services Organisation
DWO	Direct Works Organisation
EC	European Community
ECU	European Currency Unit
GAD	Government Actuary's Department
IT	Information Technology
JVC	Joint Venture Company
LAGSA	Local Authorities (Goods and Services) Act 1970
LAWDAC	Local Authority Waste-Disposal Company
LEA	Local Education Authority
LGA	Local Government Act
LGPLA	Local Government, Planning and Land Act 1980
LGR	Local Government Review
LMS	Local Management of Schools
MBO	Management Buy-Out
NACCB	National Accreditation Council for Certification Bodies
NHS	National Health Service
QA	Quality Assurance
QWA	Quality Work Assured
SLA	Service-Level Agreement
SSSC	Statement of Support Service Costs
TMO	Tenant Management Organisation
TQM	Total Quality Management
VAT	Value Added Tax
VCT	Voluntary Competitive Tendering

TABLE OF STATUTES

TABLE OF STATUTORY INSTRUMENTS

TABLE OF EC LEGISLATION

TABLE OF CASES

Chapter 1

TERMINOLOGY

This chapter explains the terminology in the main statute law applicable to competitive tendering. The major legislative building blocks are the Local Government, Planning and Land Act 1980 (LGPLA), the Local Government Act (LGA 1988) and the Local Government Act 1992 (LGA 1992). Other relevant Acts include the Local Authorities (Goods and Services) Act 1970 and the Local Government Act 1972 (LGA 1972).

COMPULSORY COMPETITIVE TENDERING

The LGA 1988 gave common currency to the phrase 'compulsory competitive tendering' (CCT) in local government. Although this phrase is not used in the Act itself, it has become a convenient shorthand for the requirement to follow a series of procedural steps before a local authority is empowered to allow its directly employed staff to carry out work in certain defined categories. In addition, the LGA 1988 contains general provisions aimed at preventing 'anti-competitive behaviour' that are relevant to all local authority contracting decisions. This means that particular tendering processes must be adhered to whenever consideration is given to the future performance of certain local authority services in-house. Even where an in-house option is not contemplated, the fair-competition requirements in the LGA 1988 will still bite. The matters regulated are the advertising process, the invitations to tender and the applicable time-limits. The specific procedures to be used are detailed in Chapter 3.

CCT is a term now applied to all services statutorily tendered, including those covered by the LGPLA 1980 and the extension into professional services resulting from the LGA 1992.

DEFINED AUTHORITIES

Defined authorities are the public bodies that must comply with CCT. Under the LGA 1988 these are mainly local authorities, but authorities responsible for urban development, new towns, police, fire services and metropolitan transport are also included. The LGPLA 1980, LGA 1988 and LGA 1992 apply to English, Welsh and Scottish local authorities and the Development Board for Rural Wales. CCT, with an amended regime, applies to Northern Ireland.

1

FUNCTIONAL WORK AND WORKS CONTRACTS

CCT catches not only the services a local authority requires to fulfill its statutory duties or to exercise its statutory and ancillary powers (functional work) but also services it provides to other public bodies where it is lawful to do so (works contracts). The distinction is not of great significance to councils neither securing services from nor providing services to other public bodies. All such an authority's tendering will relate to functional work, for which it alone has the responsibility to comply with the requirements of the LGA 1988. However, an authority proposing to enter a works contract with another public body must satisfy itself that its tender has been solicited and accepted in a manner compliant with the strictures of the LGA 1988. This may be a particular difficulty if the other contracting party is not normally bound to follow the same procedures (see Chapter 10).

DEFINED ACTIVITIES

Defined activities are the services to which the CCT regime attaches. Originally, the LGA 1988 covered refuse collection, cleaning of buildings and other cleaning, catering, grounds maintenance and vehicle repair and maintenance—all manual services. The Secretary of State for the Environment has the power to nominate further defined activities by issuing regulations, and thus the management of sports and leisure facilities, parking services, vehicle fleet management and security services have all been added as new defined activities and the exemptions for the cleaning of police buildings and the maintenance of police and fire authority vehicles proposed for repeal.

In the wake of the LGA 1992 a number of professional services have also become subject to CCT. These are construction and property services, legal services, personnel services, financial services, information technology services and also housing management.

The LGPLA 1980 does not use the phrase 'defined activities' and is limited in scope to construction and maintenance work, principally affecting highways and housing authorities.

Each of the above defined activities is examined in Chapter 2.

DIRECT SERVICE ORGANISATIONS AND DIRECT LABOUR ORGANISATIONS

Direct service organisations (DSOs) and direct labour organisations (DLOs) are the sections or departments of local authorities carrying out the defined activities subject to CCT; that is, performing as a contractor external to the authority would. They are distinct from those staff responsible for determining the levels of service required and monitoring the delivery in terms of both quality and volume specified, who perform the client role.

DLO and DSO should attach to sections providing services under the LGPLA 1980 and the LGA 1988 respectively. In practice, many authorities use the abbreviation DSO for any personnel employed in the provision of services subject to CCT, reserving the technical distinction between DSO and DLO for the statutory accounts and returns made to the DoE. A minority of councils still use the archaic term 'direct works organisation' (DWO), and others blur the terminology by allocating specific names, such as Dartford's 'Dartforce' or 'ELMS (Enfield Landscape Maintenance Services), to their DSOs.

DE MINIMIS ACTIVITY AND COMPETITION-FREE ALLOWANCES

Wherever the total estimated cost of all work within a particular activity defined under the LGA 1988 is less than £100,000, that service is exempted from CCT. The *de minimis* value set for professional services is generally £300,000. Elements of the services that are specifically exempted (see Chapter 2) do not have to be counted in determining whether the cost of an activity falls below the *de minimis* level.

Few larger authorities are able to claim that their involvement in defined service provision is *de minimis* unless the bulk of the work is already contracted out to the private sector. Smaller districts have the most chance of arguing *de minimis* levels of activity, but even for them it is rare, except for catering, as district councils have no education or social service responsibilities leading to large-scale school or welfare meal provision.

De minimis activity under the LGPLA 1980 is related not to monetary value of the service but to minimum staffing levels: workforces of less than 15 persons are exempt. However, a further provision refers to the scale of individual contracts rather than the overall level of activity. This is the competition-free allowance (CFA), by which work that would be embodied in a single contract not exceeding stated values can be awarded to DLOs without competitive tendering. The values of CFAs and the types of work to which they apply are discussed in Chapter 2.

One possible use of the *de minimis* level by local authorities not wishing to remain direct service providers is to contract out of all defined activity work but retain a small percentage of the service in-house. Provided the cost of such service is less than the *de minimis* level, the rigid requirements of the CCT regimen are avoided and an experienced nucleus remains, around which a future DSO could be formed if ever required. Such tactical use of the *de minimis* exception leaves the possibility of internal competition as a brake upon the threat of uncontrolled price rises from external companies in future tendering rounds and the threat of price-setting by rings of contractors of the type discovered in local authority glazing contracts in 1991.

ANTI-COMPETITIVE BEHAVIOUR

In addition to the prescriptive tendering conditions of CCT, the LGA 1988 attempted to ensure fair treatment of external firms bidding for any local authority contracts, not merely those interested in defined activities under the Act, by preventing 'non-commercial considerations' forming part of the basis for awarding a contract. No evaluation, short-listing or selection of tenderers or contractors can take into account the terms of employment of a firm's workforce, the use made of self-employed labour, any involvement in fields of government policy irrelevant to the contract, conduct of a firm or its workforce in relation to any industrial dispute, any foreign business interests, any political or other affiliations, any financial support for or refusal to support any institution, or any willingness or unwillingness on the part of a firm to make use of certain technical or professional services provided by the local authority under the Building Act 1984 or the Building (Scotland) Act 1959. The effect of these provisions is to concentrate an authority's consideration of potential contractors on the factors of price, value for money and quality in relation to the services offered. All extraneous matters are eliminated by law. The Secretary of State for the Environment has power, under section 19 of the LGA 1988, to specify further non-commercial considerations. This is therefore an area with the potential for increased regulation.

The intention behind the legislation appears to have been to outlaw the worst excesses of so-called contract compliance, by which certain local authorities used their purchasing power as a means of exerting influence over areas of public policy deemed by Parliament to be no legitimate concern of local government. The exclusion of tenderers with South African business connections or those not paying minimum wage rates were common examples.

One unfortunate effect of the exclusion of non-commercial considerations in the awarding of contracts is to render it more difficult for local authorities to fulfill their duty under section 71 of the Race Relations Act 1976 in respect of the need to eliminate unlawful racial discrimination and to promote equality of opportunity and good relations between persons of different ethnic groups. This consequence was recognised and section 18 of the LGA 1988 permits councils to require potential contractors to answer certain race relations questions approved by the Secretary of State for the Environment. The responses can lawfully inform the award of any contract. The questions themselves are included in Appendix II and contract compliance is considered further in Chapter 5.

The provisions relating to anti-competitive behaviour impact on one other local authority practice: that of choosing tenderers from previously compiled select lists of contractors (sometimes referred to as approved lists). Such lists have had to be reviewed in the wake of the LGA 1988 to ensure that firms have not been excluded by virtue of non-commercial considerations. All local authorities whose lists are so tainted are under a duty to readvertise and compile fresh ones.

Anti-competitive practices are self-policing, since reasons must be given, if requested, for any decision on a contract award or non-inclusion on a select tender list, challenges may be raised and the Secretary of State may intervene. Contractors' rights and the Secretary of State's powers to act are discussed in Chapter 6.

SECRETARY OF STATE

In this book 'Secretary of State' refers to the Secretary of State for the Environment unless otherwise specified.

Chapter 2

SERVICES SUBJECT TO CCT

The tendering requirements of the LGPLA 1980 and the LGA 1988 differ and therefore the statute under which a service became subject to CCT is significant. The LGPLA 1980 is self-contained in terms of the services to which it applies; the LGA 1988 is not. The Secretary of State for the Environment also has power to designate further services as defined activities, which then fall to be tendered as if they were one of the services originally specified in the LGA 1988.

THE LGPLA 1980

General highways works

General highways works cover the laying out, construction, improvement, maintenance and repair of highways as well as the maintenance of street lighting. Gritting and snow clearance were originally excluded but from April 1995 must be tendered (in England only).

The requirement to tender general highways works applies to all projects. The CFA was abolished with effect from April 1995.

Works in connection with the construction or maintenance of a sewer

CCT applies to all sewer construction and maintenance works over £50,000 in value and to 60 per cent of all activity of a lesser value. The CFA is therefore 40 per cent of all projects costing less than £50,000.

Other works of new construction

Other new construction work relates to all non-highways and non-sewer building works and civil engineering. All such work has to be tendered.

Other works of maintenance

Other works of maintenance refer to all minor renewals and improvements to structures, including minor building extensions. All such work falls to be tendered, the original CFA having been withdrawn.

5

Exceptions

A general exemption exists for works in civic parks and gardens, playing fields, open spaces and allotments unless the works relate to buildings or structures. This exemption is rendered largely redundant by the inclusion of grounds maintenance in the list of defined activities under the LGA 1988.

Work carried out by resident caretakers and persons employed wholly or mainly to service a specific building is excepted. Government approved and assisted training schemes offer another exemption and the *de minimis* exclusion applies to all authorities employing less than 15 workers in a particular type of construction and maintenance work.

The final exemption covers emergency work, which is tightly defined. It is limited to alleviating the effects, or averting the potential effects, of an emergency or disaster that involves the risk of serious danger or destruction, or the risk of danger to health or life. Even where activity meets this test, work must be required within 48 hours of the incident and be of such a nature that it can be said that work on that scale is not normally undertaken. Minor, foreseeable emergencies, such as that arising from a burst pipe, are not a permitted use of the emergency works exception.

THE LGA 1988

Collection of refuse

CCT applies to the collection of household waste (defined, in England and Wales, by section 12 of the Control of Pollution Act 1974 and, in Scotland, by section 124 of the Civic Government (Scotland) Act 1982) and commercial waste (England and Wales) or trade waste (Scotland).

There are no express exemptions from CCT, but section 2(8) includes general emergency provisions, similar to those in the LGPLA 1980. In the event of a prolonged failure of a contractor to collect refuse, perhaps due to industrial action, public-health reasons might justify invoking the emergency exemption and bringing in council labour to rectify the situation.

Cleaning of buildings

The cleaning of building interiors and windows (inside and out) are subject to CCT. Standing exemptions relate to the cleaning of any dwelling (defined as any building or part building occupied as a person's home) and any residential establishment. The latter refers to homes for children, the elderly and other vulnerable groups created under specific powers in the National Assistance Act 1948, the National Health Service Act 1977 and the Child Care Act 1980, or in Scotland under the Social Work (Scotland) Act 1968.

Police establishments are excluded under the LGA 1988, but the removal of this exemption has been proposed in the DoE consultation paper.

Other cleaning

Other cleaning relates mainly to street sweeping. It covers the cleansing of any street, emptying of gullies, cleaning of traffic signs and street name-plates, removing litter from any land and emptying litter bins. The definition of litter excludes abandoned vehicles and scrap metal so that local authorities can continue to exercise their powers to remove major environmental nuisances as they see fit. Cleaning of road markings is not included in the definition of other cleaning in the LGA 1988.

Catering: schools and welfare

Catering in this context applies to services provided for schools, residential establishments and day centres, and to the preparation of food for delivery to welfare clients, popularly known as 'meals on wheels'. It covers the provision of ingredients, the food preparation and delivery and service of meals. However, in recognition of voluntary work undertaken by charitable organisations in the meals-on-wheels field, the delivery element of this service is not subject to CCT.

Certain types of establishment are expressly excluded from the requirement to tender. Special schools maintained by a local education authority (LEA) or, in Scotland, managed by an education authority are exempted, provided that the meals are prepared on the premises where consumption occurs. The same exemption for meals prepared and consumed on site applies to residential establishments and day centres. These exemptions do not apply where food is prepared elsewhere and delivered to the place of intended consumption.

Catering services in colleges of further or higher education are not caught by CCT under either this defined activity or that of other catering.

Other catering

CCT applies to all catering activity other than that defined as school or welfare catering or exempted under that defined activity. It does not apply to further education institutions nor in Scotland to hostels used mainly by school pupils.

The principal effect of this section is to apply CCT to civic or municipal catering for social purposes or for the benefit of staff catering (such as restaurant and canteen operations) and non-food catering (such as bar provision or any other situation in which alcohol is served).

Maintenance of grounds

Maintenance of grounds covers cutting and tending grass; planting and tending hedges, shrubs, flowers and plants; and controlling weeds. Landscaping and the initial seeding or laying of turf are not included, but returfing and reseeding operations are.

The only complete exemption is for grounds maintenance relating to research projects or work aimed at securing the survival of any kind of plant.

Repair and maintenance of vehicles

Any maintenance or servicing of a motor vehicle is caught by CCT. Tendering requirements also apply to repairs, but expressly exclude those for accident damage.

Police and fire service vehicles are exempted from CCT under the 1988 Act, but the removal of this exemption has been proposed.

Managing sports and leisure facilities

The detailed definition of the services to which this extension of CCT applies is found in the Local Government Act 1988 (Competition in Sports and Leisure Facilities) Order 1989. The defined activity covers the management of swimming pools; skating rinks; gyms; tennis, squash and badminton courts; sports pitches for team games; athletics grounds; cycle tracks and centres; golf courses and putting greens; bowling greens, centres and alleys; riding centres; courses for horse-racing; artificial ski-slopes; centres for flying, ballooning or parachuting; and centres for boating or other water sports. The list appears comprehensive. The only identified omissions are greyhound stadia and skateboard facilities. Possibly there are few of these in local authority management.

Management includes a panoply of tasks, such as arranging instruction, supervision, catering, equipment hire, marketing and promotion, bookings, collection of fees and charges, security, internal cleaning and maintenance of the buildings (but not their exteriors).

Premises not used predominantly for sport or physical recreation are excluded. This saving enables the management of such buildings as community or youth centres and tenants' halls to continue as before the LGA 1988. Also exempted are premises occupied by education institutions (maintained schools and colleges in England and Wales, and managed schools and institutions in Scotland) and nursery schools, and dual or joint-use facilities to which the general public and educational institutions have access, provided that education usage exceeds 600 hours a year.

Security services

Security provision in any controlled place[1] (an airport, burial ground, common, country park, education premises, harbour or port, housing amenity land, market, open space or park or picnic site or pleasure ground or recreation ground or road playground) is subject to CCT. Museums, art galleries, libraries, civic administrative buildings, police establishments, dwellings and residential homes are not controlled places and not therefore included in the CCT requirement. The work of a residential caretaker and security work involving the enforcement of statutory council functions (such as bye-law policing) are also exempted.

---

1 The Local Government Act 1988 (Security Work) (Exemption) (England) Order 1995, SI 1995 No. 2074.

Vehicle fleet management

The provision of vehicles provided for use by council officers on official business and vehicles used by direct services organisations is a defined activity. The particular elements covered are the procurement, leasing or hiring of vehicles and their disposal as well as administration such as vehicle registration and licensing. Operational planning and scheduling of vehicles used in accordance with client needs are excluded from CCT.

The DoE has indicated that packaging this work with vehicle maintenance may be acceptable unless in an individual case the result is restricted competition. In any event the management of DSO vehicles may well form part of another defined activity such as refuse collection or grounds maintenance.

Education transport to meet home to school needs of pupils is expressly excluded.

Supervision of parking

Historically on-street parking is enforced by the police and carries criminal sanctions. Under the Road Traffic Act 1991 a local authority can be granted control by the Secretary of State for Transport, with attendant decriminalisation of the process to enable the penalties collected to finance enforcement directly.

The new defined activity is the provision of parking attendants to enforce parking restrictions on-street and to issue penalty charge notices (under section 44 of the Road Traffic Act 1991), immobilisation, removal, impounding and release of vehicles, the collection of fixed penalty charges and the related implementation of these offences (including hiring staff and operating pounds).

General exemptions

A general exemption exists for all defined activities under the LGA 1988 in respect of emergency work, defined as activity calculated to avert, alleviate or eradicate the effects of an emergency or disaster (actual or potential) involving danger to life or health or serious damage to or destruction of property. This saving permits the emergency planning functions of local authorities to rely upon in-house provision of services such as catering to evacuation or rest centres that are activated when an emergency arises or threatens.

Another exemption covers employees who carry out defined activities and are service tenants of council property. If occupation of the dwelling is a condition of employment and the accommodation is provided for the better performance of the employee's duties, then that part of those duties that would otherwise be subject to CCT is exempt.

Finally, work carried out under training agreements under which all or part of the cost is borne by the Training Commission or the Secretary of State is also exempt.

Local authority discretion

Some services potentially fall into more than one category of defined activity. In such cases the local authority has discretion to decide in which tendering exercise to place that particular element. Provided such a decision is made for sensible, operational reasons, it is unlikely that it can be successfully challenged unless it can be shown that the motivation for the decision was primarily to frustrate fair competition. However, caution must be exercised, since the DoE regards 'exotic contracts', mixing different defined activities, as anti-competitive unless it can be demonstrated that the proposal does not deter competition.

THE LGA 1992

Police support services

Rather than bringing new services into the tendering arena, this proposal relates to the removal of the LGA 1988 exemptions for police vehicle maintenance and cleaning of police buildings, as well as for police catering in London, bringing the Metropolitan area into line with the rest of the country, where such catering is already subject to compulsory tendering. Henceforth 90 per cent of cleaning and 40 per cent of vehicle maintenance will be subject to competition, the latter requirement to be reviewed in due course.

Maintenance of fire service vehicles

The removal of the LGA 1988 exemption for fire service vehicle maintenance is proposed, except in so far as the maintenance is carried out by staff employed on fire-fighting duties. Competition is not to be imposed immediately. Instead targets are to be set for market testing by 1996/7.

Housing management

The defined activity for housing management is the sum of services provided in the council's role as landlord. Essentially this eliminates client and strategic activity but the resultant competition requirement is high, being set at 95 per cent. The *de minimis* level is £500,000 and tendering will be implemented on a phased basis for local authorities with stock exceeding 5,000 properties. Further detail is set out in Chapter 17.

Various professional services

Different percentages of construction and property services, legal services, personnel services, financial services and information technology services are now subject to competition. See Chapters 12 to 16 for further details.

Deferred proposals

Home to school transport and management of theatres, arts facilities and libraries services were originally proposed for exposure to competition. To date none of these proposals has been implemented by the Secretary of State.

In addition proposals to subject corporate and administrative services (including publicity and media relations, messenger and internal mail services, building facilities management and reprographic services) to competition were abandoned by the Government in December 1994. This decision recognised the fact that such support services are in the main recharged to internal business units which are themselves already subject to competition and hence already exerting adequate pressure to ensure that support services become cost-effective.

Chapter 3

THE TENDERING PROCESS

Competitive tendering begins with some form of advertisement, continues through selection or short-listing of tenderers to submission of bids, and culminates in the evaluation of the bids and the awarding of a contract. Statute law impinges at several stages, in particular where the service falls to be tendered under the umbrella of the LGA 1988. This chapter delineates the key events in the tendering process to secure compliance with the law, summarises the elements of proscription and of local authority discretion, and outlines the main differences between the LGPLA 1980 and the LGA 1988 in this regard. It also examines the proposed refinements invoked for the introduction of competition for professional services.

TIMETABLE FOR TENDERING

The LGA 1988 deadlines for tendering, in conjunction with the setting of minimum and maximum contract periods, govern the timetabling of the tendering process and set in motion the cycle of contract expiry and renewal. Accordingly, this is the best point of access to understanding the practical mechanics of competitive tendering.

The scale of the services subjected to competition under the LGA 1988 militated against the imposition of a single date by which all authorities should tender all defined activities. To have done so would have risked swamping the market, leaving most authorities without any hope of obtaining external bids for their work. To overcome this problem six groups of English councils and five groups of Welsh authorities were set up. Each defined activity was then allocated a series of dates, a different final date for implementation being given to each group of authorities. By ensuring that no two groups of authorities, in either England or Wales, shared the same date for the same defined activity, the potential for maximising the opportunity for bids from private sector tenderers was realised.

Grounds maintenance and leisure management were treated to a variation of this strategy. For these services the requirement was for a rolling programme of contracting, each tranche of not less than 20 per cent of the total volume of grounds maintenance activity falling to be tendered at intervals no greater than six months; and two tranches of 35 per cent of sport and leisure management activity; followed by a final one of 30 per cent, tenderable at no more than six-monthly intervals. This original timetable (and the imposition of common contract lengths) ensures that retendering at expiry of the contract continues, in order to reduce market-glutting.

Housing management and the professional services brought into CCT by the LGA 1992 have produced further timetabling issues. The principal factor governing the last date by which competition must be effected is Local Government Review. The London boroughs and metropolitan authorities not caught up in LGR go to the market earliest, followed by districts for which the commission has proposed the status quo of two tiers of local council with CCT for reorganised authorities post-dating the creation of the new councils. In addition, Welsh and Scottish authorities have different timetables following wholesale reorganisation of local government structure.

Contract periods

The LGA 1988 set minimum and maximum contract periods for the blue-collar services subject to CCT and distinguished between a number of different types of authority with different contract periods for each. The only remaining distinction is made for contracts wholly or substantially performed for an educational establishment for which shorter contract periods apply and these are shown in parenthesis below.

Contracts for Grounds Maintenance will run 5–7 years (4–6), Vehicle Maintenance 5–7 years (3–4), Sport and Leisure 5–10 years (4–6), Building Cleaning 4–6 years (3–4), other Cleaning 5–10 years, School and Welfare Catering 4–6 years (4–5), other Catering 4–6 years, and Refuse Collection 6–10 years. The new manual defined activities contracts for parking supervision, security and vehicle management are all 4–6 years.

For the professional services only a maximum contract length of 5 years has been set.

ADVERTISING

The process of securing competition starts with inviting tenders. The LGA 1988 stipulates that an advertisement notifying potential contractors of the opportunity to register their interest in tendering for the provision of defined services to the authority must be published in a locally circulating newspaper as well as in a suitable trade journal. The advertisement must include a brief description of the work, details of the time and place at which the detailed specification of the work can be inspected free of charge, a statement that copies of the specification will be supplied (and the fee if one is to be charged), the specified time in which persons wishing to carry out the work should notify the authority and a statement making it clear that the authority intends to issue invitations for the carrying out of the work.

All of the details in the advertisement must be reasonable. Complaints can be lodged with the Secretary of State for the Environment if the period for registering an interest in tendering, the times for inspecting the specification or the charges for a copy of it are regarded as unreasonable. A minimum period of 37 days has to be allowed for registering interest in tendering. This accords with the European requirements.

Obviously, the authority must comply with its own notice and ensure the specification is available, and must also ensure that the names of interested contractors are recorded.

The above are the advertising requirements imposed on an authority in relation to its own functional work. In respect of works contracts, the onus of advertising in a local paper and trade publication rests with the body seeking to contract a local authority DSO. Failure to comply means the DSO cannot accept the contract if awarded the work.

SPECIFICATIONS

Access must be given to service specifications, which means that considerable preparatory work will have to be carried out before advertising. Some authorities have built into their tendering processes an opportunity to consult potential tenderers on the draft specification. This enables the authority to consider any aspects of concern to the contractor that may inhibit competition at an early stage rather than discovering them only when a complaint of anti-competitive practice is made to the Secretary of State. The consultation can result in revision of the documentation or considered reasons for retaining the original draft, which can form the basis for a well-prepared defence should a challenge materialise.

If no concerns were expressed by contractors prior to tendering, this will in itself cast doubt upon the good faith of any contractor not subsequently awarded the contract who complains to the Secretary of State that some part of the contract documentation is of an anti-competitive nature, favouring the DSO over external tenderers.

Specifications have long been the subject of contradictory complaints to the Secretary of State. On occasion different contractors have deemed the same specification overly long or lacking in essential detail to enable them to compete effectively. The guidance from the Department of the Environment, such as it is, requires a council to ensure that the specification does not deter competition by virtue of its length or complexity and that the approach taken is to specify the outcome required for each element of the service rather than specifying inputs unless it is essential to do so to achieve the service. Specifying the qualifications and experience of the staff to be employed must therefore be reserved only for those situations where the quality of the service delivery is difficult to determine objectively. Even specifying quality by reference to quality assurance systems is constrained because BS5750 will be permissible only if adequate numbers of contractors in the private sector have it already. Even the tenderers without it must be allowed to demonstrate management systems offering equivalent benefits.

Before specification is concluded, some consideration should be afforded to staffing issues. In particular the existing guidance states that it will be regarded as anti-competitive to specify a service to achieve Transfer of Undertakings Protection (TUPE) for staff. Direct specification of TUPE is therefore precluded but this simply ensures that it remains up to the individual tenderer to organise his or her own proposal and tender for the work with due regard to the employment law consequences. TUPE will, however, feature as a consequential issue following council decisions on packaging contracts. The packaging decision will necessarily determine the degree of alignment of existing staff with the contract to be let and thus the chances of TUPE applying.

CONTRACT PACKAGING

Against the background of a stated freedom for councils to package CCT contracts as they wish—the flexibility being given to ensure 'efficient service provision'—the reality is of guidance which dramatically reduces that purported independence. A local authority must not package contracts purely in line with historical internal organisation; to do so will be deemed to have prevented, distorted or restricted competition unless a reasonable field of tenderers responds. Work must be packaged so as to appeal to a range of contractors; this implies a norm in which different sizes of contract are offered within a single defined activity. Unrelated work should not be packaged together and general contracts should not contain specialist work; this seems to mean that where the private sector would not link services together to be carried out within a single team of managed staff, a council contract package should not do so either; conveyancing should not be packaged with litigation or social services advice with planning, for example.

INVITATIONS TO TENDER

While construction and maintenance work do not carry the same advertising requirements as defined activities under the LGA 1988, the same prescriptions apply in relation to inviting tenders (from February 1994 on the basis of a full specification).

If any contractors register an interest in competing for the work, the authority must issue invitations to tender, not earlier than three months and not later than six months from the date of the notice appearing in the press. This provision does not apply to the tendering of professional services.

Where fewer than four contractors, other than the DSO, express interest in tendering, they must all be invited to bid. If more than three interested contractors are registered, then the authority may select which to invite, provided at least three are asked to compete alongside the DSO. The shortlisting of tenderers is further examined below under 'evaluation'. An invitation to tender should not be construed as meaning that the tenderer has satisfied the selection criteria and faces no risk that the council will subsequently decide to reject its bid for reasons other than price—for example, for lack of adequate financial stability. A written warning to this effect is especially vital if no more than the minimum number of interested parties have registered an interest in tendering.

Under the LGPLA 1980 the three or more tenderers to be invited to compete against the DLO must be drawn from select lists maintained by the authority. Particular care must be taken to ensure that there is no suggestion that the selection of competitors has been engineered to improve the DLO's chances of winning. Giving preference to tenderers with a track record of high-cost bids or of failing to respond to invitations to tender is unlikely to find favour with the Secretary of State. Furthermore, the select

lists must not have been compiled by reference to non-commercial considerations, something to be checked if the select list is of long standing.

In relation to works contracts for construction and maintenance works
or any service defined under the LGA 1988, the body wishing to employ
the DSO or DLO of a local authority must have sought tenders from at
least three other sources. Failure to do so will preclude council staff from
accepting the contract.

PREPARATION OF TENDERS

Under the LGA 1988 the DSO must prepare a written bid for the work in
the same way and at the same time as the short-listed external tenderers.

The effect of the LGPLA 1980 is similar. It requires a written statement
to be prepared of the amount to be credited to the DLO's revenue account
in respect of the work to be carried out or of the method of calculation to
be used. This permits use of a fixed price or a schedule of rates.

A minimum tendering period of 40 days is laid down[1].

EVALUATION

Evaluation covers the vetting of tenderers and the tenders or bids submitted. The aim is to ensure, as far as possible, that the authority can demonstrate that it has selected the best, if not necessarily the cheapest, contractor
for the work, and that it has not acted unfairly or non-commercially in
reaching its ultimate decision as to whom to award the contract.

Factors common to local authority contract evaluation include tender
price; the costs to the authority of awarding the work to an external contractor, redundancy payments being the usual one; race relations; technical
considerations relating to the bid; matters appertaining to the tenderer,
such as financial standing or relevant experience; and geographical factors,
such as the contractor's local knowledge or willingness to establish local
management arrangements.

Structuring such factors into a coherent strategy for evaluation acceptable to both the local authority and the contractors bidding to provide services is essential if challenges are to be avoided. It is therefore a stage of the
tendering process that must not be rushed. Allocating a period of perhaps
two months is not unreasonable, particularly if there are several competing
contractors rather than only two or three.

Questionnaires

There is a real need to amass a range of information in relation to the
individual tenderers to ascertain their suitability to perform work under
contract for the authority. While much of the material to verify financial
stability and capacity can be obtained through company searches and
from specialist providers of business intelligence, only the tenderer can

1 The Local Government (Direct Service Organisation) (Competition) Regulations 1993,
  SI 1993 No. 848.

supplement that publicly available information with copies of updated accounts and details of other contracts completed or being carried out. Accordingly, a questionnaire addressed to potential tenderers expressing interest in the contract is worthy of consideration.

There are two important elements in the design of such a questionnaire. Firstly, irrelevant questions will annoy and deter potential tenderers, so ask only those questions whose answers will be used in the evaluation process. Secondly, avoid questions that might solicit information proscribed as non-commercial by the LGA 1988. The mere fact that non-commercial material is before the evaluators may be taken as *prima-facie* evidence that it influenced the selection of the successful tenderer.

Early acquisition of information from potential contractors enables the evaluation of tenderers to be substantially completed before bids are received. Completion of the questionnaire can be a qualification for issuing invitations to tender. Failure to provide information reasonably required for the evaluation process is hardly an indicator of a real likelihood of establishing the relationship necessary between contractor and client if the services are to be provided to the satisfaction of both parties.

Circular 10/93 makes it clear that there are limits on the information a council can require from tenderers. Excessively detailed information cannot be sought and when seeking operational information, fully worked out schedules of works or precise resourcing levels are not regarded by the Secretary of State as necessary for proper evaluation. General descriptions of the methods to be employed and general supporting evidence of proposed resource levels should suffice. Local authorities may well on specific occasions find themselves disagreeing with this guidance.

Selecting tenderers for the contract

If more than the statutory minimum number of parties who must be invited to bid express interest in tendering, the authority has discretion to determine the level of tenders it wishes to solicit. A decision to limit invitations to three other than the DSO should not be automatic. Indeed Sir Paul Beresford, as Minister for the Environment, in September 1995 revealed plans to require councils to take active steps to encourage greater levels of competition than the statutorily required[1]. Restricting competition to the minimum necessary to achieve bare compliance with the statutory requirement may be grounds for challenge unless it can be shown that there are valid reasons for that restriction. Objective testing of responses to an initial questionnaire against criteria, preferably pre-set if not actually sent to contractors before short-listing, can identify the most suitable tenderers in terms of quality and experience. This can then be linked to a judgement as to the resources required (in terms of staff time and the cost of external consultancy if utilised) in order to complete evaluation for given quantities of tenders receivable, and a determination as to the maximum volume of tenders before processing them becomes impractical. Few authorities seek more than six to eight tenders as a maximum, regarding such a short-list as one of manageable proportions.

---

1 'Services Must Seek More Private Bids', by James Fair *Local Government Chronicle*, 1 September 1995, p. 1.

Since persons excluded from tendering have a right to seek reasons, the documentation of rational explanations for each stage in the process is a wise move as part of an overall strategy to minimise the risk of intervention by the Secretary of State.

Problems of excessive expressions of interest in tendering are rare outside the south east of England, but it is useful to consider the solution employed by Richmond when faced with over 30 suitable tenderers. With no further criteria to use to refine the short-list further, it was proposed to every contractor that the authority draw lots to determine which firms received invitations to tender. When the consultation revealed no objections, the lottery duly proceeded. No known complaint to the Secretary of State resulted, underlining the lesson that if in doubt, the best policy is prior consultation with the potential tenderers.

Tenderer evaluation

The recommended general criteria for evaluating tenderers are that the company is and will remain financially stable for at least the duration of the contract to be awarded and is technically competent. Preferably, the contractor should have sufficient experience of similar work and adequate managerial acumen for the authority to be reasonably confident of its capability to deliver the services to the standards specified. A proven trading history in the field, or lack of one, may therefore loom large as an evaluation factor.

An assessment of financial stability is dependent upon professional interpretation of the company's accounts and its trading position. Any evaluation team needs access to accountancy advice to carry out its function effectively.

Equally important is professional advice for the technical aspects of evaluation. The impartiality of such advice may be problematic for some authorities if the main repository of such skills lies within the DSO.

References from other public-sector bodies will be important in assessing the potential for securing complete service delivery from the contractor, but since referees are selected by the tenderer, a requirement to submit a complete list of relevant contracts performed within a period of, perhaps, the last five years should be considered. This enables visits to reference sites to obtain first-hand knowledge of the quality of services being delivered and assess the relationship between contractor and employing authority as well as with the public served. The contractor's response to complaints may be informative in this last respect.

The questionnaire, on its own or in conjunction with site visits or even a presentation by the tenderer, can also be used to provide clarification of the contractor's management skills and service knowledge as well as any quality assurance procedures in place in the organisation.

The extent to which factors such as race relations and health and safety can be taken into account in local authority contracting decisions is dealt with as part of the broader examination of non-commercial considerations in Chapter 5. It is, however, worth expounding the general principle that compliance with criminal law by the contractor falls to be enforced by the appropriate statutory authorities rather than indirectly through contractual commitments, which are therefore largely superfluous.

In summary, the evaluation of tenderers to ensure they are suitable, reputable and capable is as important as the examination of the bids themselves, and may be carried out prior to short-listing if there are sufficient potential tenderers or postponed, at the authority's discretion, to be performed in tandem with the evaluation of the tenders actually received.

Finally it should be noted that the 1993 DSO Regulations[1] set a maximum period of 90 days for tender evaluation.

Tender analysis

Unless the DSO bid is the cheapest by a reasonable margin and there are no potential benefits in terms of enhancing quality through consideration of a higher tender, in which case the process can be truncated, it is necessary to complete the evaluation exercise with a detailed analysis of the tenders submitted.

Price is obviously the dominant factor, subject to any balancing costs or savings occasioned were the service to be contracted externally. This part of the process is therefore geared towards establishing whether there is any substantial reason that might justify awarding the contract to other than the tenderer lodging the lowest bid. There are three major facets of tender evaluation: the arithmetical check, the technical appraisal and the financial analysis.

Verification of the figures making up the overall bid price is required to identify any errors. If any exist, they should be made known to the company submitting the bid, which should be requested to consider whether it can stand by the tender notwithstanding the mistake or wishes to withdraw. Forcing the company to stand by the price quoted is an option (tender documents usually bind the contractor to enter a contract if the bid is successful), but holding an unwilling tenderer to an incorrectly compiled price is dangerous. If the error is significant, there will be a major risk of contract failure later, with the contractor tempted to cut corners wherever possible to minimise losses.

Entering negotiations on the price submitted for the services as specified as an alternative to withdrawal is equally hazardous. This time the risk is the possibility of acting in a way that may be regarded as unfair to the other tenderers. For this reason, any course of action other than dealing identically with every tenderer is not recommended. Negotiations in this context, however, need to be distinguished from those that may well take place later, after the contract is awarded, to finalise points of detail and implementation.

Technical evaluation should include an assessment of the adequacy of the resourcing for the contract proposed by the contractor and, where known, the methods of working to achieve the services within the tender price. If necessary, the bid should be clarified by a requirement that each tenderer draw up a provisional work programme in relation to the services. Even the DoE appears to view this as a reasonable requirement, provided excessive detail is not sought.

One of the problematic areas is whether sufficient allowance has been made within the tender to employ sufficient suitably qualified persons to

1 Ibid page 16 above.

perform the services. Care is needed in two respects in making this analysis. The contractor may have evolved genuinely innovatory means of rendering the services less labour-intensive without detriment to quality, and the terms and conditions upon which workers are employed by the company are non-commercial considerations. It should be legitimate, however, provided the evidence is strong, to come to the view that the tender is so low that there is no reasonable prospect of the contractor attracting sufficient staff and supplying adequate other resources to provide the full services. A loss-leader bid of this sort, unless perhaps made by a company with substantial resources and a national or international reputation, poses an unacceptable risk of contract failure to the authority and can normally be rejected on this basis alone.

Financial appraisal will include the net effect of any extra costs to, or savings for, the authority should the contract be awarded to an external tenderer. A problem arises here because the mere fact that extra costs exist if the DSO fails to secure the work does not mean those costs can be taken into account in every case. The advice available from the Chartered Institute of Public Finance and Accountancy (CIPFA), in the form of their Code of Practice[1], the Department of the Environment[2] and the Audit Commission is subject to the 1993 DSO Regulations[3], which state clearly the allowable and prospective costs that can be taken into account.

Allowable and prospective costs

Allowable costs are those elements of the existing in-house service which can lawfully be discounted from the in-house bid as part of tender evaluation. The only allowable costs relate to employing trainees and disabled persons.

Prospective costs are those foreseen by the council if a contract for services is awarded externally. The prospective costs which may be evaluated are specified as the cost of redundancies and additional payments lawfully made to staff during the period of notice of dismissal and the net costs of terminating plant hire and leasing agreements.

The allowable and prospective costs must be calculated prior to opening the bids. To do otherwise is regarded by the Secretary of State as anti-competitive behaviour.

Cost of performance bonds and indemnities

If a council requires a performance bond from external tenderers this is regarded as an additional benefit arising from contracting-out. The costs of obtaining the least expensive bond are therefore required to be added to the DSO bid during evaluation. The same is true if a TUPE indemnity is required[4].

1 Code of Practice for Compulsory Competition (CIPFA) 1995.
2 DoE Circular 10/93.
3 Ibid page 16 above.
4 Local Government (Direct Service Organisations) (Competition) (Amendment) Regulations 1995, SI 1995 No. 1336.

Costs of redundancy

Redundancy costs appertaining to council employees whose services will no longer be required if an external tenderer is selected may be taken into account in determining the selection of contractor. Originally, such costs were to be written off over the term of the contract and could not be reconsidered at the time of retendering even though actual redundancies would occur at that time if the work did not remain with the DSO. A revised method of calculating the annual impact of redundancies and all other permissible costs at evaluation now applies. This methodology is discussed below (see 'The treatment of permitted costs in evaluation'), but since redundancy costs are usually the main element benefiting the chances for continued retention of a DSO, it is worth noting that the overall effect is to reduce the influence extraneous costs can have upon tender evaluations.

The ancillary problem of authorities with voluntary severance schemes offering payments above statutory minimum redundancy payments, a practice regarded as anti-competitive in effect if not in intention, appears to have been resolved by the finding of the High Court, in the case brought by the district auditor against North Tyneside District Council[1], that such enhancements are unlawful.

Circular 10/93 makes it clear that bringing redundancy costs into account in evaluation is only acceptable for contracts spanning several years. It is anti-competitive to bring such costs to bear on contracts of one year or less in duration or for not more than £100,000 value. In such circumstances the Secretary of State believes redundancies will be absorbed and will not occur normally.

Added years of service

By virtue of the Local Government (Compensation For Premature Retirement) Regulations 1982 and the equivalent Scottish regulations of 1979, a discretion exists for local authorities to notionally enhance the number of years of reckonable service to be taken into account for ascertaining pension entitlement of employees aged 50 or over who already have at least five years' service. The chief consequence of choosing to exercise such a discretion in favour of a departing employee is a lump-sum payment from the council to the superannuation fund. Where a local authority has by custom considered granting such enhancements, it can assess the consequences of doing so for staff facing redundancy as a result of competitive tendering and bring the resultant costs into account in the relevant tender evaluation exercise. The only proviso expressed by the DoE is that the enhancement must not exceed the maximum set down in the regulations.

Payments in lieu of notice

Once the incoming regulations are in effect, payments in lieu of notice will be capable of being brought into account in tender evaluation only where the period between the selection of a contractor and the commencement of the contract is less than three months. In all other circumstances it is

1 *Allsop v North Tyneside District Council* (1992) The Times, 12 March, CA.

presumed that the council will be able to give the appropriate notice and will incur no liability for payment of wages beyond the date when the contract comes into force. The amount that can be brought into evaluation is limited to the element of the notice period that extends into the contract period.

Loyalty payments

Loyalty payments to maintain services in the transition period after the contract has been awarded to an external tenderer are an expense that ought by rights to be permitted to form part of the tender evaluation, provided that the planned expenditure is limited to the minimum necessary to keep the service running up to the commencement of the new contract and is targeted on key workers rather than applied indiscriminately to all DSO workers. Regrettably, loyalty payments of this type are not included in the list of permitted evaluation costs contained in the proposed regulations.

Holiday pay

Frozen holiday pay has been accrued by many local authority manual workers as a result of past harmonisation of conditions of employment. This is payable to workers at the time they leave the council's work-force and will fall to be paid to workers made redundant as a result of the tendering of their service. Such accrued entitlements are no longer to be considered in contract evaluations. The DoE has not given its reasons for this decision, but presumably it arises from the fact that such payments would have to be made to the individuals with those rights at various times in the future and all that redundancy does is bring forward the date of eligibility.

Hire and leasing agreement termination charges

Charges on termination of equipment or vehicle leasing agreements ought not to be a controversial factor in tender evaluations. The existence of the contractual commitments to make payments in the event of early termination should long predate the tendering process, and contractor objections should be restricted to those arrangements entered into suspiciously close to the tendering of the service.

Fixed overheads

Irreducible fixed overheads, which must be met by the authority whoever provides the service, were formerly an acceptable consideration, providing it was genuinely impossible to make savings. This related to assets and support services used partially by the DSO and partially by other council functions, essentially where there were corporate economies of scale, lost or reduced should the DSO cease to exist. Obviously, the DSO's share of such costs would form part of the in-house tender, but could be offset to the extent that the authority must continue to bear such costs irrespective of the result of the tendering. The regulations remove all possibility of considering such fixed costs as part of the evaluation process.

Monitoring costs

Additional supervisory costs can arise from monitoring an external contractor rather than directly employed staff. This is particularly so in the early months of a contract's existence. This is no longer a legitimate evaluation factor. Invoking it will be regarded by the Secretary of State as an anti-competitive practice as will bringing into account anything other than the specified allowable and prospective costs.

Apprentices and disabled employees

The extra cost to the DSO of employing apprentices, certain specified types of trainee or registered disabled persons in the interests of social policy can be an acceptable evaluation consideration, provided that a full justification is made for such claims.

The treatment of prospective costs in evaluation

The utilisation of prospective costs, such as redundancy payments, in tender evaluation exercises is the subject of a detailed method of calculation in the 1993 regulations[1]. Wherever the lowest bid submitted is not that of the DSO and an examination of costs that may lawfully permit the work to be awarded to the in-house team nevertheless is to be made, a complex, five-stage process is to be utilised. It involves a calculation of the respective annual costs of accepting the DSO and the lowest tenderer's bids averaged, on a current year basis, across the contract period. From these, the annual average savings available are drawn. The regulations then require the assumption to be made that the savings will accrue for a period of ten years (a notional period that exceeds the maximum permitted contract period for a defined activity under the LGA 1988 by a considerable margin). The value of the savings notionally available across the ten-year period is then discounted to a present-day value, using a discount rate set by the Secretary of State (currently 6 per cent). Only if the net value of the allowable extraneous costs (which are notionally assumed to be incurred at the commencement of the contract and need not therefore be averaged or discounted) exceeds the net present day value of the available savings will the Secretary of State accept that the in-house bid offers the best value for money.

Discounting on the assumption that savings will continue beyond the life of the initial contract has caused considerable council concern, which appears justified in the wake of a report published in October 1992 by the London Business School[2]. This examined the retendering of refuse collection contracts and found that savings at the first round of tendering disappeared at renewal, giving rise to the conclusion that contractors had trimmed prices and even loss-led to win the work in the expectation of negotiating renewal of the contract at a more advantageous price at the time of expiry.

1 Ibid page 16 above.
2 'Cheap Rubbish? Competitive Tendering and Contracting Out in Refuse Collection—1981–1988' by Stefan Szymanski and Sean Wilkins (London Business School's Centre For Business Strategy).

Taking other ancillary factors into account

Costs are not the only financial balancing factors to be considered in evaluation: there are also the savings that will accrue to the local authority if the DSO ceases to perform the work. Equipment and vehicles that are owned by the authority and will become redundant can be sold, and this benefit should be calculated as part of the exercise. Even more importantly, particular depots or landholdings may become surplus to requirements if the DSO ceases to exist and they are not needed for occupation by the new contractor. The generation of interest on the capital receipts that will accrue at the time of disposal should also be considered, subject to amelioration only if the assets require a lengthy marketing period.

Rather than requiring the value of releasable assets to be discounted in the way deemed proper for costs brought into evaluation calculations, it is laid down that local authorities should draw in, as a credit against external bidders not wishing to use such assets, their net current value wherever the DSO or other contractors are offered use free of charge. This will encourage local authorities to set proper asset rental charges by reference to commercial considerations for any depots, plant or equipment to be made available.

Results

Once proper financial and technical evaluation has been completed, if the lowest tender is affordable (within the authority's budget), deliverable, competitive in respect of variables governing the actual rather than the estimated value of the contract, and submitted by a reputable, capable contractor, there is unlikely to be any lawful reason for not accepting it. The fact that an authority would prefer, on policy grounds, to retain the service in-house is entirely irrelevant.

FAIRNESS IN IMPLEMENTING COMPETITION

The LGA 1988 is explicit that the authority must act fairly at every stage of the compulsory competitive tendering process. In the CCT process councils must not act in a manner having the effect of, or intended to or likely to have the effect of, restricting, distorting or preventing competition. This duty gives considerable room for questioning an authority's actions (see chapter 6).

The DOE's position on fairness is set out in draft guidance dated 11 October 1995. Councils are required to encourage competition, to package contracts to appeal to private firms and to have in place a transparently fair and open tendering procedure, including a clear methodology for balancing price against quality of service. Furthermore various stages of the process must be recorded in reports to council committees; these include packaging, contract lengths, timing of stages in the CCT process, contract requirements, performance bands, availability of assets, invitations to tender, evaluations, TUPE, contract award, performance monitoring, variations to specification and defaults.

In the interests of ensuring fairness, certain tasks within the tendering process are now prescribed client functions which cannot be carried out by anyone responsible for or involved in the calculation and submission of the in-house bid. The tasks covered are the selection of publications for advertising, selecting firms to be invited to tender, sending out tender documents, calculating prospective costs, receiving, opening and evaluating bids and deciding with whom the work is to be placed. Elected members, chief executives, chief officers and legal and financial advisers are, however, exempt from this restriction.

While it is permissible for two or more defined activities to be included in a single contract, the DoE view is that tenderers should be given the option to bid for each type of work separately if it is likely this would achieve an improved level of tenderer interest. Given that it will commonly be less expensive to monitor one contractor than two, a reasonable alternative would be to expressly permit subcontracting of the elements of the service falling into a different defined activity, giving the tenderer an alternative to direct provision while retaining the integrity of a single contract to the benefit of the council.

In relation to the evaluation process, the regulations require local authorities to inform contractors in advance of any intention to take extraneous costs into account as well as the nature of any weighting mechanisms to be used in comparing schedules of rates submitted by different contractors.

ANTI-COMPETITIVE BEHAVIOUR IN PROFESSIONAL SERVICE TENDERING

The extension of CCT to professional services has resulted in additional guidance with reference to anti-competitive behaviour issued by DoE circular letter dated 12 December 1994. In particular

  (i)   councils should not necessarily exclude tenderers for lack of relevant experience (especially if TUPE is to apply and the authorities' own staff will transfer);
 (ii)   packages of work including more than one defined activity are allowable if properly justified on service delivery grounds (subject to the duty to avoid anti-competitive behaviour);
(iii)   contracts in excess of five years' length would not normally be justified;
 (iv)   indications of likely work volumes should be supplied to tenderers;
  (v)   method statements may be required from tenderers if the specification is output-based but only in sufficient detail reasonably to assess the tenderer's competence and experience; and
 (vi)   geographical requirements should be limited to those essential to provide the service with no attempt to restrict the tenderer's placement of other staff.

EVALUATION PROCESS FOR PROFESSIONAL SERVICES

Wherever price becomes a subordinate factor to the quality of the service required, the evaluation process inevitably becomes more complex. The tendering of professional services thus inevitably involves consideration of detailed evaluation models and methodology which may have no necessary application to manual service contracts.

In the parlance of European public procurement practice, the most economically advantageous tender will be achieved when a range of factors in addition to price are brought into play. These should include compliance with tender documentation, approach to quality, methodology for service delivery, resourcing of the contract, and previous experience and scale of operation (if the extent to which the council wishes to be a pivotal client of the tenderer is important).

Apart from the normal questionnaire responses, a range of further information will be required. This will include the tenderer's quality standards and controls, qualifications, expertise and experience of key managerial and lead staff, complaints procedures and material aimed at satisfying concerns over the risk of contract failure or of conflicts of interest.

Method statements may also be required for elements of the specified service to enable an assessment to be made of specific local government expertise necessarily required for a proper standard of service. As a minimum a method statement should cover resourcing, methodology for achieving set performance targets, assuring quality procedures to be used, technical and professional inputs, interfaces with other services, client communication, complaints and monitoring.

Presentations and beauty parades may be chosen as a means of casting light on the extent to which the tenderer can inspire council trust as well as demonstrating experience and expertise. While such face-to-face meetings may be of value, an ability to present may not equate with good service and a presentation should remain only one element of the evaluation process. A good rule of thumb is to watch for an understanding of the council's needs and objectives being demonstrated rather than too much talk about the tenderers themselves. This may seem at odds with the need to collect information about the firm but usually this can be gathered and assessed more readily and without exaggeration on paper. The presentation should show that the firm has weighed the specified requirements and can adapt itself flexibly to meet them—not to demonstrate an existing structure and working methods said to be ready to take care of the council's needs. These will have evolved to meet the needs of other clients (or indeed of the firm itself) and it is their willingness to change and mould themselves to the council as client which is vital.

An alternative approach involves carefully structured interviews controlled by client officers rather than freedom for tenderers to make an advertising pitch.

The difficulty will be in demonstrating, after the event, that the judgements taken on contract award were motivated by proper reasons and that where subjective elements came into play, they were not given undue importance.

One solution is to use formal pre-set scoring and weighting mechanisms. Each criterion is set down with a score between, say, 1 and 5 allocated to differentiate between an inadequate tenderer and an excellent one. Different criteria can then be weighted by allocating longer or shorter scoring scales. Finally a relative balancing of price and quality can be made by determining a percentage for price considerations and one for quality issues. For example, 60 per cent of the available scores could be allocated to the range of prices received and 40 per cent to scoring the quality criteria.

There is a problem with pure mathematical models of this type. They appear logical and objective but the individual scoring decisions are necessarily subjective themselves and thorough documentation of the professional reason for each stage of the process must be kept.

The legislation does not tie local authorities into such evaluation systems and provided the process used is 'equitable, auditable and transparent' it should withstand challenge. The most important thing is to reduce subjective judgements wherever possible and to record rationale wherever they cannot be avoided.

POST-TENDER NEGOTIATIONS AND RETENDERING

The Secretary of State, fearing that post-tender negotiations may undermine the fairness of the tendering process, has expressed the view that such action may be anti-competitive. If such negotiations are unavoidable, a successful DSO must not be given the opportunity to reconsider its tender on the original specification or to tender for a revised specification of service unless similar opportunities are given to all tenderers who submitted lower tenders that would, price apart, have been acceptable. This somewhat confusing guidance may be taken to permit negotiations with a DSO in isolation if it submitted the outright lowest bid; otherwise, the only tenderers who need be granted the same consideration are those whose bids would have been seen as lower than that of the DSO had extraneous costs not been brought into the evaluation by the local authority.

This procedure offers strong possibilities of challenge, irrespective of the Secretary of State's pronounced position. A safer procedure would be to offer the same opportunity to renegotiate to all tenderers, without revealing the respective competitiveness of their bids, who have been adjudged to be financially sound and technically competent and with whom the authority would be willing to contract were their price to be satisfactory.

There are grounds to believe that a decision to retender following a tendering exercise may be regarded as anti-competitive and that authorities choosing to do so must be prepared to produce proper justification for their actions and to satisfy the Secretary of State that the DSO is not aware of the external bids submitted or the names of the other contractors. This test may be impossible to satisfy, given the statutory rights to information referred to in Chapter 6.

CONTRACT IMPLEMENTATION

Implementation of the decision to award the work to a particular tenderer is the last stage in the process. It covers the negotiation of any outstanding detail; the authority's transitional dispositions; the contractor's preparations, including the recruitment of staff prior to the hand-over date set down in the contract documentation; and the finalisation of the authority's redundancies, where applicable, and monitoring arrangements.

Obviously, implementation is less onerous if the DSO is the successful tenderer. The staff are already in place and there is no formal contract to be executed. An authority, being a corporate body, cannot contract with itself and it is a frequent misunderstanding to believe DSOs are somehow separate entities from their authorities, akin to wholly-owned subsidiary companies. They are not; the link between the client operations of the council and DSO is at best quasi-contractual and only that by virtue of a statutory requirement for the DSO to comply with the detailed specification in performing the services.

For a winning external tenderer, the formalities of executing the contract are less significant than the need to muster the resources and hire the necessary workers in advance of the contractual commencement date. The 1993 DSO Regulations[1] set a minimum lead-in period of 30 days and a maximum of 120 days between award of contract and commencement of work to prevent local authorities setting unfeasibly short implementation times. Subsequent statutory instruments have made it clear these deadlines will not be applied to the tendering of professonal services.

A typical timetable for preparations prior to commencing service provision on a contracted basis is shown in Appendix I.

EUROPEAN LEGAL REQUIREMENTS FOR THE TENDERING OF PUBLIC-SERVICE CONTRACTS

The consequences of European law for competitive tendering of local authority services is considered in full in Chapter 21. It is worth noting here, however, that dependent on the value of the contract to be let, advertising in the European *Official Journal* is a requirement irrespective of whether an authority is tendering voluntarily or in compliance with the LGPLA 1980 or LGA 1988.

PROCEDURAL VARIATIONS UNDER THE LGA 1992

Whilst the tendering regime of the LGA 1988 applies to all defined activities, section 8 of the LGA 1992 contains a power enabling the Secretary of State to modify the tendering regime to be applied to professional services subject to CCT. Where such modifications have been made, they are identified in relation to the implementation of competition for specific services elsewhere in this text.

---

1 Ibid page 16 above.

Chapter 4

CONTRACT TECHNOLOGY

This chapter concentrates on the nature of contracts used by local authorities for the provision of services secured through competitive tendering. The DoE maintains that, wherever possible, local authorities should use standard contract documents, such as those of the Joint Contracts Tribunal, as departures from such forms may have the effect of restricting competition. Since prepared national forms of contract suitable for all defined activities do not exist, this provision may be of greater importance in the future than at present. In the absence of nationally adopted standard contracts of the type existing for engineering and construction projects, councils have generally chosen to produce their own or to purchase model documents generated by those local authorities who have decided to tender services in advance of any statutory requirement to do so. The extension of CCT to professional services may be the appropriate time for such contract documents to be revised and improved.

An obvious danger in the use of locally produced contracts is that they do not carry the benefits of having been tested before the courts and in arbitration and thus there are no authoritative interpretations to guide both parties as to the meaning to be ascribed to key phrases that have been inserted to achieve the principal aims of the contract. Since it is the local authority, a body with sufficient power in the market-place to insist on the use of its own formal documentation, which may have to seek to enforce duties and rights contained in the contract, it must be aware that any ambiguity will be interpreted by the courts in favour of the contractor and against the local authority seeking to assert or exploit it. This is an example of the doctrine of *contra proferentem* at work in respect of contract interpretation.

Because the local authority must generate a specification for the services and in general cannot modify such a specification once tenders have been sought in reliance upon it (unless retendering occurs) it is vital to ensure that the contract documents achieve their main purpose, which is to secure the delivery of specified services of appropriate quality at a known or ascertainable price, with minimal scope for differing views as to the meaning and impact of individual clauses. In reviewing the essential elements of a local authority service contract for CCT use and the specification it must contain, reference should be made to the examples of contract documentation in Appendix III.

TYPES OF CONTRACT

There are two types of contract readily applicable to competitive tendering. The first is built around a fixed price for a specified level of service or a lump sum derived from the pricing of a bill of quantities. The second type uses a schedule of rates for individual elements of work or per working hour spent and the value of the contract is dependent on the quantity of work materialising, none being guaranteed. Other than the tender evaluation difficulties the latter approach poses, the main difference between the two types relates to the payment system to be contained in the conditions of contract.

Other types of contract common to some of the disciplines subject to CCT are really variants on the two types outlined above. They include labour-only contracts, management contracts and management-fee contracts. It is worth examining these possibilities if only to be satisfied that they are generally inappropriate for CCT.

Labour-only contracts, as the phrase suggests, are those in which only the labour element is tendered, with the local authority retaining the management of the contract. Since the defined activity subject to CCT must include direct supervision of the delivery of the services (the whole contractor function), such a contract will not meet fully the requirements of the LGA 1988, unless it is let in conjunction with a separate contract for the management element. There may be situations in which such an option yields benefits to a local authority, but in most cases it will prove an expensive separation of function from supervision.

Management contracts are the converse of labour-only contracts, but may stretch to a wider range of activity than the mere supervisional line management of the services to take in some of the design and planning responsibilities that would otherwise be retained as client functions. Unless the labour element is tendered separately, management contracts do not meet the legislative requirements of CCT either.

Management-fee contracts, which are common in catering and construction, describe the situation where the client provides all resources, including labour, or meets all such costs in total, the service being managed by the contractor in return for a percentage fee based on turnover or total cost. Unless the management contractor tenders the labour element in accordance with the relevant legislation, a local authority's DSO staff could not bid for the work, since the resulting contract would not comply with the requirements of either the LGPLA 1980 or the LGA 1988. Accordingly, management-fee contracts can exist only as a form of privatisation, with the management contractor free to obtain labour and any other resources required from the private sector, and the local authority reimbursing the cost of such acquisition in full.

For the purpose of considering model contract conditions it is assumed that the local authority will be required to make payment of a fixed annual price or a variable one, ascertained by reference to prices offered for different elements of work by the successful tenderer in relation to the full service delivery covered by a defined activity, rather than merely the management of labour elements of such a service in isolation. Such contracts offer the only means of defining costs and performance sufficiently clearly so as to provide the basis for fair evaluation between different potential contractors. This is not to exclude the possibility of contracts containing an element of retainer for a basic guaranteed service, with additional activity generating variable costs based upon pre-set rates.

It is also assumed that the contracts are awarded in accordance with the CCT regime. Negotiated contracts cannot be regarded as complying with the tender evaluation procedures implicit in the legislation and are therefore applicable only to situations in which the local authority wishes to privatise a service. In these situations the council can negotiate with any chosen contractors without regard to the statutory processes, but such activity is outside the scope of this work.

FORM OF AGREEMENT

Essentially, the form of agreement is the document executed by the parties as a contract, which must incorporate, by reference, the conditions of contract as well as the specification. It may form an integral part of the contract or appear as a front sheet or back page to it. The example included in Appendix III satisfies the main requirements.

CONTRACT CONDITIONS

The conditions of contract are the terms under which the services, whatever their nature, are to be carried out. They form a framework upon which to fall back should a satisfactory relationship not develop between the local authority and the contractor, and they should incorporate all of the global rights and duties of the parties other than the definition of the tasks and performance standards, which are properly matters for the specification of the services. The importance of clarity and of eliminating ambiguity has already been emphasised, but the conditions must also use a terminology consistent with that used in the specification. Since the latter will usually be drafted by a service professional and the conditions by a lawyer, achieving compatibility may be a tricky task.

The main heads of condition to be incorporated are discussed below.

Contract period

As outlined in Chapter 3, the minimum and maximum periods for which a CCT contract for a defined activity may last are set by Parliament. This does not mean that contracts must necessarily be made for a fixed period falling between the minimum and maximum markers. The contract can include a clause permitting it to be extended for a further period by agreement between the parties so long as the combined length of the original contract and the period of extension do not exceed the relevant statutory maximum. Hence the contract can be let for the minimum period, for example, with an option to extend it for a period of one, two or three years, provided the extension does not push the duration of the contract beyond the maximum statutory contract period for that defined activity.

Description of parties

This will normally be clearly stated in the form of agreement and repetition is unnecessary.

Description of the subject-matter of the contract

The reason for having a contract is to secure the performance of services. Words sufficient to bind the contractor to supply the services are all that need be included, provided that services are defined as including all matters referred to in the specification.

Price

The price to be paid by the local authority for the services falls to be ascertained from the tender. A fixed price can be specifically mentioned in the contract conditions, but it may be simpler to annex the form of tender, which will be necessary in any event if a schedule of rates or a priced bill of quantities has been required from the tenderers.

Inflation

In tendering for a contract, which should, all being well, span several years, it is unrealistic to expect prices to remain static. If the contractor is required to allow for the contingent risks of estimating inflation over the life of the contract, the result will be inflated costs for the local authority in the early years. Accordingly, it is sensible to make allowance for inflation of tender prices at regular intervals, using a pre-determined method of calculation. The commonest solution is to use the retail price index, but other indices are available. For instance, indices calculating inflation across a range of specific resources, as used in construction contracts[1], could be adopted.

Payment and value added tax (VAT)

The contract conditions should set out clearly the frequency and method of payment by the local authority to the contractor. The system should state the nature of invoicing and supporting documentation required from the contractor and the nature of the certification process to be completed before payment is made. The circumstances in which payment can be withheld should be clarified within the payments clauses or elsewhere in the conditions. Responsibility for calculation and payment of VAT also ought to be clarified.

Variations

The authority of individual council officers to vary the contract conditions and specification of the services must be clearly stated. Controlling the budget for a contract in which the contractor is able to claim additional payments in respect of variations made by multiple sources could be a nightmare.

1 The Monthly Bulletin Construction Indices For Use With National Economic Development Office Price Adjustment Formula Civil Engineering Works.

Emergencies

The ability to require the contractor to respond to emergencies or to switch from regular contract work to urgent work of a similar type may need to be reserved in relation to certain defined activities. It is up to the individual drafters to determine whether this is more appropriately located in the conditions of contract or as a part of the service specification.

Statutory requirements

Unless adherence to mandatory requirements is the responsibility of only the local authority in law, there is no reason for referring to statutory requirements in the conditions of contract as a general rule. If a requirement is a legal obligation upon all persons, then a contractor will be bound to act within the law and is liable to be prosecuted or subject to sanctions irrespective of whether such responsibilities are reiterated in the contract or not.

In most cases the only purpose served by the inclusion of statutory requirements is to remind the contractor of his or her duties and this should be unnecessary if suitably competent tenderers are competing for the work. Only if failure to comply with statutory requirements might reasonably be regarded by the council as a default having a major impact on the confidence in the contractor to provide the service should consideration be given to including a condition binding the contractor to comply with the law. In most circumstances a breach of the law in a contract situation will give rise to sufficient consequences to invoke ordinary default and termination powers and the statutory breach need not be actionable as of itself constituting a breach of contract.

Use of local authority assets

If the contractor is to occupy local authority accommodation or deploy council-owned vehicles, plant and equipment in providing the services, the basis for use of such assets ought to be clearly stated. In particular, any payments to be made to the council and any responsibility for repair or maintenance should be stated.

Requiring the contractor to enter a standard form lease or licence agreement offers a solution, but it is worth remembering that the Landlord and Tenant Act 1954 gives the lessee a right to secure a renewal on expiry of a lease of business premises. To avoid this it will be necessary to bind the contractor to join in an application to the County Court for the waiver of the right to seek renewal. In addition, any lease or licence must be terminable at the same time as the main contract for services expires or is brought to an early end.

Third-party work

If a contractor is operating from council premises or using council equipment, the issue of the provision of services by the contractor to parties other than the council needs to be addressed. If it is to be prohibited, the conditions or the lease or licence needs to say so; if permitted, any terms should be laid down, including the possibility of the council sharing in the receipts from such third-party work. This may be particularly applicable to vehicle maintenance operations run from council depots where the contractor's ability to tap into external sources of work may valuably subsidise the cost to the council of its own requirement.

Solicitation of council clients

Certain defined activities will bring the contractor into direct contact with paying clients of the local authority, which may well wish to protect itself against those clients being poached to become private customers of the contractor during or at the expiry of the main contract with the council. For example, a refuse collection contractor will be required to collect trade refuse for which the council levies a charge, receiving income that partially defrays or subsidises the cost of the service to the general public.

The same risk may be posed by former in-house staff if a contract for service is awarded to an external tenderer, and consideration should be given to strengthening their contracts of employment in this respect. That risk has already materialised in the London Borough of Camden. When the council awarded its refuse collection contract to Onyx, former council dustmen set up in business in their own right as Express Waste and were able to undercut the trade refuse charges levied by Onyx for Camden and to win work from commercial premises formally serviced by the council.

Conflicts of interest

There may be general and ongoing conflicts of interest in services such as legal and estate management if the contractor can act for the council as well as third parties who may oppose the council on related issues. In such cases, a prohibition clause should be justified. In legal services, the Law Society has accepted broad restraints. (See Chapter 13.)

Confidentiality

The names and addresses of paying clients may not be the only commercially sensitive information released to a contractor in the course of operating the contract. A general duty to maintain the confidentiality of such information may need to be imposed.

Control and monitoring

While effective monitoring of the completion and quality of the services is dependent to a large extent on the methodology and the selected performance indicators used in preparing the specification, the contract conditions will need to reserve the right and means of promoting proper monitoring. This means that the client's proposed system of monitoring must be determined prior to tendering. For example, rights of access to the contractor's documentation and staff will need to be expressly reserved in the contract conditions.

Health and safety

Contracting local authorities retain a vested interest in health and safety, not least because they may remain liable for injury to contractors' employees while they are on the council premises. Local authorities will therefore normally expect the successful contractor to have and to follow a suitable health and safety policy, or, in the absence of one, to use the council's policy.

Staffing

While by virtue of the LGA 1988 a local authority cannot bring factors in relation to the contractor's work-force into account in evaluation of the tenderers and their bids, it is entitled to require that competent, trained staff are deployed in providing the council's services and to reserve the right to demand that individual employees offending council clients or committing serious breaches of their duties under the contract be withdrawn from services provided for the council. Other issues such as the wearing of uniforms may also need to be addressed.

TUPE

If the parties agree that contracting-out a service constitutes the transfer of an undertaking, the complexities of staff transfer will have to be incorporated in appropriate contract terms. In particular, clauses should cover pensions comparability or compensation for shortfalls and liability for claims for redundancy or unfair dismissal made by former council staff now transferring.

Assignment and subletting

Prohibitions of assignment and subletting of contracts are common in the public sector but unqualified rejection of subcontracting may be anti-competitive. It may be preferable to require consent to subletting, such consent not to be unreasonably withheld.

Liability of contractor and council and insurance

Defining the respective liabilities of contractor and council in relation to employees and third parties and associated indemnities is unlikely to suffice without the contractor carrying a specified level of insurance for injury, death and loss of or damage to property.

Finally the Commission for Local Government investigating a complaint of mal-administration may require compensation be paid to the complainants. If the Ombudsman's finding rests on default by the contractor a clause could bind the contractor to pay.

Performance bonds

If a bond guaranteeing payment of a set sum by a third party in the event of contract failure is deemed necessary, it should be the subject of a contract condition setting the level required expressed as a percentage of contract value. The DoE states that such a bond should not be required automatically, but only where a real risk is perceived in awarding the work externally. It advises that where a requirement is imposed, it should normally be for no more than 10 per cent of the annual value of the service and its value must relate to the costs that would be incurred were retendering to occur.

The law relating to the enforceability of performance bonds is complex and careful drafting will be necessary if a bond is to secure payment of losses incurred on contract failure (on proof of the same) without set-off or long delay. See the 1994 case of *Trafalgar House Construction (Regions) Limited v General Surety and Guarantee Company Ltd*[1] involving so-called 'unconditional on demand' or 'first demand' bonds for further enlightenment.

Recovery of sums due to the council

Obviously, overpayments to the contractor or the costs of correcting poorly executed work will be recoverable under the default provisions from monies otherwise due under the contract. It may be that the council will also wish to include rights to set off debts to the council arising from other contractual arrangements against monies payable under a contract for defined activities.

Probity

Local government officers are bound by the LGA 1972 and a national code of conduct, which impose professional ethics to avoid corruption and even the appearance of impropriety. Section 117 of the LGA 1972 makes it an offence for an officer to accept any fee or reward other than his or her proper remuneration in the course of employment.

The conduct of contractors is not so rigidly regulated. Accordingly, a prohibition on accepting gifts or gratuities from the public and positive requirements in relation to the contractor's conduct may be imposed in the contract conditions.

Special conditions

Individual defined activities may give rise to specific inclusions in the contract conditions. Examples include the collection of fees and charges and building maintenance in sport and leisure management contracts. Certain service-specific conditions may cause problems. In particular, requirements relating to the location or standard of the contractor's premises or limiting the contractor to the sole use of specified materials or equipment will be regarded as anti-competitive unless demonstrably essential. Similarly, requirements to forgo private commercial work within the local authority's boundaries for the duration of the contract are to be prohibited by regulation.

A DoE requirement that councils should not demand that an external

1 [1995] 3 All ER 737, HL.

tenderer treat an awarded contract as a transfer of undertakings (the effects of which are discussed in Chapter 9) is intended to prevent one possible means of frustrating the process of compulsory competition.

Finally, requirements that tenderers shall have BS5750 accreditation, or its European equivalent, will, in the absence of widespread use in specific sectors of the external market, be regarded as restricting competition. The maximum deemed acceptable is a condition that such a quality-assurance system will be developed within a period of no less than twelve months following commencement of the contract.

Termination

In the event of total failure or fundamental breach of contract the local authority will reserve the right to terminate the contract. The conditions should make provision for the recovery of any additional costs incurred by the council in securing another contractor to perform the services.

Some local authorities have included no-fault termination clauses in contracts. Westminster's legal services tendering is one example. Whilst no specific challenge has been made to such a term, if one were made it would be almost bound to succeed since it would justifiably deter a contractor from bidding.

Defaults and remedies

In monitoring contract performance problems arise when levels of poor performance short of total failure are detected. Withholding payment for elements of work inadequately completed will not necessarily achieve the goal of persuading the contractor to improve and the temptation arises to penalise poor performance by withholding sums greater than the value of the poorly completed work, particularly if calculated from the schedule of rates or bills of quantities priced by the contractor. Danger arises in such an approach because the levying of penalties is unenforceable in law. The common-law position on contract penalties is to be reinforced by pending regulations, which will outlaw, as anti-competitive, procedures that are arbitrary or penal in their effect or impose an excessive charge in the event of a default arising or allow the contractor no opportunity to rectify a default.

The starting point for default deductions must be the true cost of rectification, which may be greater than the unitary rate for that element of work. For example, it costs more to make a special collection to empty one householder's bin than to collect the refuse as part of a round. The administrative costs of issuing default notices can also be visited upon the contractor, inflicting financial consequences upon the defaulter without giving rise to an unlawful penalty.

A further weapon may be reserving the right to hold retentions from the monies otherwise due to the contractor until such time as its performance has improved, when the retentions will be handed over.

Systems involving the allocation of the results of statistical sampling to the total value of work claimed or the allocation of default points to default notices and deductions based upon the points accumulated are also possible but are more likely to give rise to allegations that illegal penalties are being imposed. If statistical sampling is to be considered as a means of ascertaining default deductions, the testing standards set out in BS5701 and BS6000 offer the safest systems for avoiding challenges.

The important lesson is to avoid default procedures which are 'arbitrary in construction and penal in intent'. It was a clause so described which caused the DoE to require Walsall to retender vehicle maintenance contracts to take effect in April 1996.

SPECIFICATIONS

The preparation of a specification for each service subject to competition is now a statutory requirement for both LGPLA 1980 and LGA 1988 competition, and the service must be operated in accordance with the specification thereafter. This is reinforced by section 10 of the LGA 1992, which created a duty to keep the specification available for public inspection during the currency of the tendered arrangements and to publicise its availability sufficiently.

In this context a specification is an attempt to define the task to be performed in providing the service and the standard to be achieved. It will thus cover the nature of the work, the methods to be employed, where these are material to the finished result, and the quality requirement. The lack of a sufficiently comprehensive specification will prevent certainty that the lowest tenders received (with the exception of loss-leader bids) offer the best value.

The extent of specification may in itself be regarded by the Secretary of State as anti-competitive. Draft guidance, issued as a precursor to regulations, makes it clear that it will not be acceptable to specify the minimum number of persons to be employed in providing the services or the particular type of vehicles to be used. This is countered by advice to the effect that the specification must be clear, adequate and precise as to the details of the nature of the work or service to ensure that the DSO does not obtain an unfair advantage from its knowledge of the existing service. The art of specification thus treads a narrow line between two possible avenues of contractor challenge.

Finally, it must also be noted that the contents of a specification may be circumscribed by specific legislation. For example, in specifying refuse collection and street cleaning regard must be had to section 89 of the Environmental Protection Act 1990 and the accompanying litter code which essentially set the minimum levels of cleanliness and timescales for achieving them for various grades of public land.

Profile of the existing service

The starting point for most specifications is likely to be the existing level of service. It is therefore necessary to compile a database comprising the measured quantities and frequencies of work if one does not already exist. Only when such information and adequate costings are to hand can decisions be taken on the viability and affordability of improving the service or of varying or downgrading it to achieve economies for the client.

The database must examine the service from three distinct viewpoints. It must assess the elements of input, such as labour, capital and materials going into the service, the measurable outputs in terms of the service provided and the methods or process of converting one into the other. While the specification to be produced should not bind the eventual contractor to existing inputs or methods as a matter of course, for work in which measurable results or quality standards are difficult to isolate there may be no other practical means of specifying the level of service required. Restrictions on dictating matters appertaining to the contractor's workforce set out in the LGA 1988 should be noted in this respect.

Objectives

The compilation of a specification must be carried out with a number of competing ends in mind. It must be suitable to be priced by tenderers and offer the prospect of cost-effective bids, it must achieve services of adequate quality and, above all, it must be couched in such a way as to render it monitorable. For example, a frequency-based grass-cutting specification can never be entirely successfully monitored unless an inspector accompanies the operative at all times, whereas a specification based upon maximum tolerable height of grass, leaving the contractor to determine frequencies, can be monitored effectively in the course of sporadic site visits.

In a nutshell the model approach to specification is to determine the nature and extent of the work to be performed not to determine how it is to be done. This approach results in an output-based specification rather than one which is input-based.

Quality

Building quality in alongside quantity is commonly the most difficult aspect of specification, and therefore Chapter 20 addresses quality issues. It should be emphasised at this stage that specifying the quality and experience of the staff to be deployed in providing the services may be the only way around the problems of setting measurable performance indicators. This is likely to be particularly true of professional services. Furthermore, it would be impossible in most contracts to entirely dispense with subjective judgements of quality to be made by council officers during the course of the contract.

Client choice

The options for providing different levels of service to different clients have to be explored and individual requirements catered for. This is most obviously demonstrated in the case of schools with delegated budgets, but it is increasingly important in other areas, such as social services establishments.

Key tasks

Much of the necessary preparation work can be extrapolated from what has already been stated on the subject of specifications. However, certain considerations should be applied to raw data gathered as part of the process of preparing the service specification. These principally concern the format to be adopted and the supporting documentation to be supplied. Thus it will be necessary to determine whether the specification will contain merely a list of tasks, or whether bills of quantities will be necessary and whether the specification requires a pictorial dimension in the form of drawings or even a photo survey demonstrating the quality of service to be achieved at each key site.

Finally, it must be emphasised that the workload and officer time required for the preparation of a paper specification should never be underestimated.

CONTRACTOR INPUT

The wisdom of consultation with potentially interested tenderers on the specification is mooted in Chapter 3. Consideration must also be given to the response to be made to companies questioning the contract documentation and the services to be provided during the tendering process.

At the outset officers empowered to supply further relevant information and deal with tenderer inquiries should be nominated. Where further information is given, it should be confirmed in writing and supplied to all tenderers. Meetings should not take place between contractors and individual officers; another witness should always attend. Finally, contractors should be encouraged to visit the locations at which the services are to be provided. Only by taking such precautions can the most realistic tenders be achieved and the authority and its officers be safeguarded from accusations of unfair or anti-competitive practices.

CONTRACT CLAIMS

The dangers implicit in defective or exploitable specifications and ambiguous terminology can be demonstrated by examining the potential for claims to be submitted above and beyond the tender price by an aggrieved or canny contractor.

A contractor will be able to seek additional monies if he can demonstrate that he has incurred losses as a result of the acts of the local authority or of council employees. Direct and actionable losses can arise from delays in issuing instructions or providing information, delays by other main contractors upon whom the service depends, difficulties in securing access to premises, compliance with misleading instructions and breach of contract by the council itself. Client instructions conflicting with the precise terms of the specification provide potentially fertile grounds for claims for additional payments. Failure to keep proper monitoring records combined with poor contract documentation can thus result in vastly inflated costs accruing to the responsible local authority.

OTHER NECESSARY DOCUMENTATION

The completed contract will comprise the form of agreement, the contract conditions, the specification, the form of tender and bills of quantities where applicable. However, this is not the limit of the documentation required in the tendering process leading to a formal contract. Tenderers will require instructions for tender submission, an appropriate form of tender (plus standard labels and envelopes if tenders are required to be returned in such), a standard form of performance bond, a non-collusive tendering declaration and a certificate of *bona fide* tender incorporating an undertaking to contract with the local authority if the tender is accepted.

The DoE's position is that local authorities should not require excessively detailed information with tender submissions. The example quoted in current draft guidance is that tenders for building cleaning should not require prices per room but only per building. Quite where this leaves council endeavours to determine the adequacy of tender resourcing, as a means of verifying the prospects for successful completion of the contract, is uncertain. Given the dramatic consequences of contract failure in most defined activities, the guidance offered appears to ignore commercial realities.

Although the contract is the sole basis of agreement and tenderers should not be enticed to bid by misleading information, this should not prevent common information packages for tenders being made available on the clear understanding that the recipients should visit sites and verify the information supplied for themselves if considering bidding.

CONDITIONS OF TENDERING

The obvious purpose of instructions for tenderers is to ensure that everyone invited to bid understands what is required of them as part of the tendering process.

An important secondary purpose achieved by setting conditions impliedly accepted by the submission of a bid has been to tie a contractor into holding his tender open for acceptance for a period and to executing a formal contract when required by the council to do so. This has been undermined by the case of *Southampton City Council v Academy Cleaning Services (London)* in 1993. A cleaning company simply withdrew its tender after it had been accepted but the council did not succeed in the High Court in its action for damages equal to the difference in costs between Academy's bid and the next lowest. The conditions of tendering were that the bid had to be held open for 90 days and acceptance in advance of a formal agreement would constitute a binding contract. These terms accord with models used by many local authorities and the case raises obvious risks of disruption to tendering processes if firms can withdraw without penalty at any time prior to the execution of a formal written contract. If occurring late in the run-up to commencement, a local authority could be in an impossible position, having incurred significant expenditure on redundancy or transfer of undertakings consultation. It would also need to seek the urgent consent of the DoE to carry on the service in-house until retendering could be arranged, if the next lowest tenderers could not at that stage accept the work.

QUALIFIED TENDERS

The instructions for tenderers will normally prohibit consideration of qualified tenders. If such a qualification is made, offering the local authority an advantage not previously appreciated, it seems it may not be possible for a local authority to completely ignore the matter, because of its fiduciary duties to its charge payers and future council-tax payers. Only if the qualification offers the council no ready benefit should it be rejected out of hand[1]. Otherwise the appropriate course of action should be to consider retendering or to offer all tenderers an opportunity to submit an amended price incorporating the same qualification or to lodge objections to the process. Only if such action would fatally interfere with the time-scale in which the contract must be let by law should no further action be taken.

MODEL CONTRACT DOCUMENTS

The local authority associations have produced standard core contract conditions and a guide to their use in the formulation of CCT contracts; the second edition of these is available from the Association of Metropolitan Authorities.

A number of individual councils also sell copies of their draft contracts. They include the London Borough of Wandsworth and the City of Westminster. The latter's documents include a specification for legal services.

The Association of Chief Technical Officers (ACTO) has produced documents for services such as refuse collection, street cleansing, cleaning of public conveniences and grounds maintenance. Although basic, they make useful comparators with other models, especially used in conjunction with the standard specifications for such activities as grounds maintenance that are produced by the British Standards Institution.

Finally, CIPFA has established a contract specifications library as part of its competitive tendering information service.

DATA PROTECTION ACT REGISTRATION

The Data Protection Act 1984 safeguards the collection, holding, use and disclosure of personal data held on computer. Plainly if contracting-out occurs the new service provider will require access to some such information in relation to clients and to staff, if TUPE applies. The council should in such circumstances amend its registration documents to cover the potential disclosures it may need to make to the contractor. Similarly, the contractor should be required to register as a data user.

---

1 *Blackpool and Fylde Aero Club Ltd v Blackpool Borough Council* [1990] 3 All ER 25.

Chapter 5

CONTRACT COMPLIANCE

This chapter considers the effect of the LGA 1988 on the practice engaged in by many local authorities of endeavouring to further social or political ends through the selection of sympathetic contractors and by making express contractual requirements of them that do not relate directly to the subject-matter of the contract.

Contracting is an effective means of spreading compliance with social or political policies into the private sector, given that the carrot of lucrative work can be withheld from tenderers who do not toe the line or at least demonstrate their willingness to change in future. The LGA 1988, however, greatly restricts the ability of local authorities to make requirements of any contractor other than those directly pertinent to the provision or quality of the goods or services to be provided. Since the range of action open to councils is so constrained, the extent to which they can bring contracting pressures to bear in support of their duties under the Race Relations Act 1976 and upon general issues involving health and safety is a matter of particular interest.

THE CONCEPT OF CONTRACT COMPLIANCE

Public procurement as a means of achieving non-commercial or political objectives has been used in the United Kingdom in two distinctly different areas. The first relates to equal opportunities and health and safety, contract compliance in these respects having been both common and laudable. The other is the achievement of more overtly political ends, such as the boycotting of companies with commercial interests in South Africa, the nuclear industry or defence contracting, or the encouragement of environmentally sound practices, all matters in which local authorities have no express remit and in which public policy is set by central government.

The existence of the Sex Discrimination Act 1975, the Race Relations Act 1976 and the Disabled Persons (Employment) Act 1944, each with a complementary code of practice, rendered it easy for local authorities to demand strict compliance without the need to define, *ad nauseam*, the detailed requirements to be made of the contractor. Similarly, the regulation of health and safety practices, in the interests of protecting contractors' work-forces and the general public, was simplified in the wake of the Health and Safety At Work Act 1974 and the guidance on safety policies provided by the Health and Safety Executive and individual trades associations.

Full-blooded political restriction of contracting decisions was always rare. Even before the LGA 1988 such actions carried the risk of being challenged on the grounds of unreasonableness.

The nature of the actions taken in the realm of contract compliance also varied between authorities. At one extreme lurked outright refusal to purchase goods and services from contractors failing to measure up to pre-set criteria but a more sympathetic approach, in which contractors were encouraged to adopt or move incrementally towards applying minimum standards within their organisations, while reducing their involvement in activity deemed inappropriate or commercially immoral, was more frequently adopted. Indeed, the latter approach is perceived in the United States as a particularly effective way of breaking down discrimination and of enhancing workers' conditions over time. In that sense contract compliance may be preferable, as an approach, to detailed legislation.

The justification used for applying contract compliance in the fields of equal opportunities and health and safety was the presumption that public money should not be employed to create profits for those who discriminate illegally or whose competitiveness is achieved at the expense of poor and unsafe working practices.

From the point of view of the parliamentary drafters engaged in preparing the provisions that became the LGA 1988, it was necessary to determine whether any role for contract compliance could stand alongside the primary intention of opening up local authority services—a potentially lucrative market for a range of commercial interests—to fair competition and value-for-money comparison. The extent to which local authorities have lost the ability to continue to make use of contract compliance is next examined generally and in relation to specific policy concerns.

THE LGA 1988

The non-commercial considerations that local authorities can no longer take into account, as a result of the attack on anti-competitive behaviour in the LGA 1988, are discussed in Chapter 1. In broad terms they can be summarised as preventing local authorities involving themselves in matters concerning a contractor's workforce or political and commercial affiliations in the course of granting or withholding contracts for the provision of goods and services.

The list of eight non-commercial considerations set out in section 17(5) of the LGA 1988 is not exhaustive, and the Secretary of State is empowered to add further matters to the list if loopholes are identified. The effect of this section is to outlaw contract compliance for political ends at a stroke and to severely limit the extent it can be used in support of legislative requirements binding contractors, employers or local authorities. Any discussion of the effect on specific compliance issues, most of which relate to employment law, must take place against the backdrop of the relevant part of section 17(5), which states 'the terms and conditions of employment by contractors of their workers or the composition of, the arrangements for the promotion, transfer or training of or other opportunities afforded to, their workforces' to be non-commercial considerations.

RACE RELATIONS

Limited forms of contract compliance may legally continue in respect of racial equality by virtue of an enabling provision in the LGA 1988 and the nature of the duties placed on local authorities by the Race Relations Act 1976. Section 18(2) of the LGA 1988 authorises councils to require tenderers to answer certain, approved, race-relations questions. In addition, they can incorporate within their conditions of tendering and contract terms any provisions that are reasonably necessary to effect the duties created by the Race Relations Act. Such conditions are the only express exceptions to the general prohibition on interference with matters relating to a contractor's work-force.

Section 17 of the Race Relations Act places certain duties on local authorities. The first requirement is to take steps to ensure that the various functions of a local authority are exercised with due regard to the need to eliminate unlawful racial discrimination, and the second is to promote equality of opportunity and good relations between different racial groups.

The approved questions that can be put to a tenderer, but only in writing, if the council wishes to do so, cover the following issues:

 (i)   compliance with the Race Relations Act 1976;
 (ii)   findings of racial discrimination against the company;
 (iii) formal investigations by the Commission for Racial Equality (CRE);
 (iv)   the contractor's response to any adverse finding by a court or tribunal or the CRE;
 (v)   publication and distribution of the contractor's racial equality policy;
 (vi)   observation of the CRE's code of practice for employment.

The full text of the approved questions is included in the tenderer questionnaire in Appendix II.

A limited power is thus exercisable to bring race relations into consideration in soliciting tenders and selecting contractors. There is no power to terminate any existing contract if the contractor does not appear to be complying with the Race Relations Act 1976 in practice, whatever assurances were given in response to the approved questions. Given that this is the case, it is essential to seek confirmatory documentation at the time of evaluation if any responses given by, or references supplied for, the contractor give the council any cause for concern. Once the contract has been let, no action can be taken for the duration of that contract.

Notwithstanding comments to the contrary made by the CRE, there is no provision for a local authority to monitor the composition of the contractor's workforce and selection procedures. Even though such monitoring is undeniably the most effective means of ensuring compliance with the Race Relations Act, it seems that section 17(5) of the LGA 1988 precludes it in the absence of any express power. The use of contract compliance as an authorised means of achieving equal opportunities for ethnic minorities is thus largely a weapon without teeth.

Nor, within the general context of CCT advice, should a model set of racial equality terms and conditions be applied indiscriminately to all contracts for the supply of goods and services, as the right for a local authority to exercise the applicable powers is dependent on it being necessary to do so in relation to this type or scale of contract or for this specific contractor or due to factors relating to the particular industry. Fair consideration of each case upon merit and justification remains a vital step if challenges are to be avoided.

SEX DISCRIMINATION AND DISABILITY

There is no provision within either the Sex Discrimination Act 1975 or the Disabled Persons (Employment) Act 1944 analogous to the statutory duties laid down by section 71 of the Race Relations Act 1976. In the absence of any defined role to be played in the enforcement of equal opportunities generally, there is no obvious argument for permitting local authorities to invoke tendering and contracting in the cause of female and disabled employees.

The issue was tested in relation to sex discrimination in *R v London Borough of Islington, ex parte the Building Employers Confederation*[1]. In this case the contract included a clause requiring the contractor to comply at all times with the specific provisions of the Sex Discrimination Act 1975 that make it unlawful to discriminate against women when making decisions involving recruitment or dismissal. The council had deliberately not referred to the subsection covering the terms of employment offered, regarding this as being a non-commercial consideration by reference to section 17(5) of the LGA 1988. The Divisional Court found that the wording of section 17(5), referring as it does to 'composition of the work-force', is broad enough to encompass any decision or practice that will have a bearing on the future composition of the work-force. Therefore Islington's contract clause was unlawful, notwithstanding that it sought only to compel the contractor to comply with existing law.

It is probable that a contract clause based on the Disabled Persons (Employment) Act 1944 would be treated identically by the courts.

HEALTH AND SAFETY

Under the Health and Safety at Work Act 1974 any employer has to ensure that employees, service users and the general public are not exposed to risks of a health and safety nature. The contracting-out of a service means the local authority ceases to be a direct employer of staff, but may not release the council from its duties under the Act, not least because retained council employees will on occasion continue to work alongside or monitor the employees of the selected contractor.

Consideration can be given to specifying compliance with the parent legislation, regulations or codes of practice so as to make them directly enforceable, with the option for the council to terminate the contract in the event of severe or persistent safety infringements. The proviso must again be made that the contract should not attempt to place any obligation on the contractor relating to the terms and conditions or composition of the workforce.

In addition, at an earlier stage, as part of the evaluation process, the adequacy of the tenderer's safety record and existing safety policy can be taken into account. It will be reasonable to exclude from consideration

1 [1989] IRLR 382.

any tenderer who has not demonstrated an ability and willingness to provide a safe system of work. However, the local authority cannot insist upon its own safety policy being substituted for the contractor's existing policy.

In *R v London Borough of Islington*[1], the Divisional Court was required to consider the lawfulness of the council's contractual health and safety conditions. Unlike the sex discrimination conditions, these were upheld. It was argued successfully that the phrase 'terms and conditions of employment' in section 17(5) of the LGA 1988 relates to contractual terms between the employer and the workforce and is not wide enough to cover the physical environment in which the contractor's employees are expected to work. Lord Justice Parker stated:

> I do not . . . intend to hold that a local authority is not to include in its contract provisions requiring the contractor to comply with the general law. It is only to the extent that there are specific obligations so included which cover such matters as pay, hours of work, what a particular employee is or is not to be permitted to do and so on that there would be an infringement.

This provides a fairly narrow interpretation covered by this subsection of the LGA 1988, which may yet prove useful in other arguments as to what can constitute anti-competitive behaviour.

CONCLUSIONS

For all practical purposes the LGA 1988 has brought about the demise of contract compliance within local government procurement of goods and services. Contractual attempts to require companies to comply with existing statute law in realms in which local authorities have no legitimate enforcement interest or statutory duty will be struck down by the courts. The one clear exception is race relations, for which a quasi-enforcement function exists together with approved questions to be asked of potential tenderers. Even in this area, however, it remains advisable to justify and document decisions made and actions taken.

Health and safety issues are not explicitly exempted from the LGA 1988 prohibitions in the same way as race relations, but the courts will not necessarily strike them down as non-commercial considerations.

1 Ibid.

Chapter 6

CONTRACTORS' RIGHTS AND CHALLENGES

This chapter explores challenges by staff and cartels but concentrates on the ramifications of the statutory requirements placed on local authorities to furnish reasons for contracting decisions, details of the tenders received and such additional information as the Secretary of State may request. The rationale for the existence of such rights is to simplify the policing of anti-competitive practices and can lead to the Secretary of State issuing directions to councils in relation to contract awards or DSO performance. These instructions can have draconian consequences for an in-house contracting organisation.

Officers and councillors will be well aware that apart from setting statutory processes which must be followed for CCT, the 1988 Act places an absolute duty upon them to refrain from anti-competitive behaviour, which is widely defined as anything that has the effect of preventing, distorting or restricting competition. All decisions taken by a local authority in the cause of implementing statutory competition for council services must be grounded on this principle.

The importance of this provision in relation to any stage of the competition process in which different options are open to the council, is that challenge by the Secretary of State provides a swift and effective remedy to an aggrieved private company which costs the complainant nothing to implement. The Secretary of State's powers are broad and largely unchallengeable and, if convinced that the effect of a council decision is to prevent, distort or restrict competition, he may well exercise his discretion to demand that the council retender the service. If he does so the DSO will face an increasingly impossible task in securing the work in-house.

The odds are stacked against in-house success on retender because of two provisions in the 1988 Act, which have been comparatively little used to date, but are likely to be picked up and utilised by professional service contractors. Both provisions relate to the statutory provision of information by the council following a tendering process. Section 20 of the Act requires that reasons for decisions taken at each stage of the process must be made available to the parties affected by the decision. This may well now enable a tenderer to question the reasons for packaging and specifying services in a particular manner. The more important provision is section 12, which permits any person to demand a statement of a council's decision on receipt of tenders and the 'financial provisions of each offer to carry out the work' with the DSO's financial provisions specifically identified.

The width of the wording used in section 12 means that where a tender is other than a fixed sum for a set volume of work, the full schedules of rates for different types of work will have to be released. Armed with full and current details of the pricing strategy employed by the DSO, which must bid to recover its costs and overheads in full, an external competitor will be ideally placed to win if a subsequent complaint results in an instruction to the council from the Secretary of State to retender the service.

It must therefore be emphasised that it is in the local authority's interest, if it wishes to maximise the chances of retaining jobs in-house despite the requirements of CCT, to take all reasonable steps to avoid complaints from aggrieved tenderers, or rather to minimise the risk of the Secretary of State's intervention. This means exercising great care in selecting, specifying and packaging services to be tendered and wherever possible disarming retrospective criticism by embarking upon consultation which affords the potential external competitors every chance to make representations before the relevant decision is taken. After all, even the Secretary of State has refused to entertain complaints where he has accepted that the complainant had the opportunity to influence a council decision before it was made and chose not to do so.

STATUTORY RIGHTS TO RECEIVE INFORMATION

The source of rights to contracting information is the LGA 1988, sections 12 and 20. The former is specific to the tendering of services defined for compulsory competition by the LGA 1988 itself. Section 20 has broader application: it relates to all contracts for goods and services entered into by a local authority and thus gives rise to a major departure from the usual practice of maintaining confidentiality and withholding relevant information in reliance on section 100B and Schedule 12A of the LGA 1972. This is the provision under which reports can be exempted from the principles of access to information by which the public and press are enabled to view council committee reports and background papers.

Section 12 of the LGA 1988

Henceforth any person can request a statement from the council in relation to the decision taken on the tendering of any functional work that is a defined activity under the LGA 1988. The statement must be in writing and must include certain specified information: the authority's decision (presumably the name of the successful tenderer), the financial provisions of each offer to carry out the work and the financial provisions contained in the DSO bid. There is no requirement to name any of the tenderers other than the DSO and the successful bidder.

Any individual, company or other corporate body, such as a fellow local authority, can avail itself of the right to demand this information and there is no time-limit or statutory period in which the statement can be sought. The opportunity is therefore available for potential contractors, whether submitting tenders or not, and for other local authorities seeking market information to secure valuable information on the pricing strategies of their competitors, including the DSO of the contracting council. Such requests for statements could even be submitted at the time contracts for defined services come up for renewal and retendering has to take place.

The DSO of the local authority at whom such requests for information are aimed will not be in a position to retain commercially sensitive information as to its costs and will be vulnerable to well-researched predatory bids in the second round of tendering where contracts are initially retained in-house.

The same consequences may deter external contractors from submitting bids unless they perceive themselves as having a good chance of securing the contract, since to bid will be to release their prices to their competitors in the same market. This will be especially true where contracts are let upon a priced schedule of rates for different works elements rather than for a fixed annual sum. The reason for this is that, arguably, the only way for a council to discharge its obligations and comply strictly with the duty to supply the financial provisions in each offer is to release details of all the rates upon request. Since the evaluation of a schedule-of-rates tender is dependent on weighting the different items of work with the anticipated level of usage or demand, a statement showing only the estimated annual cost for each contractor using their schedules of rates and the authority's weightings would be meaningless without the detail upon which it was based. Furthermore, the attempt to pass off the evaluated estimates of annual cost would not satisfy the specific duty relating to revealing the financial provisions shown in the original offer or tender.

It may even be argued that to notify the local authority's decision on a contract award involving a schedule of rates is meaningless without the weightings applied to the scheduled items. Since most authorities are wary of revealing this information voluntarily, it will take a complaint from an aggrieved contractor to the Secretary of State, persuading him to exercise the powers of inquiry referred to below, or case-law to determine where the right to contracting information under section 12 ends.

Section 20 of the LGA 1988

Whereas section 12 covers only the awarding of a contract, section 20 confers rights to secure reasons for decisions taken at each stage of the tendering process for any contract for the supply of goods or services to a local authority, and not merely contracts for defined services covered by the LGA 1988. This is because non-commercial considerations are unlawful if applied by an authority to consideration of all tenders received for the supply of goods and services.

The following decisions taken by a council during the tendering process can be interrogated using section 20:

  (i)   exclusion from an approved list from which potential tenderers will be selected;
 (ii)   refusal to invite to tender a person who has previously expressed an interest in doing so;
(iii)   refusal to accept the submission of a tender;
 (iv)   refusal to contract with a particular tenderer;

(v)   refusal to approve any person or company to act as a subcontractor for the purposes of any existing contract;

(vi)   termination of an existing contract.

The rights granted by section 20 go beyond the ability to demand details of the local authority's decision; the full reasons may be sought as well.

Section 20 rights are narrower than those in section 12 in only two ways: the class of persons who can use them is restricted and strict time limits apply to their exercise. The rights in section 20 benefit only those persons who are directly affected by the decision taken by the local authority; that is, the contractor or tenderer. Such a person is entitled to be notified as of right, and thus without having to lodge a request for it, of any decision of the type referred to above taken by the council concerning that person's continued involvement in the tender process or in performing the services. The recipient of such a notice then has 15 days from the date of the notice to require the local authority to issue a written statement of the reasons for the decision taken.

A contracting council must therefore inform every affected party of the decisions taken at each stage of the tendering process, and must also ensure the explanations are fully documented against the possibility of contractors seeking reasons or the Secretary of State intervening.

Councils and tendering companies alike seem largely ignorant of the extent of the duties and rights contained in section 20. As the competition to provide services to local authorities increases, the advantages of making greater use of these provisions to reduce the scope for protectionism of in-house council service organisations, and of section 12 to maximise knowledge of the competition, will doubtless dawn on all involved.

The case of *R v London Borough of Enfield, ex parte T. F. Unwin (Roydon) Ltd*[1] illustrates the full import of the duty to give reasons for contract-related decisions. The issue here was the temporary suspension of a contractor from the local authority's approved list of tenderers while corruption allegations were investigated. The removal from the list was deemed to give rise to the right for the company to receive the reasons for the action taken, notwithstanding police advice to the council that such revelations could prejudice the criminal investigation.

INTERVENTION BY THE SECRETARY OF STATE

Sections 13 and 14 of the LGA 1988 give the Secretary of State for the Environment specific powers in relation to local authority contracting for defined services. The same sanctions were created for construction and maintenance work by the LGA 1988 and incorporated into the LGPLA 1980 as the new sections 19A and 19B.

Section 13 of the LGA 1988 and section 19A of the LGPLA 1980

If it appears to the Secretary of State that a local authority has acted anti-competitively or irrationally in its tendering procedures or has failed to

---

1 [1989] 46 BLR 1.

fulfil any of the conditions in the LGA 1988 or LGPLA 1980, he or she can issue a notice requiring a written explanation of the council. Such a notice is colloquially known as a section 13 notice in local government circles, irrespective of the service to which it relates.

The notice has two parts, the first stating the alleged contravention of the CCT regime and requiring the recipient authority to prove that the facts are not as understood by the Secretary of State or to justify the actions taken, the second demanding specified information to be supplied. A period of one month is given for compliance.

The basis for the issue of a section 13 notice is commonly a complaint from an aggrieved contractor, since the process instigated by the Secretary of State provides an effective mechanism whereby marginal decisions by local authorities can be investigated and remedied effectively without the costs inherent for a contractor in mounting any other form of legal challenge.

The primary complaints resulting in section 13 notices are the costs loaded on external tenderers' bids under the evaluation process, contract packaging (in the main relating to overly large contracts for which only the largest companies in the country could practicably bid, rather than multiple smaller contracts, which for most services pass without contractor comment), onerous contract conditions or specifications and the compulsory requirement to use an existing council depot or vehicle fleet or the lack of a facility for all tenderers to make use of existing council buildings and plant.

The one issue giving rise to section 13 notices at the unprompted behest of the Secretary of State is the failure of a council DLO or DSO, having been awarded work in compliance with the CCT regimen, to achieve the regulated rate of return (or surplus) on their accounts, which have to be submitted annually by every local authority, or, worse still, incurring overall losses.

The Department of the Environment and the Scottish or Welsh offices that have responsibility for notices issued under these powers outside England seem to have adopted a practice of informal contact with authorities before considering the preparation of a formal notice. Nevertheless, a substantial number of section 13 notices have been issued since 1988, without any apparent regard for the political allegiances of the recipient authorities. In the main the explanations given or the assurances provided as to future activities appear to have satisfied the Secretary of State and further intervention remains the exception. Hence the exploration of section 14 notices below is a study of the worst cases of anti-competitive practice and DSO failure, rather than any indicator of the response of the average local authority to CCT.

One response to a section 13 notice is noteworthy for local authority tender evaluation. York City Council have argued, successfully, since no further intervention resulted, that among other financial factors that may legitimately be taken into account are the additional supervision and monitoring costs arising should the contract pass to an external tenderer. The DoE has since made it clear that only fully justified costs of this type can avoid being branded anti-competitive.

Section 14 of the LGA 1988 and section 19B of the LGPLA 1980

Further powers to intervene exist wherever the Secretary of State is dissatisfied with the explanation offered by a local authority in response to a section

13 notice or no response is forthcoming within the time limit. The range of actions available to the Secretary of State is very broad. Retendering may be ordered, an in-house bid can be precluded and a DSO can even be closed down as soon as it ceases to keep its accounts in surplus; previously under the LGPLA 1980 only financial failure over two successive years could justify an instruction to close a DSO.

These powers are being invoked increasingly frequently to enforce the closure of loss-making DSOs. The London boroughs of Camden, Kingston-upon-Thames and Hillingdon and a number of district councils have received section 14 notices for failure to achieve the required rate of return. Other local authorities have been forced to retender contracts as a result of complaints about costs taken into account in the evaluation process. The London Borough of Haringey's refuse collection contract was removed from the DSO in consequence of anti-competitive behaviour by the council in awarding the work in-house in the face of bids lower than that of the DSO (see below). Boston, Chester, Doncaster, East Lindsey, Gosport, Hammersmith and Fulham, Langborough-on-Tees, Liverpool, South Tyneside, Stockton-on-Tees, Thurrock, Waltham Forest and Woodspring are further examples of forced retendering for manual services while Lambeth and Portsmouth are recent examples in the field of housing management.

The extent of the Secretary of State's powers has been tested in the courts following the service of section 14 directions. The impact of the judgment[1] against Knowsley is assessed below.

Analysis of complaints to Secretary of State

From 1994/5 statistics of the complaints of anti-competitive behaviour received by the DoE, 48.5 per cent concerned TUPE issues (applicability of the regulations or staffing information supplied by councils), 8.7 per cent related to onerous contract terms, 7.7 per cent were allegations of mis-attributed or exaggerated costs taken into account in evaluation, 5.9 per cent were about resourcing disputes, 3.9 per cent related to contract packaging decisions taken by the council and 3.9 per cent were general inferences of misconduct arising from the acceptance of other than the lowest bid. For the mathematicians, this leaves 17.5 per cent as unclassifiable complaints.

The Knowsley Borough Council case

Knowsley Borough Council, Leicester City Council and York City Council each received bids for refuse collection lower than the prices submitted by their respective DSOs. Each authority chose to award the work to its own DSO. The Secretary of State formed the view that some of the financial factors brought into the evaluation exercises conducted by the authorities, including the value of enhanced severance terms voluntarily agreed by the authorities with their work-forces and the loss of profits that would be generated were the services to be secured from the DSO and the appropriate

1 *Regina v Secretary of State for the Environment, ex parte Knowsley Borough Council* (1991) The Times, 28 May QBD.

rate of return achieved, should not have been taken into account, in consequence of which the councils' actions had distorted fair competition. Section 14 notices were issued requiring the councils to retender the contracts and to obtain the Secretary of State's consent before taking any decision to award the work in-house again.

The three authorities began judicial review proceedings against the Secretary of State. They argued that they had acted reasonably and in good faith, and that any cost falling to them as a consequence of the contract being awarded to an external tenderer could properly be evaluated and considered.

Mr Justice Popplewell in the High Court determined that the only issue for the court was not whether the councils had acted reasonably but whether the Secretary of State had acted reasonably and within the constraints of the powers granted to him by Parliament. He found the Secretary of State had been entrusted with the responsibility to determine what constituted anti-competitive behaviour and no fetters had been placed on his discretion. He, not the local authorities, was the arbiter of whether any given action restricted or distorted competition, and his decisions in the circumstances under consideration must stand, however reasonable might be the arguments of the authorities that they were being precluded from considering the true costs of an external contract. The judgment was expressed in terms sympathetic to the predicament in which the authorities found themselves, but in only one respect did the judge find against the Secretary of State. He ruled the requirement to seek express consent before reawarding the work in-house was *ultra vires*.

The matter was subsequently considered following appeals lodged by the authorities and the Secretary of State. The arguments of the former were again rejected, but the cross appeal of the Secretary of State succeeded. The prohibition on considering DSOs' bids without his consent was held to properly serve the purposes of the empowering legislation and thus such a proviso could lawfully be included in a section 14 direction.

The lesson to be drawn from the case is that if the Secretary of State forms a hostile view of an authority's actions in relation to any part of the tendering process, the requirements of any section 14 notice are unlikely to be challengeable, given the breadth of discretion granted by statute, and must be obeyed, however unpalatable.

This view of the Secretary of State's powers was subsequently upheld by the Court of Appeal in 1994 in a challenge by Haringey to a section 14 notice requiring retendering of a refuse collection contract and a prohibition on awarding in-house without consent.

Avoidance of intervention

The existence of the powers of intervention is yet another reminder of the need for local authorities to use demonstrably impartial evaluation practices and to adequately document the process. For DSOs, the willingness of the Secretary of State to consider invoking his powers and close loss-making organisations demonstrates that underbidding may be as dangerous, given the short-term focus on achieving the winning tender, as overpricing in the face of external competitors.

In closing, it is worth noting that the LGA 1992 (Commencement

Number 2) Order 1992[1] clarifies any uncertainty as to the Secretary of State's ability to intervene prior to DSO commencement of the service. The Order empowers intervention as soon as the relevant decision upon tenders is taken.

Challenges by in-house staff

It has generally been assumed that the only actions open to local authority staff displaced by contracting out are to allege unfair selection for redundancy or unfair dismissal in a TUPE situation.

Staff of Brent's refuse collection operation have found a new avenue by requiring the District Auditor to investigate the award of a contract to a company submitting a tender £1 million higher than the in-house bid. This raised an external examination of the council justification which was founded in the need to achieve improvements in quality over the low standards perceived to attach to the DSO's performance.

A more unusual argument still is to be found in the case of *R v Walsall Metropolitan Borough Council, ex parte Yapp and Another*[2]. The council, following tendering, awarded building work to its in-house workforce. Subsequently economic pressures and the apparent downward movement of building prices persuaded the council to retender much of the work. Two affected employees claimed that the action was a breach of a public duty to act fairly to its workforce. The Court of Appeal found the council's actions were not in breach of such a duty, if any existed. The council's statutory responsibilities to its community charge payers and tenants and the rational grounds for reviewing its earlier decision were sufficient to defeat the employees' claims. In essence if the council had sound reasons for a contracting decision affecting its workforce, and providing it undertook proper consultation, it was secure from challenge of this type.

Complaints to the Ombudsman

An alternative for small firms who are more interested in seeking compensation than retendering may be to complain to the Ombudsman rather than to the Secretary of State. Initial hurdles will be the need to demonstrate maladministration in a procedural sense and to produce a reasoned argument to demonstrate that it would be unreasonable to expect them to pursue a remedy (if any) through the courts. Once these have been surmounted, complainants may find the Local Government Ombudsman receptive to recommending that a council pay compensation. While such recommendations cannot be enforced unless the council agrees, they have strong evidentiary value if court proceedings then follow.

By way of example, in a complaint brought against the London Borough of Barnet (reported as case number 26/A/1233 in JPL May 1989) a small building firm which had for years, apparently satisfactorily, carried out small building works for the council, was excluded from the council's new list of approved contractors. The council refused to give reasons (this was prior to the duty to do so contained in the LGA 1988) but to the

1 SI 1992 No. 3241.
2 Times Law Reports, 6 August 1993.

Ombudsman cited poor performance. The Ombudsman found little evidence to justify exclusion and deemed the failure to carry out a thorough open investigation before removal from the select list was maladministration. Compensation was recommended and secured together with an apology for the complainant firm.

CARTELS

Lest it be thought that it is only ever local authorities who may be accused of acting anti-competitively, mention must be made of price-fixing by cartels. Essentially this involves companies organising themselves to agree who should bid for which contract and at what price.

An investigation into contracts let by the government's own Property Services Agency (reported on 30 January 1994 in the *Independent on Sunday*) concluded that eleven companies which had won 40 per cent of the PSA's grounds maintenance contracts had entered into an illegal restrictive trading agreement operating from 1976 if not earlier. Seven of the named contractors were also significantly active in the local authority market place.

This is not the only area in which cartels are known to have operated. The supply of windows and glass is another which is believed to have cost councils hundreds of thousands of pounds since 1980.

While proving the existence of cartels is difficult even using the Local Government Management Board's contract index to determine patterns across the whole country, a local authority suspecting price-rigging should not hesitate to contact the Office of Fair Trading.

Chapter 7

CLIENT AND CONTRACTOR SEPARATION AND ORGANISATION

It is considerably easier to deal with private-sector companies at arm's length than to demonstrate fairness and impartiality in reaching contracting decisions when an in-house service organisation is involved. A DSO or DLO is part of the council, its staff are council employees and the surpluses it generates are the council's to use as it deems fit. Given these factors, it is unsurprising that contractors tend to assume councils will be biased in favour of their own service organisations.

This chapter explores the nature of DSOs and DLOs with particular reference to the extent of separation from their parent local authority's client function (carrying out specification and monitoring) that is necessary to minimise conflicts of interest and allegations of anti-competitive behaviour. It takes into account that there is no specific legislative requirement for services provided in-house prior to the documentation of CCT to be subject to a hard-and-fast division of staff into those performing client functions and those performing services or supervising others doing so, but that both the DoE and the Audit Commission have stated a preference for a clean split between the two types of function. Indeed, regulations will henceforth enforce complete separation of responsibilities for the process of organising and evaluating tendering from those who are submitting bids.

THE FUNCTIONAL IMPLICATIONS OF COMPETITIVE TENDERING

The normal hierarchical structures in local authorities are based on individual divisions or directorates, each responsible for the strategic management of allied groups of services and for the actual performance of those services. The role of a director or chief officer and of manual workers employed within such a structure can be clearly defined as that of either a strategic planner and monitor (client) or a service provider and supervisor (contractor). In between lurks a range of officers whose functions blur this distinction. Even senior managers tend to provide direct services within their professional expertise to other departments or the public and to have a supervisory role over other direct service staff as well as performing corporate or strategic tasks on behalf of the council. Competitive tendering is targeted on the delivery of the service, including the deployment of resources and the supervision of staff, rather than the management of the function itself, the need for which will persist regardless of whether the service is provided in-house or contracted out.

The duty placed on the local authority is to cost its in-house service delivery in isolation from functional management and to compare such costs with external competitors through the tendering process in order to obtain the lowest price practicable for the future execution of the work. This necessitates achieving a workable and justifiable separation of management costs from those of service delivery, but does not necessarily require that individual in-house employees dedicate their working hours entirely to either the client functions of the council or to service delivery. The only requirement is that a fair apportionment of the cost of employing each officer with dual responsibilities is undertaken. Such an officer with client as well as contractor responsibilities is commonly referred to as one wearing two hats and thus one apparently facing conflicts of interest in the course of performing his or her job. The more staff who are twin-hatted, the greater the risk of challenge to the accuracy of the individual trading accounts required to be created and maintained in respect of each defined activity under the LGPLA 1980, LGA 1988 or LGA 1992, or of accusations by external contractors of favouritism towards in-house service organisations.

For reasons of practicality, it becomes incumbent upon local authorities to consider disentangling client and contractor functions as far as possible while balancing the benefits of any consequent structural changes against the potential increase in costs that may result. There is a range of options between the two extremes of maintaining the existing structure (while isolating the management cost from service delivery by apportioning all affected officers between the two functions) and of creating completely self-contained client and contractor units. The absolute separation of responsibility is commonly referred to as a hard split, in which no officers below director or chief officer level wear two hats. A discussion of the merits and disadvantages of separating client and contractor to differing degrees follows the analysis of the functions and responsibilities of client and contractor set out below.

THE CLIENT FUNCTIONS

The client's interest should lie in the strategic planning of future services and their nature, not with operational detail; essentially addressing the questions why, what and where, rather than how and when—concerns that should, in the main, be left to the contractor.

Having determined the public need for the service and balanced it against predicted affordability, the client's main task is to specify the level of service to be contracted and, having tendered it, to monitor the performance of the successful contractor and ensure the council receives, so far as possible, the full services specified to the proper standard.

In preparing for competition client officers will determine the level of service required, set clear and well-defined standards for the service, specify the times and frequency of services where these are important and set any organisational requirements or working methods essential to maintaining the standard of the service, while attempting to minimise any restriction of possibilities for innovation and cost saving by tenderers that may produce financial benefits for the council.

The client will obviously then be responsible for preparing the contract documents, determining the contract period, setting the measure of inflationary uplift to be applied periodically to tender prices, determining the treatment of existing council assets, settling the default and termination safeguards to encourage maximum contractor compliance with the contract and reviewing the advisability of seeking collateral guarantees or performance bonds from successful tenderers.

These duties run on into controlling the tendering process from advertisement to evaluation and contract award. The client will determine the criteria for selection of tenderers, handle the taking up of references, provide the contact point for communication with tenderers, check the legality of other local authority bids (the contracting authority having the same duty to act lawfully in order to avoid the risk of challenges or surcharge as the authorities wishing to submit cross-boundary tenders; see Chapter 10) and ensure there is no distortion of competition.

Following the award of a contract to an external tenderer or the decision to retain the DSO or DLO to perform the work, the tasks of creating and managing a contractual relationship (or quasi-contractual if the work is awarded in-house) fall to the client, who must establish appropriate monitoring arrangements to verify compliance with the specification without incurring excessive costs.

None of the functional tasks outlined above can be controlled by officers whose allegiance is owed to a DSO or DLO tendering for the work. The extent to which DSO or DLO staff can be utilised to assist the client side will be discussed after the principal functions of in-house contracting organisations have been examined.

THE IN-HOUSE CONTRACTOR'S FUNCTIONS

The DSO or DLO facing competitive tendering will have to adopt an attitude increasingly akin to that of a private-sector commercial undertaking, but one with an intensity of focus, if not desperation, to win the one tendering exercise that will determine its continued existence or demise. Its main interest will therefore lie in assessing the workability of the draft specification, reducing the costs of wages, control of expenditure and recharges for council support (such as legal, personnel, financial and computer services) and gathering market intelligence as to its likely competitors.

Prior to tendering, managers will concentrate on assessing the existing cost of direct service provision, consider means of reducing net labour costs by improving productivity, reduce absenteeism and, if necessary, negotiate changes to contractual conditions of employment, examine the use of assets and re-examine all overheads.

After achieving a competitive level of operation, the next task is to cost the specification to be tendered and submit a bid. If the DSO tender is accepted, functional tasks will then revolve around operational contract management and maintaining or improving financial viability so as to fulfil any mandatory measure of performance, such as the rate of return on capital employed, which has been specified as a target for individual defined activities. Thereafter essentially the contractor functions as a simple service provider and is excluded from all activity that would continue were the contract to be awarded to a private concern and the local authority to cease to employ staff on direct service provision.

PRACTICAL CLIENT AND CONTRACTOR SEPARATION

Bearing in mind the goals of arm's-length arrangements and independent inspection and quality control to allay external tenderers' suspicion of bias, local authorities are likely to wish to effect a client-contractor split such that no DSO staff retain significant client responsibilities and only the most senior officers on the client side continue to be twin-hatted. If this is done prior to tendering and the contract is awarded externally, the need for further hurried restructuring in the run-up to the new contractor commencing provision of the services will be avoided and the DSO's management will be free to concentrate on operational matters, productivity and costs, and will be empowered to pursue a more commercial approach with less corporate restrictions on initiative.

Purity of separation will not be achievable in all cases. Decisions on timing and extent of separation will require a degree of pragmatism to be exercised if increased costs are to be avoided (especially within services employing small numbers of staff) and if the client side is to be enabled to call upon the full range of available professional expertise for the purpose of initial specification activity. To separate contractor functions too early or too completely will serve only to disable the client officers from producing the best contract documents to protect the council's interests. Even the use of external consultancy support cannot replicate the expertise and geographical knowledge of those staff who have already been performing the service for a length of time.

A strict separation of client and internal contractor will not normally be effected until the first draft of the specification of the service is complete. The need will arise to demonstrate that the input of officers later transferring to the emergent DSO properly serves the interest of the council in securing a quality service rather than being designed to render external companies less likely to tender or prove competitive. The fact that finalising the specification is controlled by officers remaining on the client side may be insufficient. There are two other ways to demonstrate impartiality. The first is to secure an overview of the adequacy of the draft specification from specialist external consultants and the second is to secure the views of the potential tenderers themselves by building in consultation on the draft contract documentation, as outlined in Chapter 3.

Even then the level of staffing may not lend itself to absolute separation and the cost implications for small functions, including professional support services, may be dramatic. It may remain necessary for the client function to use contracting staff, having due regard to the possibility of such actions being misinterpreted, or for structures to be evolved combining the client functions for two or more disciplines or merging potential service organisations to create multidisciplinary DSOs within which economies of scale may be achieved.

ORGANISATIONAL SOLUTIONS FOR CONTRACTING FUNCTIONS

After the necessity of some degree of separation between client and contractor has been determined, the respective position of each within the local authority needs to be considered. The starting point for most local authorities is a situation in which DSOs or potential DSOs are part of a professional directorate or department that also fulfils the fledgling client functions it is endeavouring to define for the first time. Such situations may remain cost-effective in larger local authorities, but the need to achieve economies of scale and establish the cultural change implicit in implementing CCT may force consideration of integrated DSOs, bringing together multiple functions or service responsibilities under a single director or manager. The main options, other than retaining independent DSOs or keeping them within the same department as the client function, are to integrate like functions that can be effectively managed together or to integrate all of the services subject to competition into one contracting organisation. The latter approach may suffice in respect of manual functions, but is unlikely to prove as effective a means of managing professional services.

Multifunctional or integrated DSOs

Multifunctional DSOs are common in shire district councils because the scale of the individual operations is frequently too small to attract or justify the employment of skilled business managers otherwise. Integrated DSOs in district councils appear to be no larger in terms of the number of staff employed than most of the individual DSOs within London, city and other metropolitan authorities, and are usually considerably smaller than such operations as catering, cleaning, grounds maintenance and highways DSOs within county councils. An examination of such authorities as Rochdale, Bradford, Wolverhampton, St Helens, Southampton, Northamptonshire, Sutton, Hammersmith and Fulham, Bromley, Greenwich, Camden, Hillingdon, Newham, Nottingham, Sheffield, Thameside, Kirklees, Stockport, Northumberland and Manchester, which are the main local authorities in England and Wales with established multifunctional DSOs (although the Kirklees approach is markedly different from the others), identifies a number of relevant factors in the timing and method of creation of the structure that has materialised.

Timing and method of integrating contractor functions

Many integrated DSOs started to evolve when the LGA 1988 came into force, with the contract activity passing to them as services prepared for tendering or contracts were won. In such cases all of the cost implications of the contracting directorate structure were apportioned into the contract bids rather than being imposed as an additional unforeseen cost for a successfully tendering DSO. However, some integrated DSOs have been created more recently as a response to particular contractor–client difficulties or following worrying failure to secure adequate work by winning tenders.

Some authorities appear to have political reasons for creating integrated

DSOs, either to establish robust and very strong contracting organisations with otherwise unavailable freedom of operation and decision, or to create commercial organisations to expand beyond the confines of local authority work, resulting in eventual management buy-out or sale to the private sector.

Nature of activities subject to integration

The nature and diversity of the activity performed by integrated service organisations is also of interest. The majority of integrated DSOs within the identified authorities cover all of the services subject to compulsory competition except for leisure services. Each authority appears now to face the decision whether to bring in leisure, to create a stand-alone leisure DSO or to create a separate multifunctional white-collar DSO for all tendered professional services.

There are, of course, exceptions to this. Bromley Contractor Services has a narrower spread of activities than most as a result of the loss of several contracts to external tenderers and the fact that catering has not moved across while the leisure contractor has become a stand-alone DSO. Other authorities, such as Manchester and Nottingham, have chosen to have two DSOs, each with directorate status, one for housing maintenance (because of the scale of their operations) and another for other compulsory tendered activities. Nottingham is particularly unusual in that certain legal, financial, audit and information technology services are integrated into a single DSO alongside catering, cleaning and central supplies services. The professional services appear to be in existence primarily to support the other DSO activities, with spare capacity being sold to small council departments unable to justify their own devolved professional functions.

Integrated DSO structure and costs

All integrated DSOs appear to be headed by a manager with directoral status, and the pivotal importance of retaining a person of the right calibre is borne out by the level of salary paid. While the need to restrain costs is recognised, support staff including personal assistants and a number of general managers or assistant directors are common and each activity is almost invariably headed by a contract or service manager.

Wherever possible, DSO support services have been brought into the directorate. Most have in-house financial, personnel and computer staff. One or two have dedicated lawyers. All claim to have covered part of the cost of the directorate structures by savings in central recharges, which are commonly claimed to be greater than the cost of employing the same staff within the DSO. There is no empirical evidence to justify this supposition.

Most of the integrated DSOs expect to be permitted to bring in-house at least some of the services formerly provided centrally and DSO directors need to be empowered in relation to standing orders and financial regulations to a degree otherwise unusual in local authorities. They expect to be able, without reference to committee, to re-invest a percentage of surpluses in the service, to subcontract works (up to £100,000 was a figure mentioned by three authorities), without requiring further consents and to negotiate their own conditions with their workforces. Integrated DSOs claim varying degrees of success and attribute this greatly to the importance of building bridges with client departments to replace those lost in a structural client–contractor split.

Advantages and disadvantages of integration

The principal advantage claimed is a clearer separation of client and contractor than is possible where both are situated within the same department. That said, there are authorities that now believe that the emphasis on strengthening an integrated DSO has been achieved only at the cost of the service provision, so that generation of financial surpluses, rather than enabling service quality to be maintained or increased, becomes the driving factor of the authority. Thus the advantage seen by some authorities becomes the disadvantage identified by others.

Economies of scale have been claimed by some authorities, in particular in relation to the provision of services formerly provided centrally. No real evidence is available that such economies existed, let alone of sufficient magnitude to cover the expanded costs of employing an integrated DSO director and relevant support staff. However, improving the quality of management is a claimed benefit that is supported by the extent to which some authorities, who were previously unable to do so, have reviewed staffing levels, labour rates, bonus systems and restrictive practices, overcoming the previous stranglehold maintained by trade unions or councillors.

Cross-fertilisation of trading practices between DSO activities may yield benefits, and some authorities claim a new level of flexibility between work-forces. Such flexibility may be extremely limited in practice, given that each defined activity must maintain a self-supporting trading account.

The one almost universal advantage claimed has been the devolution of far greater control to the integrated DSO. Freedom to operate commercially appears to have been frequently embraced with enthusiasm, but there is a negative side in that disputes between client and contractor within a local authority can become more frequent and increasingly bitter. Concern about the relationship is common and is often blamed on an overzealous client side endeavouring to demonstrate impartiality towards the DSO.

Integrated DSOs may benefit from increased freedom to establish their own relationships with other semi-autonomous authority services, particularly schools, where the need to channel their services through third parties ceases. The ability to offer packages of services, usually combining catering, cleaning and grounds maintenance, might appear a particular advantage.

To an extent the concept of responsive service is under threat, as is evidenced by the increasing withdrawal of integrated DSOs from neighbourhood offices and depots in search of new economies, but this tends to be a feature of competitively tendered services, however delivered.

In summary, the main advantage claimed was the clarity of the separation from the client, and the main disadvantage was the costs implicit in an integrated DSO structure.

Success and failure of integration

Examining the measures by which the success or otherwise of an integrated DSO is judged yields lessons in itself. From the DSO viewpoint, success can be judged only by in-house retention of contracts and thus survival, and then by the rate of return achieved and the surpluses generated. Client-side officers appear to perceive these surpluses to constitute monies extracted from the services and not necessarily returned corporately when surpluses are redistributed. The commonest view is that creating an integrated DSO increases rigidity within the organisation and impedes alternative methods of service provision through such mechanisms as management buy-outs and privatisation. These are seen as best achieved in single specialisms where low costs or a niche product or service is the order of the day.

In a larger authority with few obvious problems from historic staffing levels or working practices, the functions subject to CCT may require no major upheaval beyond clarification of client and contractor roles and the existing DSO will be able to produce winning tenders with the complementary thrust of willing staff input and trade union co-operation. Where historic problems exist, compulsory tendering itself may be sufficient to secure trade union agreements in relation to revised conditions and pay systems where necessary.

In such an authority, while it would be possible to examine central service recharges to determine the likelihood of economies of scale if a multidisciplinary DSO were to be considered, the insuperable problem is funding the cost of a new director and support staff when the individual DSOs have obtained a fixed income from contracts secured in competition and there is no obvious room for sufficient increases in productivity to cover additional organisational overheads. In essence, the risk in creating an integrated structure is that the additional cost will not be balanced by achievable economies of scale or business efficiencies and the loss of individual contracts by such a cumbersome merged operation will artificially inflate the overheads to be borne by other areas of work within the organisation, which would be likely to lead to further contract failures in a domino effect.

An alternative to a completely integrated DSO has been established in Kirklees. There the organisation comprises a handful of directorates managing a number of individual business units. Each has a high degree of empowerment in its own specialism. Some of the business units are DSOs, others are not. Most of the DSOs are grouped for convenience under a particular director, a solution that does not have heavy cost implications, since the directors were already employed, and which offers the possibility of impartial directors over the DSOs since the client responsibilities of each relate to other services. It is perhaps surprising that more authorities have not experimented with such an approach.

CLIENT ORGANISATION

The notion of integration may be applied to client responsibilities as well as to DSOs. Indeed, creating multidisciplinary client teams for monitoring contracts may yield not only economies of scale but also useful flexibility. For example, if particular contracts are progressing smoothly, monitoring resources can be concentrated for periods of time on a single or problematic service in the hope that intensive monitoring will turn it around and secure fuller compliance with the specification in the longer term to the benefit of the council and its customers.

COMMITTEE ORGANISATION

Local authority structures and democratic processes have inevitably been dominated by the mechanisms and minutiae of service delivery. CCT can be a tool to break into that stultification. As has been demonstrated, it necessitates a degree of independence for DSOs from detailed control or restriction and forges a new client mentality, concentrated on the larger picture, the future of service needs, proper specification and adequate monitoring systems.

A similar separation of client and contractor functions or of corporate and strategic issues from service delivery applied to councillor involvement in local authority decision-making is an obvious development from such processes. Some local authorities have already set up a client–contractor split at member level, with small contract services boards comprising members who are not chairperson, vice-chairperson or opposition leaders on service committees.

In a circular letter dated 16 June 1992 the DoE put forward detailed proposals for future regulation of CCT, which included a requirement that elected members who sit on a DSO board or a committee with a responsibility for the preparation or approval of the DSO tender should not henceforth be members of a committee or subcommittee that has responsibility for, or takes decisions in relation to, the selection of publications for advertising the tendering of the service, the selection of contractors, the distribution of tender documents, the receipt of tenders and tender evaluations.

These proposals were not brought into effect. Instead guidance was issued by the DoE on 12 December 1994 to the effect that councillors should treat any involvement in overseeing the activities of a DSO as if it were a private or personal interest. Under the National Code of Local Government Conduct, when a councillor is serving on a committee with decisions to make on awarding contracts, the existence of such an interest should lead to formal disclosure and if appropriate withdrawal from the discussion. Responsibility is thus pushed back by the DoE on to the individual members of a council and the officers charged with advising them.

Chapter 8

INTERNAL COUNCIL CONSIDERATIONS IN THE IMPLEMENTATION OF CCT

Apart from special tendering requirements and the potential separation of client and contractor functions, much of the internal impact of CCT on local authorities arises from changes in attitude implicit in or consequent on the LGPLA 1980, LGA 1988 and LGA 1992. Despite a paucity of explicit mandatory requirements, sufficient strands of commonality occur within the range of responses made by local authorities to demonstrate steps clearly viewed as necessary to comply with, or, so far as it is lawful to do so, to avoid, the government's intentions for the future provision of council services.

This chapter outlines the further structural and conceptual changes brought about by the implementation of CCT and the divergent goals for direct service provision and for contract management, whether the work is awarded in-house following tendering or not. The chapter is divided into issues for DSOs and those for client functions, followed by an examination of the shared interest in improved financial management information.

DSO CONSIDERATIONS

The perspective of a DSO towards CCT is necessarily focused on producing a tender able to win the work from other external bidders and, having done so, to keep the costs within the limits of its own tender while achieving any financial objectives specified by the Secretary of State. Accordingly, this section concentrates on factors affecting the viability of DSO tenders. In particular, it examines the types of cost falling to be met by the DSO and the relationship with the client function once it has competed successfully and must work in a quasi-contractual manner within the parent local authority.

DSO costs

The primary costs to be taken into account will be the wages and salaries of the staff directly employed in providing the service and their line management, together with the additional costs of their employment. Taken with the other overheads the DSO must bear, including administration, transport, buildings and support services, whether provided by central service department staff or other DSOs, these constitute the debits to the trading account.

Staffing costs will comprise the total of all DSO wages and salaries, national insurance and the employer's superannuation contributions, and the costs of payroll services and essential training.

Additional overheads fall into three broad categories: those resulting from accommodation, those arising from use of plant and equipment, and those pertaining to support services. Accommodation costs will cover the office and depot space given over to DSO use, business rates, electricity and gas, service contract expenditure, furniture, telephones and fax, cleaning, security, reception and possibly other services if an integrated facilities management package is offered. Plant and equipment costs should bring into the equation fuel and other travel costs as well as consumable items. Support services will include accountancy and audit, advertising, computors, legal services, personnel, postage, printing, stationery and typing.

Additional overheads may arise from any departmental costs, including any time spent by the chief officer or director on management of the DSO, and any of the democratic costs properly attributable to committee involvement in DSO activity.

Compiling bids

Present costs, including overheads, are only the starting point in the compilation of a tender for submission as part of the competition process. The next task is to assess the extent to which the specification represents a departure from the present levels and types of service. Any changes to known frequencies and programming, the identified level of capital works, set standby arrangements and the consequent fixed overheads should pose no pricing problems. Unplannable changes to routine and emergency works pose the greatest difficulties in setting sustainable staffing levels and thus estimating likely future costs.

Consideration can then be given to any productivity savings that may be achieved and any scheduling or procedural means of reducing costs that could, in return, provide scope for reducing the price to be submitted if the pre-tender costings appear to the DSO management to offer a less than acceptable chance of winning the work.

Next, any contingency sums and the calculation of the statutory rate of return that has to be achieved must be added, together with any loading for risks arising from potential variations to the volume of work in the contract specification and consequent loss of contract income.

Finally, any income accruing to the tenderer as a result of performing the services can be netted off the total price. In this context local authority client officers can choose to allow fee income paid by the public in relation to the tendered services to be collected and retained by the contractor, thus effectively reducing all the bids to be received, or to have the contractor account for such income and return it to the council.

Hopefully, the result is a DSO tender that can bear comparison with the private sector. If not, attempts will have to be made, immediately prior to submitting the tender, to reduce staffing costs and any other overheads capable of variation.

Tendering will be easier if a schedule of rates is to be completed by each tenderer, as riskier items of work can be individually loaded. However, if high-risk work constitutes more than 20 per cent of the overall cost of performing a given contract, private-sector companies are likely to deem the contract poorly specified and not a commercial proposition for anything other than perhaps an overly inflated price.

Specification reviews

Careful consideration of the specification is a vital prerequisite of tender preparation for a DSO. It is only too easy to bid on the basis of the level of service currently provided or the level that the DSO believes the client wants rather than on the basis of the precise wording of the service as specified. This is an instance where inside knowledge is a positive drawback which can lead to loss of the contract by overbidding.

In addition it is vital to adopt a principle which will be followed rigidly by the private sector. This is to treat the minimum standards set by the specification as the maximum which will be priced. Even then most tenderers will shave something off in recognition of the reality that the council's monitoring staff will not be resourced sufficiently to catch and default every single instance of under or non-performance.

Finally every requirement of the tendering process should be followed slavishly. It cannot be assumed that a DSO will be allowed to evade any requirement imposed on private-sector competitors as part of bidding and evaluation and staff time and resources within the DSO should be allocated accordingly.

Assessing hourly rates

Simple measurement of outcomes may suffice to assess the productivity of workers performing manual tasks for the purpose of submitting a bid for such an operation. With professional and other white-collar services, measurable results are not so readily assessable, so that tender preparation is less a matter of breaking down the service into unit costs than of estimating the number of chargeable hours achievable by staff handling particular types of work, and then ensuring that the hourly rate charged for each service element or the number of hours allowed for given tasks enables the recovery in full of all non-productive or lost time.

For example, in relation to legal services, the standard expectation of a solicitor or legal executive in private practice is 1,100 chargeable hours per year out of a total of 2,000 or more hours spent at work. In a local government context an officer employed full time for 52 weeks, working a 37-hour week (note that in London boroughs the working week is only 36 hours for white-collar staff), would be paid for 1,924 hours a year. An average of 270 hours would be lost to annual leave and public holidays, average sickness absence could account for another 37, training for 20, other non-productive time for another 106 and elections for 10 hours. This leaves 1,481 chargeable hours as the maximum achievable. Such a calculation, once overheads, so-called on-costs, are added, dramatically inflates what might at first appear the reasonable cost of employing a local government officer by comparison with the hourly rates charged by private-sector agencies.

Perhaps unsurprisingly in such circumstances, the key to recovering the full costs incurred in a professional DSO lies in proper time-recording so that chargeable hours are accurately assessed and the maximum legitimate income realised. Failure to account for time lost to particular clients, on travelling for example, could be particularly detrimental to the calculation of hourly rates to support a tender standing a reasonable chance of winning work and sustaining an in-house team.

Market intelligence

Gathering information as to the nature of the likely competition is an essential task for DSO management in the time immediately prior to submitting a bid for work. The vital consideration will be the level of wage rates paid by competing contractors already operating locally in the private sector, labour costs being both a major element of most local authority bids and also the single element most readily capable of being addressed by managers if the in-house team appears presently uncompetitive.

In the absence of minimum national wage rates there is no substitute for seeking information from large employers of in-house staff exercising similar functions and organisations buying in such services from external providers on the basis of set hourly rates. For example, all local companies occupying office and shop premises will require cleaning services and will either employ their own cleaning staff directly or deal with contract cleaners. Such organisations may well be prepared to exchange cost information, particularly if they are companies with which the local authority has established a relationship in respect of other services. For obvious reasons contractors likely to be in direct competition will be unlikely to provide such information; nor should they be approached lest it be assumed by a contractor that any information obtained will reach those client officers concerned with tender evaluation, in whose hands wage rates and conditions of service would constitute non-commercial considerations.

The gathering of such external cost comparisons with internal wage rates will enable managers to determine whether changes to contracts of employment and conditions of service need to be negotiated with staff groups. The process for, and consequences of, doing so are covered in Chapter 9.

Containment of support service costs

DSOs have to bear the true cost of support services provided to them even if the authority could not reduce its overall staffing and overheads to save all such costs were the contract to be let to an external contractor. The argument that DSOs should bear only the marginal costs of providing such support services receives no support from local authority codes of accountancy practice nor from the DoE. The elements of cost that cannot be saved no matter to whom the work is awarded are no longer even permissible evaluation factors for the client function to take into account.

This leaves open for review and discussion the level and quality of support services required by or imposed on a DSO and whether the recharges made for such services are a proper reflection of the true cost of providing them. Such reviews may well result in service-level agreements or service statements of the type discussed later in this chapter.

It must be appreciated that a DSO may be in a position to reduce its overall reliance upon support services, but cannot evade a fair recharge for other council officers ensuring propriety, such as the council's monitoring officer and the treasurer acting in fulfilment of the responsibilities laid down by section 151 of the LGA 1972. Nor can the DSO management necessarily expect the freedom to purchase support services from external providers, especially if the consequence is an overall increase in the costs of the local authority as a whole because the surplus capacity likely to be created would not result in commensurate redeployment or redundancy to achieve savings of the same order as the recharges formerly levied upon the DSO.

Purchasing

The acquisition of goods and services from external providers is frequently organised centrally within a local authority, and all departments, including their DSOs, may be required to use centralised ordering and stores. This may mean that a DSO is prevented from purchasing directly and may incur additional overheads attributable to the corporate operation that exceed any economies of scale achieved.

The corporate arguments for continuing such practices are likely to be similar to those deployed in respect of internally provided support services. If in the longer term the majority of users could achieve savings through direct purchasing, however, local authorities may have to accept that large purchasing and stores functions can no longer compete with the terms offered by suppliers of goods and services seeking to survive economic recession.

Contingencies

Inevitably, it will be necessary to build into the tender price some allowance for remote or unforeseen eventualities. For example, some allowance might be made for the extent to which the client side could cause cash-flow problems by withholding payment or requiring deficient work to be rectified without further payment. After all, organisations are seldom, if ever, likely to achieve absolute perfection in following a specification, not least because of the inevitable existence in service contracts of areas in which subjective decisions will fall to be made by monitoring staff.

The most serious consideration for a DSO is reserved for the interrelationship between pay settlements and any periodic tender price uplift for inflation set by the contract documents. It could be regarded as anti-competitive for contract arrangements to require tenderers to hold their prices static for the duration of an arrangement expected to last several years. The risk of insufficiently inflating the tender to generate sufficient profits in the early years to offset the inevitability of losses in future years as wages rise would tend to deter proper competition. Accordingly, most tendered contracts will include an objective measure of inflation by which prices will be raised at set intervals, usually on the anniversary of the agreement. The use of the retail price index is common, although certain trades use specialist inflation indices compounding different elements, such as labour, fuel and other particular materials or goods significantly utilised in providing the service, into an annual rise.

Unless a DSO has negotiated out of national conditions of service, it will have to contend with annual local authority pay bargaining geared towards other public-sector pay rises. This may lead to fluctuating levels of settlement in different years, depending on the comparable bargaining strength of the employer's and trade unions' positions. National pay increases for local government staff over the last 10 years show no constant correlation to the retail price index and if the latter forms the basis for determining tender price inflation, a local authority pay settlement even 1 per cent higher in any given year can significantly imperil a DSO's trading position unless a contingency exists for such fluctuations. The same is likely to be true whichever measure of inflation is utilised in the contract unless the uplift is geared to local authority pay settlements, a proposition that might be unacceptable to private-sector tenderers and may be questioned by the Secretary of State if it is made the subject of complaint.

The effect of any difference between the date on which council pay settlements are implementable or to which they are backdated and the date set in the contract documents for tender price uplift also needs to be assessed. DSOs will have to budget for the effect of pay increases in the period prior to the addition of the inflationary uplift to payments for the services.

Use of DSO surpluses

Whenever a DSO generates surpluses on its statutory accounts, whether through improvements to productivity, non-materialisation of contingencies allowed for in the bid or merely by achieving any applicable mandatory rate of return, it is for the council to determine how these are used. In the present climate of serious budgetary restrictions on local authority expenditure there will be pressure to divert such surpluses into corporately set service priorities. There are, however, arguments for maintaining at least part of those balances for the benefit of the DSO generating them. These include the payment of productivity-related bonuses to staff to stimulate further surpluses, reinvestment in equipment, cover for future risks and opportunities for research and development.

DSO image

The opportunities for a DSO to expand are limited by the restrictions upon carrying out work for authorities other than the parent local authority (see Chapter 10). Nevertheless, the chance of exploiting such openings as do exist and influencing other in-house departments to offer new work to the DSO may be improved by new logos and smart uniforms. These will present a confident face to everyone coming into contact with the DSO and its operatives. Such action linked to a sympathetic approach to persons for whose benefit services are provided may go a long way towards defusing, if not eliminating, complaints.

Contract management

From the DSO standpoint, contract management means satisfying the officers of the client function in respect of their reasonable expectations of service based on the specification while controlling costs and ensuring that all income to which the DSO is entitled accrues to its trading account.

With these aims in mind, once a DSO has been awarded the work following the tendering process, it will have to monitor carefully the services demanded of it and ensure that client requirements exceeding or departing from the specification, whether through formal variation orders or not, are appropriately costed by reference to the DSO's tender price and rates, and result in due payment being credited to the statutory accounts.

Variation orders may, of course, remove or diminish work covered by the specification, and in those circumstances the DSO management may wish to argue that a *pro rata* reduction in the monies payable in accordance with the tender is an inappropriate measure of the reduced reimbursement to which the DSO is entitled. It could be argued that the tender price should only be reduced by reference to the marginal cost of performing the work to be taken away if the DSO cannot achieve savings in labour and resources to compensate in full for the income to be removed. Clients need therefore to consider carefully before removing significant volumes of work from a DSO, just as for any external contractor, since any postulated savings may be offset in large part by lost economies of scale and dissent as to the level of clawback to be made from future DSO income. This underlines the fact that even a quasi-contractual relationship with a DSO brought about by formal tendering to a specification is far more rigidly incapable of being significantly amended than the former arrangements.

DSOs as subcontractors

Situations can arise where a local authority wishes to contract out works or services as one contract, some part of which could be carried out by a DSO. In those circumstances local authorities have within the main contract either treated the DSO as a nominated subcontractor or, if the subject matter is a defined activity, allowed the main contractor to include the DSO on its list of tenderers for the subcontract.

Local authority organisations have blithely assured councils that a DSO can act as a subcontractor to a private-sector company undertaking work for a local authority provided that the competition requirements of the LGPLA 1980 and LGA 1988 are met (broadly, that the main contractor solicits tenders from at least three parties other than the DSO). This view is based on the assumption that the DSO can be regarded as providing work or services not to the private-sector main contractor but to the parent local authority as the ultimate beneficiary of, and paymaster for, the contract.

Such a view relies on robust common sense, but may not be adequate protection in law against alleged *ultra vires*. The DSO in such a situation will have no quasi-contractual relationship with the council, as would be the case if it had tendered directly to the local authority. Instead, the only contractual links will be that tying the main contractor to the council and that binding the DSO to the main contractor. The strictly legalistic view may well be that the DSO can be regarded only as providing work or services to the private sector and thus needs to demonstrate that such work is a minor part of the total defined activity and one that can be carried out using spare capacity rather than constituting an arrangement entered into with profit as a prime motive (see Chapter 10 for a more detailed overview of the legal complexities affecting local authority provision to other bodies).

The safest course may be simply to tender any element of the work for which a DSO wishes to compete separately from the main contract and to accept the contractual risks inherent in having more than one main contractor on site (in particular, the loss of clear responsibility for all activity on the site and the possibility of claims for loss and expense occasioned by the actions of the other contractors involved).

Accounting requirements

The principal requirement of a DSO under section 9 of the LGA 1988 is to maintain a separate account for each defined activity. It is not a requirement to establish an account for each DSO. In consequence, if a particular defined activity is performed by more than one DSO, a single merged account can be kept; and if a DSO is multifunctional, it will have to maintain more than one separate and self-balancing account. It is equally true that if work falling within a single defined activity is obtained from different sources or from more than one tendering exercise, perhaps for other public bodies as well as the parent local authority, the costs attributable to all the activity and all the income can be amalgamated in one account. This gives the possibility of cross-subsidy, with potential losses from one arrangement recovered through further work in the same category.

Rates of return

Section 10 of the LGA 1988 empowers the Secretary of State to specify financial objectives to be achieved by DSOs for different defined activities. These targets take the form of a rate of return to be made on the value of capital employed in performing the service or, in some cases, a simpler requirement that costs shall not exceed income.

All services tendered under the LGPLA 1980 and most of those subject to competition under the LGA 1988 are required to break even after allowing for a 6 per cent per annum rate of return on capital assets employed by the DSO at current value. A circular letter from the DoE, dated 27 March 1991, requires the cost of leased assets (normally treated as revenue expenditure rather than as capital in local authority accounting) to be included for the purpose of calculating the return required.

Capital assets retained by the client side, such as buildings and vehicles, whose use is offered free to all potential tenderers, whether in-house or private sector, are not included in the valuation upon which a successful DSO has to achieve the rate of return. Similarly, where assets are offered to all tenderers at a subsidised cost, it is the actual charge levied, not the current value, that is brought into account.

Certain activities are not required to achieve a rate of return on capital employed, but must ensure that income equals or exceeds expenditure. This applies to building cleaning and leisure management. In the latter case, the income received includes any subsidy to the service made available to any tenderer.

Redundancy costs

DSO accounts have always had to bear the costs of making employees redundant during the currency of services won under CCT. Accordingly it has always been sound practice to make any structural changes to organisation before commencing the CCT process for the first time since there will be no DSO account in existence to charge those costs to and they cannot therefore adversely affect the future trading position. However, the same is not the case where a DSO submits a bid based on employing fewer staff than the number currently employed and notified to external contractors under the TUPE rules (see Chapter 9); the cost of these redundancies will fall on the trading account in the year the redundancies are made.

Annual reports

In each year a report on each defined activity under the LGA 1988 must be prepared and must include summary accounts. It must be available not later than six months after the end of the financial year to which it relates (that is, by 30 September) and the Secretary of State and District Auditor must receive copies not later than one calendar month after that. The report is a public document and must be open to inspection by any person free of charge. Its availability for inspection must be advertised and copies must be made available on request at a reasonable charge. The relevant statutory provisions regarding annual reports are to be found in sections 11 and 12 of the LGA 1988.

The Secretary of State has a power to define the form of report required for defined activities under the LGA 1988, but no equivalent power for LGPLA 1980 services. The DoE has stated its desire to obtain a degree of uniformity in annual reports by consent and has circulated local authority organisations with proposals to achieve this end.

The proposals for common information on LGPLA 1980 services cover a description of work, the contract start date, the level of combined work (work treated as construction and maintenance work by the council, using the powers in sections 18(1A)a and 20(5) of the Act to draw into tendering related activity not caught by the definitions in the Act), income and expenditure, the surplus or deficit achieved, the capital employed and the rate of return, the value of any emergency work or other functional work not won in competition, the values of functional work and works contracts won in competition, the value of work carried out by external contractors, the value of non-lowest tender work won by the DLO, the total staff numbers, the number of manual employees and, finally, a description of the action being taken wherever the rate of return has not been met.

The proposals for LGA 1988 defined activities are very similar. There is no reference to emergency work or functional work not won in competition, which are inapplicable, nor to the value of work carried out by external contractors. The only additional requirement is a statement of the level of duplicate activity undertaken (anything potentially falling within more than one category of defined activity which has been placed in one particular contract by virtue of a council decision under section 2(5) of the LGA 1988).

If a consensus is reached the DoE intends to issue a circular letter applying the new standardised annual reports to services provided in the municipal year 1993/4.

Standing orders and corporate policies

DSO managers and staff remain council employees and are bound to observe council standing orders and financial regulations as well as any applicable corporate policies. Consideration will have to be given to amending standing orders in favour of greater freedom for DSOs if they are presently overly restrictive.

A different problem arises from the creation of new corporate policies intended to apply to all council employees. A DSO will have tendered on the basis of known policies and their attendant costs at the time of preparing bids. DSOs must ensure that they are adequately consulted about any planned policies that may have the effect of increasing DSO costs, since the client side will be unable to intercept such increased costs unless they would bear similar *de facto* price increases from an external tenderer.

CLIENT CONSIDERATIONS

The client emphasis so far has rested on the processes of specification, inviting tenders and awarding contracts. When these tasks are completed, in many respects the client function has a narrower focus of interest than a DSO. Within the parameters of a requirement to act reasonably in maintaining a workable relationship with the successful tenderer, be it DSO or an external agency, client officers need have no particular regard to the effect of their requirements on the selected contractor's costs. The tasks are to assess the extent to which the contractor is fulfilling the contract specification and require action to rectify defaults based on the rights retained in the conditions of contract. This section addresses the key decisions, other than specification, falling to be taken by client officers prior to tendering and examines the differences in monitoring a DSO as opposed to the pure contractual relationship existing with a successful external tenderer.

Use of assets

An issue to be determined before inviting bids for a service is the extent to which assets are to be regarded as retained by the client or placed at the absolute disposal of the DSO. There is considerable merit in making such assets as depots, plant and specialist vehicles available to any successful tenderer wishing to use them on equal terms. DoE guidance is that, so far as practicable, external contractors should not be precluded from using council assets nor forced to do so. Even potential redevelopment should not prevent consideration of short-term usage of depots by successful external tenderers, since inability to quickly establish a local base of operations in a new geographical location is deemed a common impediment to many firms who might otherwise consider tendering for local authority work.

Since any rental value placed upon tenderer use of council assets will only bounce back in the form of an increased cost in the bids (presumably with an added element for profit), consideration can be given to allowing use at no cost. The bonus to the DSO, which will not have to generate a rate of return upon such assets, is offset by the evaluation consequences discussed in Chapter 3 and the new draft guidance which encourages commercial asset rentals.

Contingency planning

Whereas for a DSO contingency planning relates to the risks of pricing the specification, the client side must plan its chosen courses of action and be in a position to react in the event of: an unsuccessful in-house bid, a relationship having already been built up with the DSO officers; the failure of the successful tenderer to perform, leading to consideration of terminating the contract and retendering; or the closure of the DSO consequent upon losses due to the intervention of the Secretary of State. Each of these scenarios requires the evolution of mechanisms for ensuring continuity of service provision while retendering occurs.

Contract Supervision

Contract supervision covers control of quality and quantity of work and the budgetary effect of any variation orders it is necessary to issue which omit elements of the services as originally specified but no longer required, or add new elements with the consent of the contractor. In addition, consideration will be given to monitoring safety procedures and customer relations. In fact, customer complaints can constitute a very effective monitoring tool, providing the complaints are verified for accuracy before assuming that the contractor has defaulted on specific obligations.

Monitoring performance must strike a balance between two very different potential approaches. The first is based on sanctions, seeking failure through rigid adherence to specification, and the second on establishing trust in a clear working relationship with the contractor, characterised by good communication and agreed informal and formal contract procedures. The second approach avoids unnecessary confrontation but need not jettison sanctions entirely as long as both sides understand the circumstances in which they will be utilised and that the client will not immediately resort to them on discovering defaults unless the contractor has a history of non-rectification or corner-cutting through misconduct or inefficiency.

Whichever monitoring ideology is employed, maintaining adequate records of performance checks and failures will be an essential prerequisite to any attempt to successfully implement contractual sanctions or to terminate the relationship for fundamental breach of contract.

The post-tender relationship with a successful DSO

If a DSO is successful in competing for its work, it will not enter into a binding contract as would any other tenderer, simply because it remains a part of the local authority, which, as a single corporate body, cannot contract with itself. The LGA 1988 requires the DSO to perform the services tendered in accordance with the specification and for the contract conditions to be complied with even though they cannot be enforced using the same legal mechanisms as for an external contractor. The relationship between the client side and a DSO is thus placed on a quasi-contractual basis, with both sides reliant on a finalised document that will be treated as though it created a binding contractual relationship.

Since there is no contract in existence the local authority can decide to remove work from the DSO and place it externally without fundamental breach by, or the consent of, the DSO. Likewise, the services can be retendered before the date on which the arrangements would have expired had they been the subject of a binding contract running for a set period of years.

In any contractual relationship the client will be able to issue variation orders, providing that the sum total of work removed from the contractor does not fundamentally alter the nature of the contract as tendered and let. The contractor's consent is needed for any additional work, especially if the order is more than simply a substitution of new examples of the same type of work. Variation orders removing work from a DSO are straightforward, but if they place new tasks on the DSO, there is a risk of legal challenge on the basis that the DSO has not won such work in competition. It may be permissible to change the locations at which services are provided and make minor additions, but orders placing substantially new tasks on or effecting significant increases in the volume of work carried out by a DSO should be approached with extreme caution. Wherever possible, such additional work should be separately tendered, or placed externally if tendering is impractical because of the time-scales for compliance with the LGPLA 1980, LGA 1988 and LGA 1992.

Citizen's Charter

The client responsibilities in relation to the Citizen's Charter requirements of local authorities are to ensure the specific levels of service are publicised and that proper mechanisms exist for dealing with complaints in relation to lack of service or poor-quality work.

FINANCIAL MANAGEMENT

The key concerns for client and contractor in awarding work in competition are cost and quality. Both are simplified in the contractual relationship between a local authority and an external provider of services. This section analyses the more complex financial relationship between DSOs and other services preparing for competition on the one hand and those parts of the local authority that supply support services on the other. In particular, it must be appreciated that support services may themselves be seeking to apply the disciplines of trading accounts and will in turn be obtaining services from others.

Understanding the existing mechanisms for allocating identified costs of support services within local authority accounting procedures is essential to the creation of such internal mechanisms as service-level agreements and service statements, which endeavour to define both the costs to be borne by business units within a local authority and the quality of support services supplied to them.

Recharges and overheads of support services in local authority accounting

Local authority accounting procedures are not the subject of rigidly detailed statutory regulation, and in the main councils produce their accounts in accordance with voluntary codes of practice produced by the CIPFA. The goal for accounting staff is to allocate the cost of all support services to the departments and service units receiving such internal professional, technical and administrative support. To this end it is necessary to keep sufficient records of the purpose to which the chargeable hours worked by support staff are put. Analysis of these records enables salary costs and the on-costs or overheads attaching to the employment of any individual to be allocated on a percentage basis to different users.

Time spent on section management is separated and becomes an overhead on the support function, to be allocated *pro rata* to those benefiting from the service. The sum of all such allocations becomes the end-of-year recharge to each department and its subdivisions. Service management within a front-line department is similarly handled. The overheads carried by support services will be similar to those for DSO costing. They include accommodation costs and computer costs alongside administrative support and departmental management. It must also be recognised that front-line services will obtain some logistical support from other units in the same department and support-service recharges are not therefore an issue confined to central departments.

The potential for cyclical recharging is obvious, unless recharges are built up from the central local-authority costs through the support services to the front-line functions serving the public. Additionally, CIPFA has recognised the need to distinguish corporate management and regulation.

Corporate management and regulation

Corporate management is defined as those activities in which local authorities engage specifically because they are elected, multipurpose authorities. It includes the costs of council meetings and those of corporate policy committees (but not the democratic costs relating to other committees charged with the management of specific services), elections, corporate budgeting and accounting, annual reports and management costs that arise 'over and above the costs which would be incurred in managing all the various services if they were run by single purpose authorities'. It also covers the costs of employing a chief executive (other than those relating to the performance of specific services), officers carrying out the duties for which they have mandatory responsibilities by virtue of section 114 of the Local Government Finance Act 1988 and section 5 of the Local Government and Housing Act 1989, subscriptions to local authority associations, flat-rate member allowances and the staff employed and services required to support the above-mentioned officers and meetings.

Regulations cover the duties that the council or specific officers are statutorily required to perform to maintain the standard of services or the probity of staff. This would include the statutory officers such as the director of social services, who is appointed to secure compliance with section 6 of the Local Authority Social Services Act 1970.

In recent times CIPFA has accepted that corporate management and regulation should be exempt from the principle that all support services and service management costs should be apportioned to users[1]. It is presumed that such costs should be 'charged to separate heads'; that is, identified but not apportioned and recharged between individual business units. Instead, the costs of corporate management will be allocated to a separate budget head and not recharged between departments and services, while the costs of regulation will be divided between service departments but not apportioned between sections or service units.

Trading accounts

Unless created to satisfy the statutory accounting requirements for defined activities subject to CCT, or for statements of support service costs, internal trading accounts are merely a form of basic account showing the direct costs and overheads of services, together with any income, apportionments or recharges and any direct subsidy, from which a surplus or deficit balance can be derived as a means of evaluating the performance and competitiveness of the operation and of demonstrating cost containment within pre-set parameters.

Outside DSOs there is no common terminology in use and trading accounts are variously referred to as practice accounts, memorandum accounts and shadow trading accounts, depending on the purpose to which the accounts are put.

Practice accounts and operating accounts form an integrated part of the council's main accounting systems; operating costs are debited to the account, which is also credited with charges due, which are, in turn, debited to the service users. Such a system requires the whole or greater part of the council to operate on a trading-account basis.

The other approach is to maintain the main council accounts as the public record, with separate trading accounts operated for management purposes only. Such an account can, if desired, reflect the cost of support services on some basis other than that of the end-of-year recharges as shown in the official accounts. This is the approach reflected in CIPFA's present attempts to formulate a draft code of practice for trading accounts, whether the cost of support services is governed by a service-level agreement or a less formal arrangement. The draft implies that trading accounts are professionally perceived by accountants as inherently insufficient to secure compliance with the long-standing statutory requirement for the council's main revenue and capital accounts to reflect actual expenditure (now to be found in the Local Government and Housing Act 1989).

The value of trading accounts is that they enable the potential competitiveness of an operation to be tested without indulging in full-scale tendering. Isolating the costs of a service in this way provides a practical means of preparation for compulsory competition.

1 *The Management of Overheads in Local Authorities*, CIPFA, 1991.

The danger is that the process can degenerate into an extensive and wasteful paper-chase if every front-line function and support service is required to operate a trading account. Furthermore, it cannot serve any long-term useful purpose unless budgets for all support services are devolved to service users. This in itself would create complexities for support services requiring additional support from other units in the course of their normal operations.

Where trading accounts become part of a local authority's main accounting systems and are 'live' as opposed to paper accounts, it will be necessary to determine how any balances on such accounts are to be handled. Surpluses can be returned to the general fund or to service users, distributed to employees in the form of bonuses or profit-sharing or carried forward to future financial years. Deficits cannot be carried forward and if passed on to users would have an immediate impact upon all other extant trading accounts. It seems probable that some provision would have to be made for such losses to be borne from some central provision.

Internal markets

Different internal departments and business units already trade with each other in so far as they provide services to and receive them from each other without regard to departmental demarcation lines. While such activity merely reflects the actual usage made of resources already employed and paid for by the council, the cost of support services must be allocated to specific functions for accounting purposes, as has already been demonstrated.

The level of recharges for support services will always be open to criticism as long as it is determined from calculations made by the staff themselves of the percentage of their time to be attributed to different functions. Hence a demonstrable need exists for reliable time-recording systems to eliminate the perceived unreliability of manually completed time-sheets. Fully computerised time-recording, with staff operating desk-top systems and allocating chargeable hours to clients as the time is worked without the need for manual inputting of information in arrears, has been successfully implemented by the London Borough of Enfield's legal service. The advent of networked technology in such fields as word processing, printing and telecommunications enables itemisation of actual usage as the basis for unimpeachable recharging of support service costs to multiple users.

Nor is the accuracy of recharges the only area to be addressed. The pressure of trading account disciplines and of pending CCT calls for the costs of support service usage to be identified and reported more frequently than at the end of each municipal year so that managers are not faced with unforeseen debits from their account when it is too late to recover them from any other source. In the case of a DSO such a scenario would enable the Secretary of State to consider ordering complete closure of the operation.

DSOs must know the basis for support services at the outset and need to be kept informed of the costs incurred at regular intervals as the current year unfolds. This increased requirement for management information is bound to lead to additional expenditure on support service administration. While no substitute for regular periodic financial monitoring reports, a useful discipline developing in local authorities, for both recipients and providers of support services, is the preparation of service-level agreements or service statements as a means of estimating support service costs more accurately prior to the submission of bids for work under CCT, when, of course, such costs must be included.

Service-level agreements and service statements

Service-level agreements and service statements are two forms of agreement made between an internal supplier of support services and a DSO or business unit requiring such services. Both seek to specify the services required by the trading operation or to be imposed on them by virtue of corporate policy requirements, and thereafter to utilise the document as a quasi-contract between the parties. The difference between the two arises in their treatment of the costs to be borne for support services.

Service statements seek to identify the means by which recharges are to be calculated for the support services provided. They will therefore include the chargeable hourly rates for different grades of support staff who will provide the services covered by the agreement and the unit cost of services to be provided on a piecework basis (for example, the cost per page of typing or printing).

Service-level agreements attempt to go further by estimating the quantities of support service to be supplied and seeking to bind both parties to a set total cost for the provision of that level of service, while recognising the need for both sides to monitor the quantity and quality of services sought or imposed. Service-level agreements may seek to agree a basis for support-service charges other than one geared towards the actual cost of staff time and service usage, for example by averaging the hourly rate to be charged or by setting retainers for a basic level of service or by introducing costing mechanisms differentiating between simple and more complex tasks, whatever grade of staff ultimately performs the work. In other words, a service-level agreement steps away from local authority recharging procedures and seeks to adopt systems akin to those that would be used by external commercial organisations, including loss-leader and profit-generating elements.

The problems with service-level agreements are that they cannot bind the parties in the way a contract can and may conflict with local authority accounting practices, in particular, on the residual responsibility claimed by the council's treasurer to ensure that the official accounts reflect the true cost to the authority of services, which carries with it the power to rectify or amend the accounts, without reference to any existing service-level agreement, if the result of the agreed costing mechanisms does not ensure the recovery of the true support service costs. Thus a service-level agreement can be operated by the parties as a means of calculating recharges to DSOs or trading accounts only with the grace and favour of the local authority's treasurer, which will, in turn, be exercised in accordance with the CIPFA codes of practice for local authority accounting. Until recently these did not permit anything to be recharged other than the best estimate of the actual cost of the support services.

However, the CIPFA guidelines on accounting for overheads in local authorities open the door to users paying 'for support services by negotiating SLAs with service providers and by paying charges in accordance with these agreements'[1]. This is subject to the proviso that the cost of 'all other support services should be apportioned over the accounts of the users . . . The basis of apportionment adopted should be used consistently for all expenditure heads to which apportionments are made'[2]. In summary, CIPFA are backing reliance on service-level agreements provided that a common basis for recharge is utilised in respect of all the users of the particular support service subject to the agreement. Separate charging mechanisms for different recipients of the same service are not permissible.

The accounting problems posed are clear. Nevertheless, service-level agreements and service statements both offer an opportunity to experiment with specifications for support services in advance of those services themselves being subjected to compulsory competition. Efforts spent in developing them are therefore not wasted so long as endeavours are made to generate adequate descriptions of the services and target performance measures rather than concentrating solely on the costs to be recharged.

1 Ibid, page 31.
2 Ibid, page 31.

Chapter 9

STAFFING MATTERS

At first blush the primary staffing implications of CCT appear to be exclusive concerns of the local authority. After all, it is the council's employees whose conditions of employment will be under threat in the period leading up to competition and who will become redundant if the DSO's bid for tenderable work is not accepted, and the authority, not the contractor, who will pick up the costs of severance.

The contractor's initial interest in such matters stems from the fact that the local authority may use redundancy costs as a reason for not awarding work to an external tenderer who might otherwise be regarded as the lowest bidder. The only other obvious employment-related issue for the contractor is the need to increase the size of its existing workforce if it is awarded a new council contract, and, on occasion, encouraging the original DSO staff, or a proportion of them, to take up offers of new employment, will best achieve that end.

Alternatively the council and the contractor may find themselves in a situation to which transfers of undertakings law applies. The ramifications of TUPE for CCT are particularly complex but the interests of staff and the risk of claims for damages mean that careful exploration of such issues is essential for each contracting opportunity.

Attempts have already been made by trade unions to tie contract-winning companies into the redundancy process, using the argument that CCT gives rise to a transfer of an existing undertaking to a new employer. Such efforts have not succeeded to date, but contractors need to be aware of the possibilities inherent in these situations and extract safeguards from the contracting council against the risk of incurring financial liabilities to former council workers.

Furthermore, local authorities may endeavour, within their contracts, to specify matters relating to staff to be employed by the contractor in providing services to the council; the possibility of unreasonable requests, in breach of the anti-competition provisions of the LGA 1988, rears its head once again.

This chapter illustrates the balance to be struck between the interests of the council and its intended contractors in relation to redundancy and staff transfer, and examines the legitimacy of employment-related contract terms imposed upon contractors.

THE POSITION OF DLO AND DSO STAFF

To avoid any lingering doubts as to whether a DSO remains an integral part of the local authority and its staff part of the council's workforce subject to the constraints and benefits as enjoyed prior to competitive tendering, reference can be made to the attempt by a former employee of South Somerset District Council to secure damages from his ex-employer. David Woodland, in February 1995 at Yeovil County Council, alleged that the council and its DSO, South Somerset Contractors, had conspired to dismiss him. Throwing out the claim, Judge Cotterell ruled that South Somerset Contractors and its managing director were not third parties and therefore they could not conspire with each other because they were one and the same. The acid test was whether the DSO could sue and be sued in its own right and South Somerset Contractors could not pass this test. The fact that the DSO had separate statutory accounts and tendered for contracts under its own name did not make it autonomous or independent of the council.

LOCAL AUTHORITY EMPLOYMENT PRACTICES

Local government has generally prided itself in performing the role of good employer. Over the years much effort has been put into treating employees equitably, adopting the best staffing practices, paying reasonable wages, upgrading terms and conditions and furthering equal opportunities. The reasons for this are not entirely philanthropic. Such an approach serves to attract and retain high-calibre staff and engender loyalty among those who might well be lower paid working outside the public sector. Those authorities that have gained reputations as mediocre, dispute-riven organisations experience difficulties in recruiting key managerial and professional employees, not least because they will be perceived as stressful and frustrating working environments. Additionally, given local authorities' statutory duties in respect of race relations, sound recruitment and disciplinary practices help to minimise embarrassing allegations of discrimination and unfair dismissal.

In the context of CCT the one negative consequence of enhanced terms and conditions is increased staffing costs. Since labour is the single largest element of most service budgets a danger for in-house provision is posed in those areas where external contractors can offer labour at reduced rates, achieving this by paying lower hourly rates and providing inferior terms, conditions and benefits to employees than are available to local authority workers. This is plainly not universally applicable to private-sector contractors tendering for local authority work, but is sufficiently prevalent that councils have been forced to consider negotiating reductions in wages and other terms of employment to increase DSO competitiveness prior to implementing CCT. This tendency is exacerbated where loss-leader bids from external tenderers are anticipated as a means of obtaining footholds in new local authority markets.

NEGOTIATING REVISIONS TO TERMS AND CONDITIONS OF EMPLOYMENT

The first point worth reiterating, because it is frequently misunderstood, is that competitive tendering, whether the DSO wins or loses work as a result, does nothing to alter the status of its workforce. All staff remain council employees with all the contractual rights that status conveys. Continuity of service is preserved for all purposes, including the calculation of redundancy entitlement, and all other accrued rights, such as frozen holiday pay, remain intact unless negotiated away. The starting point is thus a workforce whose wages may exceed the minimum necessary to recruit similar staff outside local government and whose bonus schemes, holiday entitlement and sick-leave allowances may be the factors rendering the DSO potentially uncompetitive.

Once it is accepted that in service areas subject to CCT rigid adherence to existing pay and conditions may turn a local authority from a fair employer into a non-employer, negotiating revisions to existing contracts of employment may well be in the interests of both the council and its staff. That said, it may be that local authorities are not prepared to countenance employing anyone other than on contracts incorporating their own concepts of minimum acceptable conditions. If staying competitive involves driving wages down to levels at which the council doubts it can obtain employees of satisfactory quality, it may simply prefer to award the contract externally and pass the problem to the contractor while dissociating itself from practices contrary to those of a good employer. Alternatively the staff may believe that if the contract is lost, TUPE will protect their positions and they will refuse to negotiate.

The aim in negotiating must be to strike a balance between sensible, agreed changes to contracts of employment to improve DSO competitiveness and pressing for unreasonable reductions in terms and conditions, which will demotivate the workforce and damage industrial relations should the DSO end up winning by an overly large margin.

Organising negotiations with the whole workforce will be easiest where strong trade union affiliation is the norm, but there will always be individual employees who are not union members and the safest course is for the authority to seek to obtain the signature of each and every worker, rather than relying on collective agreements signed by shop stewards on behalf of their members, if the risk of later industrial tribunal applications is to be minimised.

Moving away from annual national pay awards towards local bargaining may be particularly helpful to DSOs. Pay increases can be linked instead to the criteria by which a DSO's tendered price is uplifted. Normally, this will be in accordance with the retail price index or some specific form of inflation index for labour costs geared to the needs of a particular service or industry.

Existing bonus schemes may be expensive to administer, requiring excessive record-keeping and analysis. Simplified schemes may save the council money, and may prove even more beneficial if linked to increases in productivity or the overall DSO results. Effective profit-sharing motivates employees by giving them a stake in the level of success achieved by the DSO beyond the mere fact of continued employment. Alternatively, if absenteeism is a factor escalating costs, a bonus paid in whole or part on actual attendance of employees, or paid to teams so that peer-group pressure reduces malingering, may be a preferred solution.

Another area in which local authorities have traditionally been generous towards employees is in allowing time off for trade union activities. DSO managers will have to consider whether such allowances should be constrained to merely the statutory rights.

Finally, the addition of confidentiality clauses to contracts of employment may be appropriate. These make explicit the existing duties at common law of an employee to maintain the confidentiality of information received in the course of the employer's business, but may go further and prohibit the holders of commercially valuable knowledge concerning the employer from seeking positions with rival contractors for a stated period after leaving the council. Obviously, such clauses will be struck down by the courts if deemed to be unreasonable in their extent. The period for which they apply and the definition of competitors need to be carefully thought out and justified if the restriction is to be enforceable.

An undesirable side-effect of negotiating different wage levels and rises for particular groups of employees within a large organisation like a local authority, which has previously graded posts using impartial job-evaluation criteria, is the creation of new forms of inequality. This brings with it the risk of actions brought under the equal-pay-for-equal-work provisions of the Equal Pay Act 1970. The reality of this danger is borne out by the case of *Ratcliffe and Others v North Yorkshire County Council* in which the House of Lords gave judgment on 6 July 1995. Having lost one of its contracts, the council cut wage levels for female school-meals staff as part of the preparation for further catering tendering under the LGA 1988. In consequence of this action the DSO was able to win four further contracts. Claims from employees for the reinstatement of equal pay followed, using selected male council employees as comparators. Their Lordships ruled that the revision of conditions resulted in unlawful discrimination and rejected the argument that the pressures of competitive tendering could justify wage differentials between female staff and their male counterparts.

Whilst the DoE has stated that action will not be taken against DSOs failing to meet financial targets because of such back pay requirements a victory of this kind may prove pyrrhic for the staff if the DSO is driven into long-term deficit.

The final option for a local authority finding it impossible to agree changes to contractual terms and conditions of employment is unilateral imposition. This is really an action of the last resort since it carries a high risk of employees claiming they have been constructively dismissed. Even if individual workers have begun to work the newly offered contracts under protest, tribunals have on occasion found them to have been unfairly dismissed in such circumstances.

Contingent revisions to terms and conditions

One of the problems for a DSO facing the bidding process is that in a TUPE situation changes to contractual conditions of employment will not necessarily achieve an improved margin of in-house costs over external tenderers because a successful private-sector bidder will inherit the staff on the same amended terms.

Two solutions present themselves. The first is to tender on the assumption that it will be possible post-award to negotiate changes especially if the staff have been consulted and indicate a willingness to treat after the event.

The other alternative is to enter into a contingent agreement whereby the conditions of employment will change only when a condition precedent is satisfied. The condition precedent would be the award of the work in-house by the council. To be sure that a contract is enforceable there should be valuable consideration given by each side to the other. Obviously the DSO will be securing cost reductions. The gain to the staff is less readily pinpointed. However, the benefits of being able to continue within the Local Government Superannuation Scheme (commercial organisations are precluded from being 'admitted bodies' whose employees can contribute to pensions under the scheme), rather than risk the personal benefits comparability of any rival pension plan, might be one. Changes to working conditions or flexitime could be seen as an alternative carrot. The contingent agreement could also be time-limited to the length of the contract whereafter the staff would revert to national conditions or their previous basis of employment. This would secure a continuing edge at retendering.

The fact that the staff are prepared to reduce costs to their personal prejudice ought not to be grounds for a successful challenge to the Secretary of State by an aggrieved external tenderer, since it achieves the very thing competition was intended to do: drive down costs. The fact that the private-sector bidder cannot similarly cut future costs with an expectation of reducing terms and conditions across the workforce is one of the advantages a DSO gains through employment law as it presently stands and one which should be exploited.

LOYALTY PAYMENTS

If the tendering process results in the contract being awarded externally, problems may arise for the local authority in maintaining the service during the lead-in time before the new contract commences. This could well be a period of between three and six months, during which council staff, who may have no more than a few years of local government service and thus no expectation of substantial redundancy payments, will be tempted to seek alternative employment if opportunities become available. This will be particularly true of employees who are not likely, or do not wish, to be hired by the successful tenderer.

The solution may well lie in making loyalty payments to those key staff prepared to remain until the new contractor takes over. Because such action is divisive and may stir resentment, and because the district auditor has the right to challenge expenditure he or she regards as unnecessary, local authorities will have to consider whether it is truly vital to maintain a full staffing complement to the very end and whether certain types of employee can be replaced by temporary or agency workers at a lower cost than making special retention payments. For long-serving staff, the refusal of the authority to release them with their redundancy payment earlier than the commencement date of the new contract (presuming this to have been notified as the effective date of redundancy) ought to be sufficient to deter premature departure, if not to maintain motivation. Doubtless, the action to be contemplated will vary according to the profile of the workforce in terms of average age, length of service, skills and employability in the prevailing jobs market.

REDUNDANCY

An overview of the notice requirements and the key issues in redundancy situations arising as a result of competitive tendering is given below; the detailed legal provisions for redundancy are contained in the Employment Protection (Consolidation) Act 1978 and the Trade Union Reform and Employment Rights Act 1993.

The statutory consultation periods when a potential redundancy situation occurs are 90 days where 100 or more employees are affected and 30 days where 10 or more are affected. Adequate consultation is prescribed for less than 10 redundancies, but is not defined. Agreements with trade unions may grant rights to more time for consultation.

A decision to go out to tender automatically produces a potential redundancy situation. To avoid having to continue payments to staff after the intended commencement date of the new contract because of the consultation requirements and notice periods, redundancy notices should be given at an early juncture. Failure to do so may cause the local authority to be accused of wasting public funds and may attract the attentions of the district auditor. The notices can always be withdrawn if the DSO submits the winning tender for the provision of the services.

A new European directive is proposed to amend the existing Directive 75/129, with which British redundancy legislation broadly aligns. It calls for the provision of specified information to potentially redundant employees and worker participation in the process. It will place a duty on the employer to include in early consultations a statement of the means whereby agreement can be reached to avoid the need for collective redundancy or to minimise the number of workers affected, and any other consequences. The employer will also have to state the means of selection for redundancy. Much of this already constitutes good practice in local government circles and ought not to impose overly arduous variations to existing procedures.

The consequences of failing to consult are currently limited to the levying of fines and damages, but additional compensation is available to individuals whose allegations of unfair dismissal are upheld by an industrial tribunal.

Redundancy situations pose another problem for those local authorities that have redeployment agreements with the trade unions, whereby the council is bound to consider alternative positions for any employee desirous of such a move. Such a policy is easy to implement for *ad hoc* or small-scale redundancies, but is wholly unrealistic in a competitive tendering context. The increasing futility of attempting to effect redeployment in large-scale redundancy situations must persuade management and unions alike to waive rigid adherence to such agreements, but the issue may be a hard fought one in some councils.

Other local authorities retain non-compulsory redundancy policies despite the doubt thrown on their *vires* by the North Tyneside case[1]. Since enhanced severance terms to persuade staff to voluntarily accept redundancy were themselves held to be unlawful in that case, the ground seems fertile for further dispute.

Redundancy causes trauma and distress, in particular to older employees. The provision of specialist redundancy counselling is therefore an action a good employer can and should implement.

---

1 *Allsop v North Tyneside District Council* (1992) The Times, 12 March, CA.

PAY IN LIEU OF NOTICE

In the past local authorities have, on occasion, sugar-coated the pill of redundancy by making payments in lieu of notice of termination of employment. This ensured the employee received normal wages up to the date of termination and an additional lump sum at the end. Payments in lieu of notice were regarded by the Inland Revenue as non-taxable, and thus had an increased value in the hands of the recipient employee.

Two factors now militate against local authorities giving pay in lieu of notice except where it is genuinely impossible for the employer to give the proper statutory or contractual notice of termination so that it expires no later than the date on which the employment will come to an end. The first is the increasing interest paid by the district auditor to severance payments generally. If notice could reasonably have been given earlier and the consequence is a higher cost to the local authority than should have been necessary, a critical report or even consideration of surcharge becomes a possibility.

The other factor is the current position of the Inland Revenue. Tax inspectors now require to be satisfied that the payment is genuinely pay in lieu of notice that special circumstances have prevented being given. Otherwise the payment is treated as a device attracting deduction of tax. Failure on the part of a local authority, as employer, to deduct income tax properly payable entitles the Inland Revenue to pursue not only the payee but also the council for the tax due and for penalties.

ENHANCED SEVERANCE SCHEMES

Further to the North Tyneside case[1], the Local Government (Compensation for Redundancy and Premature Retirement) Regulations 1994[2] have clarified local authority powers to offer severance terms in excess of statutory minimum redundancy payments. Providing such lawful enhancements are adopted as a common practice, it will be possible to add them to basic redundancy costs in determining the prospective costs to be brought into evaluation of tenders (see Chapter 3).

TRANSFER OF UNDERTAKINGS (TUPE)

Where a commercial venture is taken over by another employer, the transaction may cause the successor employer to inherit the duties and responsibilities for the acts and omissions of the original employer in relation to the staff. To affect any given activity, the Transfer of Undertakings (Protection of Employment) Regulations 1981[3] require that there must be an actual transfer of a going concern. The Trade Union Reform and Employment Rights Act 1993 removes the additional requirement that the venture must be commercial in nature on the grounds of non-compliance with the

1 Ibid page 88 above.
2 SI 1994 No. 3025.
3 SI 1981 No. 1794.

Acquired Rights Directive[1]. Public sector employees are thus to be granted unambiguously equal rights to their private-sector counterparts.

The wording of the Acquired Rights Directive, which in the original French requires a contractual transfer ('une cession conventionelle') to be effected if the employees are to have the rights conferred by the Directive, raises the argument that unless there is a contractual transfer of the whole business neither the Directive nor the 1988 Regulations are applicable. Revisions to the Directive are planned but whether they will really clarify matters remains to be seen.

Notwithstanding these legal arguments, the rapidly evolving case law makes it clear that transfer of undertakings rights will regularly arise in CCT situations wherever it can be argued that a going concern can be identified as potentially passing across with a contract for services.

Testing for potential TUPE situations

Viewed simplistically, TUPE situations arise whenever an operation, having changed ownership, remains sufficiently similar to its previous incarnation for it to be argued that a whole entity has transferred. The type and volume of work undertaken, the customers served, the organisational arrangements, the use of premises, vehicles and equipment and other factors, not least the staffing requirement, fall to be assessed on a case-by-case basis. This is to determine whether a definable entity in fact continues to exist, but no single element will have the over-riding edge in determining whether TUPE applies or not. The further fly in the ointment is that although it can never be ascertained until after the event whether a transfer of a going concern has occurred, during the tendering process, the parties must make an educated guess whether the 1981 Regulations are likely to apply. To do so they will have to predict whether a successful tenderer could perform the specified services other than with a similar scale of workforce, using similar methods and organisation and with similar requirements for plant and equipment. The greater the likely degree of commonality, the more likely it is that a TUPE situation will exist with the commencement of a service on a contracted-out basis.

Staff transfer

Whenever a TUPE situation arises, the secondary question to be addressed is the indentification of staff having the right to regard their employment as continuing with the new owner on the pre-existing terms and conditions.

At law only employees allocated or assigned to the service can invoke statutory transfer rights. Staff who work full time on the services which are the subject of the tendering process will have no difficulty in meeting this test. It is also probable that a small, *de minimis* margin of work performed outside the entity would not negate TUPE rights but it would seem unlikely that an employee could claim to be associated with the contract service if he or she had spent less than say 85 per cent of the working week in it.

There is as yet no case law on this point and commentators, argue both

1 EEC/77/187.

for and against the possibility of 51 per cent being sufficient to ensure transfer even though this would lead to the absurd result that the transferee organisation would have to inherit employees without enough work to employ them and would have to consider redundancies immediately. Notwithstanding this, it appears that Wolverhampton Metropolitan District Council in June 1995 reached an out of court settlement with a former employee of Brophy's, the outgoing grounds maintenance contractor, who argued that his employment should pass to the council's DSO with the contract for services notwithstanding his solicitor's acceptance that he only spent about 65 per cent of his time on the contract although 'there were times when his percentage was a lot higher'.

Employees who work inside a transferring entity but also perform other services, or 'split' employees, will remain with the council with insufficient residual work to fully occupy them. Redeployment or reorganisation must be considered but in many cases there will be little choice but to effect redundancy.

If the redundancy of employees straddling the entity is the bugbear of the employer, the contrasting problem of loss of the prospect of an immediate redundancy payment is the lot of employees who might, if TUPE did not apply, wish to take redundancy benefits and retire or seek alternative employment for themselves. With TUPE, staff associated with the transferring entity have no such choice. Their contracts of employment pass across and an employee must go to work for the new owner unless willing to resign forthwith, there being no right to any compensatory payment upon doing so. This is particularly hard upon persons aged over 50 who would have been entitled to immediate payment of pension, frequently with enhancements to notional length of service from the local authority.

The Trade Union Reform and Employment Rights Act 1993 reaffirms the legal position that no redundancy payment is receivable by a former employee who declines to transfer and it would be *ultra vires* for a council to make a voluntary payment.

Consultation

Prior to the transfer of an undertaking, the council and the transferee organisation have to provide information to and consult with staff and their representatives. The legal requirements, as set out in the Trade Union Reform and Employment Rights Act 1993, arise once the council recognises a situation has arisen in which measures are being considered which will affect workers represented by a recognised union. The aim of the employer must be 'to seek their agreement to measures to be taken with respect to affected employees'. In fact the safest course is to notify all staff as well as the trade unions. Even if the council believes that TUPE will not apply it would be best to consult on the alternatives of both redundancy and transfer to avoid the risk of compensation claims should an industrial tribunal or court subsequently differ from the council's view on the inapplicability of transfer of undertakings rights.

Inadequate consultation can give rise to compensation claims to a maximum of four weeks' pay per employee without the opportunity to net off other payments made by the employer, such as pay in lieu of notice. This liability does not transfer with the employees in a TUPE situation but remains with the council as former employer.

Consultation must include reasons for the transfer, estimated dates of occurrence and the implications for all the employees.

Staff rights on transfer

As has been demonstrated, the practical consequence of TUPE is that the contracts of employment of staff employed in the transferring undertaking pass automatically to the new owner. The rights and duties inherited include primarily the maintenance of the existing terms and conditions of employment, liability for outstanding grievances, equal pay claims and unpaid arrears, and honouring the benefit of collective agreements applying to the workforce.

Staff with transfer rights cannot be dismissed arbitrarily in the run-up to the change however much the transferee might wish to select employees for re-engagement. In such cases dismissal will be deemed ineffective and the contracts of employment remain in existence for the purposes of transfer.

Transferring employees wishing to remain in work do not necessarily retain their terms and conditions indefinitely. The new employer can immediately negotiate changes in the present economic climate, staff may be reluctant to jeopardise their positions and feel constrained to agree changes. Alternatively, the new owner can change contracts of employment unilaterally if able to demonstrate that a change to the composition, skills mix or size of the workforce is necessitated by economic, technical or organisational reasons. New working methods or the introduction of information technology leading to requirements for less staff or different qualifications could therefore justify redundancies or changes to conditions of employment which would not be deemed unfair.

There is no minimum time before the new employer can endeavour to effect changes to terms and conditions by negotiation or in reliance upon ETO grounds. The common belief that a period of a year must elapse is an illusion.

As well as inheriting the contracts of employment, the transferee organisation will also be entitled to the personnel records of the transferring employees including their disciplinary records. The only exception will be matters unconnected to the contract of employment such as information on personal circumstances.

A further uncertainty is posed by geographical considerations. The compulsory competitive tendering of manual services covers work physically to be undertaken within the relevant council area. Most professional services, however, can be delivered from remote locations provided staff can travel to attend key meetings with client side officers. This raises the possibility that firms tendering for professional service contracts will accept that TUPE applies but will require former council staff to relocate to places from which the tenderer already operates or plans to do so. These could be considerable distances from the base of the former local authority. Unless it can be argued that geographical location is a term of the contract of employment or can be implied into it (in itself a tenuous argument because the new employer could not insist on using the existing council offices), staff unable to relocate (for example, due to family commitments or negative equity) will lose both their jobs and the cushioning effect of a redundancy payment. Even those willing to move may suffer financially in the present housing market notwithstanding that the new employer will have complied strictly with TUPE.

One recent instance offers a measure of protection from geographical transfer to female staff. The Court of Appeal in the case of *Meade-Hill v British Council*[1] has ruled that a mobility requirement can amount to unlawful sexual discrimination since in practice a higher proportion of women would find it impossible to move house than men. However, the judgment goes on to say that the discrimination can be justified if the employer can show a requirement for mobility irrespective of the sex of the person to whom it applies. Furthermore it has been suggested that the requirement could cease to be discriminatory if compliance would not be forced upon an employee who was unable to comply with it in practice, as opposed to merely finding relocation inconvenient. The extent of the protection by implication afforded to council staff in TUPE situations remains unclear since leave is being sought to appeal the judgment to the House of Lords.

Finally, TUPE rights apply only to the actual staff transferring. There is no requirement to maintain terms and conditions when replacing any staff who resign or are lawfully dismissed post-transfer.

Pension rights

The Acquired Rights Directive 1977 expressly states that a transferee shall have no responsibility in relation to pensions. Accordingly it is probable that a requirement in national law that a transferor must offer comparable pensions or compensate the transferring employees for not doing so will attract the attention of the European Court of Justice and ultimately be ruled to breach Community law.

However, the British Government has adopted the stance of requiring transferee organisations to offer pensions comparable with those of the transferor.

As the case of *Walden Engineering Co Ltd v Warrener*[1] in the Employment Appeal Tribunal in July 1993 made clear, there is no requirement to offer identical benefits and contribution arrangements to those of the transferor. This is as well given that commercial organisations are precluded from being granted admitted body status to enable the employee to continue in the Local Government Superannuation Scheme. This is due primarily to the profitable tax breaks offered to local government and charitable bodies on US investments which would be lost if trading organisations were brought into the scheme.

Achieving comparable pensions may still not be particularly easy given the generosity of index-linking in the Local Government Superannuation Scheme and the issue would become thorny if staff were to seek damages, post-contracting-out, for new pension scheme deficiencies. While the responsibility should rest solely with the transferor, a local authority would be well advised to seek indemnification from the successful tenderer for a CCT contract to which TUPE may apply and this is the line promoted by

1 The Times, 14 April 1995.

DoE guidance. This is so notwithstanding the contrary view, that for a council to restrict competition to firms guaranteeing comparable pension schemes for transferring staff would be *ultra vires*. Tony Childs, the former solicitor to the Audit Commission, has expressed this view in print.

The issue may be further clarified once the test case commissioned by the GMB against Sefton Metropolitan Borough Council and its transferee grounds maintenance contractor, Brophy plc, in respect of failure to provide comparable pensions to about 60 former council staff, comes to court in 1996.

The present position is that with the support of the DoE, expressed in circular letters dated 15 March 1995 and 28 June 1995, a local authority can require contractors to provide comparable pensions in TUPE situations and may exclude tenderers who do not or alternatively seek indemnification from them. This is said to be a justified measure to prevent claims of constructive or unfair dismissal against the transferor notwithstanding the obvious flaw in the logic which is that case law clearly shows the responsibilities rest with the transferee not the transferor.

The task for local authorities is to put in place procedures to ascertain the comparability or otherwise of tenderers' pension schemes.

The Government Actuary's Department (GAD) currently assesses the pension schemes of applicant contractors and offers an overall annual certificate of comparability with either the Civil Service or the Local Government Superannuation Schemes, referred to as a GAD passport.

A local authority could, as part of its conditions of tendering, give preference to holders of the appropriate GAD passport but that certificate is indicative only for the scheme as a whole. To be sure that a pension scheme is comparable, an actuarial check must be made in relation to the specific group of individuals who are likely to transfer in the event of contracting-out. Councils are unlikely to have such expertise in-house and are best advised to employ an external actuary to perform this task. The London Borough of Hammersmith and Fulham is a leading authority in this field and warns that the start-up costs are significant but can be avoided if the council uses an actuary already involved in such work for local government.

The information required of both the council and contractors is significant. It will include scheme eligibility, contribution rates, benefits, pension increases, value of specific benefits (such as ill health retirements or death in service), discretionary benefits (such as early retirement without penalty, injury allowances, spouse and children's pensions and purchase of added years), transfer of benefits and scheme administration, decision making and benefit security (funding and investment management).

TUPE within the tendering process

Guidance from the DoE on handling TUPE in a competitive tendering process contained in Circular 10/93 has been overtaken by rapid developments in the understanding of the implications of the Acquired Rights Directive and the 1981 Regulations. Accordingly, on 21 January 1994 the DoE released an issues paper recognising that the local authority must be able to take a position on the applicability or otherwise of TUPE rather than leaving matters to the tenderers to state their position in their bids.

A local authority can now express a preliminary view on TUPE in relation to the contract it is letting but it must not require that TUPE shall apply and must not prevent tenders formulated on a non-TUPE basis. If tenderers do not agree with the council's preliminary view then their reasons for disagreeing must be sought and considered. If the council stands by its view then tenderers must be invited to revise their bids to take TUPE into account. If they decline to do so their tenders can be eliminated from further consideration.

The council could believe that TUPE might apply but then be presented with a strong case that it will not apply to a particular tenderer. This might be because the tenderer's bid is based on very different organisational solutions to performing the services, and these solutions break the strands of probable commonality before and after the contract is let. In such a case the council must consider accepting the bid (if it is the lowest or most economically advantageous) but may seek appropriate indemnities from the tenderer against future claims from ex-employees.

If TUPE is likely to apply, a local authority may also enquire into pensions comparability for transferring employees, as already stated. The risk for the council is that the tenderer may allege that the authority's stand on TUPE is taken for anti-competitive reasons. The need to justify the initial view taken to the Secretary of State will then arise but a more dangerous related issue will be whether the council has deliberately aligned its selection of activities for competition and contract packages to secure TUPE rights. Such action would breach the guidance on packaging and render a challenge likely to succeed.

The AMA suggests that a suitable warning to tenderers to be placed in initial adverts would be as follows:

> The Council feels that in the event of a private sector tenderer being awarded this contract, then the terms of the *European Acquired Rights Directive, Number 77/187 and/or the Transfer of Undertakings (Protection of Employment) Regulations 1981* could potentially apply. If the Directive or the Regulations are held to be applicable then tenderers should take into account the following requirements:
>
> (a) the need to consult with recognised trade unions;
> (b) the need to maintain existing rates of pay and conditions of employment of employees; and
> (c) the need for a successful tenderer to accept liability in respect of claims for redundancy payments, unfair dismissal and all other claims related to previous employees of the Council.
>
> You are advised to seek independent professional advice as to the effects of the Directive and/or Regulations on your company, should you be in the position of being the successful tenderer.

As far as contract conditions are concerned, model clauses governing the applicability and non-applicability of TUPE to a contract are included in Appendix III.

Supply of information to tenderers

If the council takes the view that TUPE is likely to apply or a contractor produces a reasoned argument that it will, then on request the council must

issue relevant staffing information to tenderers. The supply of TUPE information to a contractor does not, however, permit the council subsequently
to refuse to consider any non-TUPE bid made by that contractor.

The DoE issues paper of 21 January 1994 contained an annex setting out
the main items of information usually relevant to transferring staff. These
include the principal terms and conditions of employment which are the
probationary period (if any), retirement age, periods of notice, current pay
agreements, any agreed pay settlements yet to come into effect, working
hours, annual leave entitlements, sick leave arrangements, maternity/pater-
nity leave arrangements, special leave arrangements, terms and conditions
of transfers, and such things as season ticket loan schemes and car leasing,
if these are provided by the council.

Also to be supplied are base data on the staff who would transfer including the numbers of staff and in respect of each affected employee their age,
sex, salary rates (with the number of staff on each rate), reckonable service,
input hours, regular overtime and wage rates, other factors affecting redundancy entitlement and any outstanding industrial injury or other claims.

Finally there is the requirement to supply other general information
which may be asserted to be employment benefits of staff and any facility
time and facilities provided for trade union officials and health and safety
representatives.

It is also made clear in the annex that the above information is no more
than the common requirement but any other relevant information must be
supplied. Tenderers are already using this provision to seek a wide range of
additional material from councils. The only sound advice is to treat each
case on its merits and see whether withholding particular information
could reasonably be said to impact upon the tenderers ability to cost his bid
so as to include all TUPE liabilities. If the answer is affirmative then the
data should be supplied.

There is no requirement that the information be personalised. Accordingly, individuals' identities and addresses can be withheld and there is no
requirement to give commercially sensitive information on the DSO's
working practices unless this relates directly to TUPE liabilities. Data protection considerations are rendered irrelevant by the fact that the council
can change its registration to include the revelation of information to contractors and tenderers (see Chapter 4).

The information supplied must necessarily be speculative. Nobody can in
fact determine the exact transferring financial liabilities until the date of
transfer (the commencement date of the contract). Until then only staff in
post and their wages and accumulated redundancy liability can be identified. Calculations are thus based upon the unrealistic presumption that the
workforce is static; that no one will leave voluntarily for another job, take
early retirement or even die. In fact the time-scales explicitly laid down for
the receipt of tenders, for evaluation, award of contracts and pre-com-
mencement preparations mean that TUPE information furnished in good
faith is liable to become inaccurate prior to the contract's commencement.

Since newly appointed staff have fewer rights, will not have accumulated
wage increments and will have less service to bring into account on redundancy, the likelihood is that the TUPE consequences for the transferee
employer will be reducing over the period prior to the date of a transfer. If
the change is significant, firms will be free to lodge a complaint with the DoE
based upon the premises that had they known the true liabilities they would

have elected to submit a tender or to have submitted a more competitive price. Questions will then be asked as to whether the timing of the changes reducing TUPE liability were such that the council should have renotified invited tenderers or allowed an extended tendering period to obtain more competitive bids. This could create an unbreakable cycle of postponement and poses enormous risks to the integrity of the tendering process.

Ideally the DoE ought either to take the view that the statutory timescales involved preclude later revision of the costings supplied by local authorities in good faith or issue guidance as to the last point in the tendering process at which it is reasonable for tenderers to expect to see revisions. To date the DoE has done neither.

In an attempt to deter competition, some local authorities have sought to overstate likely TUPE liabilities which must be ruled anti-competitive behaviour if brought to the Secretary of State's attention. An example is the attempt to include the payment of frozen holiday pay as a transferring liability. Since the historic agreement with manual workers calls for the value of the frozen holiday pay to be paid to staff leaving the authority's employment, responsibility can hardly pass across to the transferee organisation. Payment will have to be made immediately prior to transfer. To argue otherwise is to seek indefinite deferment of payment which the staff and their trade unions would be certain to oppose.

The dangers from providing misinformation on TUPE are illustrated by BET's 1995 action against Humberside County Council. Interim damages of £3 million have been paid for 'grossly understated' employment liabilities on a catering contract.

TUPE case examples

Fundamental case law on the principles embodied in transfer of undertakings is largely derived from the European Community. The applicability of TUPE rights to staff in non-commercial entities is established by the case of *Dr Sophie Redmond Stichting v Bartol and Others*[1] (dealing with the transfer of a local authority subsidy for services to drug addicts to a new centre) and it covers contracting-out by the ruling of the European Court of Justice in *Watson Rask and Christensen v ISS Kantineservice*[2] (concerning the award of a contract for canteen services formerly performed in-house).

The case of *Christel Schmidt v Spar- und Leihkasse*[3] demonstrated that a single cleaner associated with a continuing requirement for a cleaning service could constitute a transferable entity. Conversely in the so far unreported case of *Rygaard v Dansk Arbejdsgiverforening*, the European Court of Justice ruled that a carpenter with a short-term contract to complete was not a stable economic entity. Thus specific works contracts are unlikely to lead to TUPE situations.

In addition *Katsikas v Konstantinidis*[4] upheld the rights of each county to determine the fate of the contract of employment of employees who choose not to transfer. Accordingly, the British position in treating such staff as having elected to resign is a legitimate exercise of discretion.

1 [1992] IRLR 366.   2 [1993] IRLR 133.
3 [1994] IRLR 302.   4 [1993] IRLR 179.

In the UK in the prominent case of *Dines and Others v Initial Health Care Services and Pall Mall Services Group Ltd*[1], the employment appeals tribunal set a detailed check-list of factors which should be considered in assessing whether an entity, retaining its identity, in fact transfers giving rise to protection of terms and conditions of employment.

The unreported case of *Bates v Amber Valley District Council* demonstrates that TUPE can apply not only to a council contracting-out but when taking back staff, in this instance to ensure a leisure centre remained operational following the financial collapse of a contractor. In this case the council was liable for the arrears of wages owed to the staff by their former employer, a liability transferring with the staff to the council.

In another recent landmark Employment Appeal Tribunal judgment, *Milligan and Bailey v Securicor Cleansing Ltd*, the Tribunal ruled that TUPE protection applied even if the employee had not fulfilled the two year qualifying period of employment to bring an action for unfair dismissal before an industrial tribunal. The case remains to be reported.

The Court of Appeal, in the case of *Newns v British Airways plc*[2], held that an employee has no legal right to secure an injunction to prevent the employer from transferring a business or entity. Prior to the 1981 Regulations the common-law position was that a contract of employment is personal to the parties and cannot be transferred to a third party without the employee's consent. The case accepts that the common law is no longer applicable but the court went on to state that even where the regulations do not apply, the employee's interest are safeguarded by a right to seek damages for unlawful termination of the contract of employment and an injunction will not be available to prevent the intended transfer of the operation.

Finally in March 1995 in a Scottish Court of Session case, *Stirling District Council v Allen and Others*[3], it was established that the transferors duties and liabilities all pass to the transferee and cannot be viewed as joint responsibilities for the purposes of bringing legal proceedings. Accordingly allegations of unfair dismissal at the time of transfer could not be brought against the council which had issued the offending redundancy notices but only against the transferee contractor who inherited the problem.

CONTRACT CONDITIONS RELATING TO STAFFING

As will be clear from earlier chapters, the extent to which a local authority can consider factors relating to the contractor's workforce in evaluating tenders is limited if accusations of anti-competitive practices are to be avoided. This does not mean the local authority cannot include within the service specification the qualities or skills expected of those of the contractor's staff to be deployed in providing services for the council. Contract conditions or clauses in the specification that concern the matters set out below ought to be acceptable, providing the council can demonstrate a genuine need to include them:

1 [1994] IRLR 336.
2 [1992] IRLR 575.
3 [1995] LRLR 30.

(i) the level of skill and training of relevant staff (in particular, those in a supervisory capacity);
(ii) the need to verify that staff in sensitive areas have no convictions involving sexual offences, violence or dishonesty;
(iii) safety procedures on council premises;
(iv) race relations (see Chapter 5).

Examples of specific contract drafting to achieve the ends discussed can be found in Appendix III.

DISABLED EMPLOYEES

Local authorities have frequently employed persons with physical disabilities or learning difficulties in such manual services as street-sweeping as part of their social responsibility to the community they serve. To the extent that the DoE recognises that the nature of the initiatives taken by local authorities on this front gives rise to increased costs or lower productivity, an estimate of this factor can be taken into account in tender evaluation.

It is debatable whether external contractors can lawfully be cajoled into employing such persons when DSO staff are considered for new positions with an incoming contractor after the in-house bid has failed.

STAFFING ISSUES FOR SUCCESSFUL DSOS

Since the cost of employing sufficient staff is likely to be the prime element of the DSO tender, the emphasis placed on reducing staffing, increasing productivity and negotiating revisions to terms and conditions prior to bidding tends to overshadow the need to continue to control expenditure on the workforce once the service has been retained in-house.

DSOs have to be self-sufficient and produce a set rate of return on their trading accounts, out of which all their costs are deducted. The only corresponding credit they are given is their tender price, which is normally adjusted annually, in the same manner as would have been allowed to the external tenderers in the contract conditions, by way of an allowance for inflation. Broadly speaking, this means that the ability to pay governs whether pay awards can be implemented, bonuses paid and new benefits or personnel policies created for council staff generally applied to the DSO's workforce if the cost implications are not to threaten survival.

All of the issues raised above concerning negotiations remain applicable, and the threat of equal-pay-for-equal-work claims may be particularly problematic for DSO managers who secured revised wage levels in workforces with staff who may be able to make legitimate comparisons between their positions and those of staff employed elsewhere in the council. Since the local authority, rather than the DSO in isolation, is the employer the fact that all other DSO workers are employed on the same conditions is irrelevant to allegations of inequality.

The best strategy, therefore, must be for the DSO management to endeavour to win the full support of all their staff by open and frank communication while seeking empowerment from the council to grant all staff a share in any surpluses generated by their efforts and productivity.

Chapter 10

LOCAL AUTHORITY SERVICE PROVISION TO OTHER BODIES

This chapter examines the problems posed should a local authority wish to provide services to another public body within the context of CCT, an issue commonly referred to as cross-boundary tendering. The material is also relevant to the supply of goods and services by a local authority to the private sector.

The Audit Commission, in a letter dated 9 October 1991 and addressed to the local authority associations, cited work for the private sector and situations 'where an authority's work for other authorities or public bodies is not reasonably related to the capacity necessary for the tendering authority to carry out its own functions' as the categories of arrangement causing most difficulty to district auditors. Hence the need to explore them further.

Prior to the implementation of CCT it was by no means unusual for local authorities to contract with each other for the provision of services. Economies of scale and utilisation of excess capacity are only the most obvious reasons for such contracts. While statutory authorisation continues to exist, the Audit Commission and others are questioning the extent of that authority in the belief that cross-boundary tendering may be beyond a local authority's powers, or *ultra vires*. The stance taken is that councils have no general power to trade for profit nor to bear the risk of losses impacting on the authority's council-tax payers. However, the LGA 1988 envisages circumstances in which an authority will perform works contracts for others as well as its own functional work. The risk of challenge is present as long as the current uncertainty lasts, but it can be narrowed by careful consideration of the powers and duties giving rise to contractual arrangements and of the reasons for invoking them. Furthermore in December 1995 the DoE wrote to the AMA stating that it now believes councils may have the power to trade for profit and take on staff for such purposes. The difficulty in relying on this advice is that it does not overcome the well-argued body of case law used by the Audit Commission to justify its position.

To be safe, a local authority must determine, firstly, whether it can consider contracting for the provision of services to or the receipt of services from another council and, secondly, whether it should. Put another way, is it lawful to contract and, if so, is it reasonable to do so? These decisions must be considered in light of the general fiduciary duty owed by a council to those individuals liable to make up any losses incurred in performing work for another authority through their council tax. The payments sought under a contract must be sufficient to cover the costs and contingent liabilities and may therefore generate surpluses if foreseen risks do not materialise. Such surpluses must be distinguished from trading for profit, which is *ultra vires*.

Empowerment is the cornerstone of the arguments surrounding cross-boundary tendering and an examination of the statutory provisions that may legitimise inter-authority contracts, or those with other public bodies, and an overview of the concept of *ultra vires* are the starting points for this chapter.

THE DOCTRINE OF *ULTRA VIRES*

A statutory body, such as a local authority, may pursue only such objects, however advantageous to the community, and use only such powers as are expressly laid down by Act of Parliament or can be reasonably implied from the provisions of an enactment. This is supplemented for local authorities by a common-law power, now embodied in section 111 of the LGA 1972, authorising anything to be done that is calculated to facilitate or is conducive or incidental to the discharge of any function. Before section 111 can be relied on, it must be harnessed to a purpose or power expressly authorised by statute. Without a substantive duty or power, ancillary or incidental powers do not exist. Local authorities in Britain are thus in a very different position to those in other European countries. In France, for example, anything can be done that is deemed to be in the interests of the public.

The doctrine of *ultra vires* developed as a means of protecting the rights of shareholders from abuse by company directors. Its applicability to local government was established in a series of nineteenth-century cases and stems from the need to safeguard those who would have to bear the financial consequences of any arbitrary or unlawful action by their representative authority. Since then any decision of an authority, any exercise of its powers and any expenditure incurred can be tested and overturned by the courts if deemed *ultra vires*. The consequence if a contract is found to be outside an authority's powers is that the transaction is void and the parties to it stand to be returned, so far as possible, to the positions they would have been in had the contract never existed.

In relation to the provision of services to other bodies, it is obviously incumbent on both parties to satisfy themselves that a relevant statutory power exists. The issue is further complicated by the fact that the existence of a power may be insufficient to save a transaction or contract if the object served by exercising the power is itself improper. It is well established, for example, that the pursuit of profit is not a purpose for which local authorities were created and that they cannot 'endeavour to trade to make a profit'[1]. Indeed, it has recently been rendered clear that a council cannot volunteer services that are ancillary to any statutory function and expect to levy a charge for them on the public or companies unless expressly authorised to do so[2].

Profit and the creation or maintenance of employment are two of the principal objects prompting the Audit Commission to attempt to impeach the practice of cross-boundary tendering by local authorities. Before turning to an examination of the Audit Commission's position, an analysis of the powers apparently available to a council wishing to provide services to other bodies is necessary.

---

1 *Attorney-General v Smethwick Corporation* [1932] 1 Ch 563.
2 *McCarthy and Stone (Developments) v Richmond-upon-Thames LBC* [1991] 4 All ER 897.

THE LOCAL AUTHORITIES (GOODS AND SERVICES) ACT 1970 (LAGSA)

The LAGSA 1970 was passed to remove uncertainty as to the legality under the common law of vital and frequently large-scale arrangements between authorities for services such as computer facilities. The Act permits co-operation and agreements between councils and with other designated public bodies for the supply of goods and materials, the provision of administrative, professional or technical services, the use of any vehicles, plant or apparatus owned by the local authority and the performance of maintenance work on land or buildings. Among other things, the Act thus authorises maintenance contracts, consultancy arrangements and vehicle hire.

Designated public bodies for these purposes include police committees and authorities; new town development corporations; passenger transport executives or metropolitan county passenger transport authorities; schools and other education establishments, including non-profit-making private schools; health authorities and hospitals; housing associations; fire and civil defence authorities; water authorities; the five 'City Challenge' companies for Bethnal Green, Bradford, Deptford, Hulme and Nottingham; HM Inspectors of Schools in England and Wales; and the School Curriculum and Assessment Body. The change in status of water authorities to limited companies may affect their continued designation as public bodies, but new powers exist for contracts or agency agreements between the new companies and local authorities.

The effect of the Act is to provide clear statutory authority for certain types of arrangement between councils and other public bodies. Such contracts for services are not, in principle, *ultra vires*. This does not preclude the possibility of impeaching the motivation for entering such a contract.

The powers set out in the LAGSA 1970 were neither increased nor restricted on the implementation of CCT. The LGPLA 1980 and LGA 1988 only place new procedural requirements on the tendering processes for works contracts where the service is defined as one to which CCT is applicable.

The final issue in relation to the LAGSA 1970 is the possibility of attempts to limit authorities in exercising their powers other than for the purpose of using surplus labour or other resources. The Act makes no reference to spare capacity, but the Audit Commission has questioned whether power exists to employ additional staff for the purpose of supplying services to another authority or public body. This matter is dealt with below as part of the examination of the LGA 1972.

THE LGA 1972

Several sections of the LGA 1972 are relevant to the subject of cross-boundary tendering, notwithstanding that it contains no powers similar to those found in the LAGSA 1970.

Section 111

The first reference people are wont to make when statutory authorisation for action is unclear is to section 111, which empowers an authority 'to do anything . . . which is calculated to facilitate or is conducive or incidental to the discharge of any of their functions'. Pleading section 111, however, will not achieve anything unless a primary power exists to which the planned incidental actions have a reasonably direct relationship. Section 111 cannot be used to justify anything merely because it is in the interests of the council or local inhabitants, even if everyone would find the action desirable or profitable.

The section does have a direct and obvious use where lawful functional work undertaken by a local authority necessitates employment of staff or plant and gives rise to a genuine surplus capacity. For example, seasonal fluctuations in workload or the need to employ sufficient staff to cover holidays and sickness may well lead to under-utilisation of some employees. Alternatively, unforeseen eventualities, such as a temporary drop in demand for the service, can occur that require short-term alternative activities for staff to be found rather than effecting expensive redundancies until the longer term needs can be predicted.

In such circumstances the spare capacity could be placed at the service of another party and there is no obvious reason to restrict that use to other public bodies since the LAGSA 1970 would not be invoked as authority for the arrangement. Naturally, this is not an unfettered option. Where express powers exist to second staff to private-sector organisations, as in section 65 of the Health Services and Public Health Act 1968, section 111 cannot be used to further extend the possibilities for employing surplus staff or to avoid any statutory restrictions placed upon such activity.

The work undertaken for the third party must be of the same nature as the authority's own work or the spectre of *ultra vires* may rear its head again. It has been held, for example, that a ferry company had no power to charter out a reserve boat for the purposes of pleasure cruises, the objects of the company being limited to the effecting of river crossings. A long line of cases confirms this logic.

Section 112

Section 112 gives the main power for a local authority to employ staff for the purpose of carrying out its functions. Once a power to provide services to other public bodies is established under the LAGSA 1970, there is no reason why the providing authority should not employ staff in reliance on section 112 specifically to perform those services. The only difficulty is the extent to which carrying out the provision of services to another public body is genuinely in the interests of the authority. If the number of staff to be employed is large in comparison with the scale of the council's own operation, the use of the LAGSA 1970 power may be deemed irrational or unreasonable, and the subsidiary power to employ staff will also constitute an abuse of authority.

Section 101

Section 101 empowers a local authority to discharge the functions of another local authority. If such an agency agreement is made, the work undertaken will become functional work rather than a works contract, in the hands of the agent authority. The importance of this distinction lies in the fact that the agent authority will be able to invite tenders from its own DLO or DSO, providing the relevant tendering requirements of the LGPLA 1980 or LGA 1988 are met, without any of the potential risks of challenge pursuing cross-boundary tendering activity reliant on the powers in the LAGSA 1970.

Provided that the agent authority's in-house contractor can demonstrate cost-efficiency and win the work in competition, the use of section 101 offers a viable alternative approach for larger scale contracts or those for services not expressly authorised by the LAGSA 1970. The only arguable drawback is the necessity for the agent authority to perform the client function, specifying, tendering and monitoring the work, rather than merely providing the direct-service element of the function.

Section 137

Section 137 enables a local authority to spend limited monies on projects not otherwise authorised by statute that are in the interests of the inhabitants of the borough or county.

The Local Government (Miscellaneous Provisions) Act 1982 added new subsections permitting financial assistance to those carrying on commercial or industrial undertakings. It may be that the provisions of section 137 allied to section 111 could authorise limited service provision to other bodies where no other identifiable power exists.

MISCELLANEOUS POWERS

It should not be overlooked that the provision of services to other public bodies or the private sector may be expressly authorised in the case of individual activities. For example, section 33 of the Local Government and Housing Act 1989 empowers the provision of certain services to specific sections of the community, the Civic Restaurants Act 1947 authorises certain catering operations to the public, the Highways Act 1980 allows local authorities to carry out work on highways for private companies and section 38 of the Local Government (Miscellaneous Provisions) Act 1976 authorises the sale of surplus computer capacity to any person.

SERVICES FOR COLLEGES AND GRANT-MAINTAINED SCHOOLS

The achievement of corporate status for colleges with effect from April 1993 and the increasing numbers of schools seeking to opt out of local authority control in favour of grant-maintained status have created a new range of bodies in the public sector that may wish to purchase services from their former parent authorities or, indeed, from other councils. While the LAGSA 1970 provides that services can be provided to public bodies, the definition of which includes schools and colleges, recent specific education legislation and Department for Education (DfE) guidance complicate matters.

The Further and Higher Education Act 1992 makes it compulsory for local authorities to provide cleaning services for colleges. However, it is also compulsory for college staff to transfer to the new corporate institution. This anomaly is now to be resolved by an express exemption from the duty to transfer staff for any employees working for a council DSO performing a defined activity for which it has had to bid under the LGA 1988.

In respect of defined activities (other than cleaning) and support services not yet subject to compulsory competition, there is no duty for the council to provide services and, if it wishes to do so, it must justify its decision within the context of the general restrictions covered in this chapter.

Local authorities may continue to provide services to grant-maintained schools, until the enactment of the Education Bill 1992. Clause 244 restricts the provision of support services to those specified by the Secretary of State for a maximum period of two years within the area of the LEA or any adjacent council.

THE AUDIT COMMISSION'S VIEWS ON CROSS-BOUNDARY TENDERING

Since to run counter to the Audit Commission's advice on cross-boundary tendering, issued as 'Technical Release 23/90 to District Auditors' on 10 October 1990, is to incur the risk of challenge, an examination of the advice and the validity of the views it contains is a vital step in the consideration of service provision to other public bodies.

It should first be emphasised that the Technical Release does no more than offer an interpretation of the law embodied in the LAGSA 1970 by the solicitor to the Audit Commission and his counsel. As is always the case, it is for local authorities to form their own view of the legality of any proposed action before they proceed. A district auditor, or an individual with the necessary legal standing, such as a charge-payer, may, however, challenge the course of action taken by the authority.

The Audit Commission's Technical Release has seen considerable critical analysis in local government circles. In its attempt to impeach the use councils have made of the LAGSA 1970 it has even been characterised by Roger Morris, writing as Chief Executive of Northampton Borough Council, as creating 'unlawfulness by rumour or innuendo'.

The position taken by the Audit Commission is that 'local authorities have no general power to engage in cross-boundary tendering for the purpose of deriving a profit therefrom or to provide/maintain employment'. This has been extrapolated from the proposition that local authorities were established to discharge functions expressly vested in them; that there is no express warrant for endeavouring to trade for profit (so-called municipal trading), since to do so is to risk losses, not to the local authority but to its council tax payers; that a local authority's powers to employ staff are limited to those necessary to discharge its functions; and that there is no general power to provide or maintain employment.

There is little, in fact, meriting disagreement in any of this. Only if the primary purpose of a service-providing authority in reaching an arrangement with another public body is to generate profit or to employ more people is the contract *ultra vires*. Since such motives would taint the contract, they would constitute an improper use of otherwise lawful actions. The purpose renders the action impeachable, but not the power.

It is even accepted by the Audit Commission that the materialisation of a profit on a contract is not unlawful, only making it the purpose of the arrangements. Presumably, by the same logic, if there were acceptable reasons for entering a contract, the fact that employment was created as a by-product would not matter either.

The only disturbing aspect of the Technical Release is its brash assertion that the LAGSA 1970 confers no additional power to engage staff but 'merely allows the services of staff already engaged for other (proper) purposes who may not be fully employed to be provided by agreement to other public bodies'. This attempt to impose a requirement that local authorities use only spare capacity in exercising LAGSA 1970 powers to provide services has no basis in the Act nor any other legitimate justification. As already postulated above, once a lawful reason for invoking the LAGSA 1970 powers arises, they may be linked to section 112 of the LGA 1972 and staff employed as for any other functions. Reasonableness in exercising those powers may be questioned in any case, but this should not be allowed to obscure the possibility of entirely lawful uses being made of them.

As will be clear from these arguments, the Technical Release does not appear to carry the sweeping effect on cross-boundary tendering claimed for it. If it had, it would be in direct contradiction to the Audit Commission's Occasional Paper Number 7, *Preparing For Competition*, issued in January 1989, which includes an acceptance of cross-boundary activity as a legitimate strategy option for DSOs.

The Technical Release does include guidance on the use made of the LAGSA 1970 powers as well as the material discussed above. It suggests auditors should examine whether the work to be undertaken outside the local authority bears a reasonable relationship in terms of capacity (staff, plant and vehicles) to the resources required for the councils's own functions. The implication is that if most or all of the resources are needed for external services, the legality of the use being made of the LAGSA 1970 powers needs close scrutiny. Undoubtedly, such an approach will identify the most extreme situations where powers are being abused, but the guidance does little to assist responsible authorities in drawing the line between sensible use of cross-boundary tendering and unreasonable or excessive reliance on external activity.

PROPER USE OF LOCAL AUTHORITY POWERS TO PROVIDE SERVICES TO OTHER BODIES

Wherever powers to act exist, a council remains under a duty to exercise those powers in a reasonable manner, reasonableness in a local authority context being interpreted in the Wednesbury sense[1]. Thus a restatement of the principles of local authority decision-making is useful.

In reaching its decisions a local authority must take into account all relevant matters and must disregard irrelevancies. It must have proper regard to its general fiduciary duty to its charge-payers or council tax-payers. This involves an analysis of the risks inherent in taking each action and, in particular, the possibility of incurring losses or of so diverting its resources to

---

1 *Associated Picture Houses Ltd v Wednesbury Corporation* [1947] 2 All ER 680, CA.

the provision of external services that the council's own internal needs might fail to be met in full.

Furthermore, the authority must act honestly and in good faith. It must not seek to conceal its dominant motives, and if these involve the creation of profit or maintaining employment, the authority should not proceed, since to do so would constitute an abuse of power.

Finally, there is the issue of proportionality: there must be a reasonable and direct correlation between the local authority's goal and the action it considers appropriate to achieve that end.

The local authority associations, in urging prudence by local authorities in the area of cross-boundary tendering, suggested careful consideration be given to the capability to manage the work, the existence and availability of suitably skilled staffing resources, and the adequacy of the preparation of costings for external work and the management information and control systems available to the DSO.

In contracting, the risk of losses can be minimised by careful identification of possible contingencies and pricing for them, in the knowledge that if the hazards do not materialise, surpluses will accrue to the council from the arrangements. Plainly, a council cannot set out to subsidise loss-making services and a DLO or DSO must make the set rate of return on defined work, so that tendered bids must, to a great extent, err on the side of financial caution.

Notwithstanding the spectres of district auditor challenge, DoE intervention (in CCT contract awards), judicial review at the instigation of an affected party or council tax payer and even of surcharge if illegality is found, a local authority acting reasonably should have little to fear. The important specific considerations that should inform cross-boundary tendering decisions are discussed below.

Relationship between an authority's internal and external services

The greater the proportion of external work undertaken by a local authority, the greater the risk that the existence of these operations cannot be justified by the needs of the council for services to fulfil its primary functions. The ratio of services provided for the council itself and to external bodies is therefore one of the tests that will be used by district auditors in coming to a view as to whether the further exercise of powers to enter contracts with other bodies is reasonable.

It is impossible to provide absolute percentages of external work that can be safely contracted; they depend on the individual case put forward by the authority. However, the nearer the proportion of external work draws to 50 per cent of the total activity, the closer will matters be watched by the district auditor. A small-authority service expanding dramatically to bid for the work of a larger district or county is not likely to be regarded sympathetically.

In extreme cases the council's own contracts may be won under CCT by other tenderers. It will be lawful in those circumstances to retain a DSO to complete existing commitments to external bodies, but it is difficult to argue that tendering for further work would be a reasonable exercise of the relevant powers. The only motivation would be to secure the survival of the DSO and retain employees, which would constitute an unlawful purpose.

Geographical limitations

There is no absolute geographical limitation on cross-boundary tendering in the LAGSA 1970, but relative locations ought to inform the extent to which it is reasonable for a local authority to provide services to another council or body. Much depends on the nature of the service. On-line computer facilities can readily be supplied from and to geographically remote sites. With the provision and management of physical services, such as grounds maintenance and refuse collection, the constraints of distance become more problematic. For such work, the fact that the service provider and recipient are near neighbours and the supplying council has conveniently situated depots from which to operate could be significant factors in assessing the reasonableness of any proposed arrangement. Non-neighbouring authorities will tend to be less able to justify inter-authority contracting.

Levying charges for work

Even where a local authority believes it is lawful for it to carry out work for others, unless the work is for a public body so that recharging cost is done under the LAGSA then the council must identify an express power to levy charges. This is the result of the case of *R v Richmond-upon-Thames LBC, ex parte McCarthy and Stone (Developments) Ltd*[1].

Government contracts

Central government departments now routinely bar council DSOs from tendering for government contracts, even where there is a history of such activity. Richmond, Lewisham, Greenwich and Westminster were prevented from tendering for grounds maintenance in London's Royal Parks for example. Arguments that spare capacity would be used, so rendering the award lawful, have been rejected. A Scottish Office spokesman made the position clear when Strathclyde was barred from bidding for a catering contract: bids from councils for government work were 'unacceptable', it was said.

ACTIONS TAKEN BY INDIVIDUAL DISTRICT AUDITORS

The role of the district auditor is to consider the legality of expenditure appearing in a local authority's accounts, rather than the wisdom of particular courses of action, and, if councillors have not been properly advised or have ignored the advice tendered by officers or auditors, to weigh the possibility of pressing for surcharges.

No threatened challenge to cross-boundary tendering has yet come before the courts, but on several occasions district auditors have used the danger of such intervention to persuade local authorities to refrain from

1 Ibid page 101.

entering contracts or to withdraw from concluded arrangements. For example, South Northamptonshire District Council won Daventry's refuse-collection contract but did not take it up, because of the threat of intervention from the district auditor. One fairly extreme case arose in September 1991 involving Milton Keynes Borough Council. Its catering DSO had tendered for contracts with sixteen Northamptonshire schools. The contracts represented 70 per cent of the DSO's projected income and involved recruiting extra staff. The first ten weeks of operation resulted in deficits. The contracts were said to be outside the scope of the LAGSA 1970 and *ultra vires*, as individual parents rather than the schools or the county council were paying Milton Keynes for the services. Unsurprisingly perhaps, John Thomas, the district auditor, was able to persuade the council to open negotiations to withdraw from the contracts in the spring of 1992. A more recent example in 1993 was the award of grounds maintenance work for Charnwood Borough Council to Nottingham City's DSO. The parties have had to withdraw by mutual agreement following the district auditor's intervention.

Another possible challenge with potentially far-reaching consequences arose in relation to the activities of Walsall Windows, the Walsall Metropolitan Borough Council's uPVC-window-fabrication operation. The DSO supplies a number of other councils, health authorities and housing associations as well as its parent borough, and external work has at different times accounted for between 10 and 60 per cent of its output. The district auditor sought to persuade the council to cease or scale down the supply to other public bodies.

OTHER CONSEQUENCES

No local authority has yet sought to argue in court the potential illegality of a contract entered into with another public body as a reason for seeking to terminate an existing arrangement, but it may be only a matter of time before one does.

THE FUTURE OF CROSS-BOUNDARY TENDERING

The uncertainty of the existing law is unsatisfactory. Even the Audit Commission, which is opposed to any broad power for local authorities to trade, accepts the existing legislation 'could constrain sensible and prudent arrangements'. Audit Commission Controller Howard Davis wrote to the local authority associations on 11 December 1990 that

> increased competition from different DSOs could lead to lower prices and better value for money. Local authorities might incur lower redundancy costs. And there is an argument that broader powers for local authorities would be consistent with Government policy in the National Health Service where authorities are actively encouraged to bid for work outside the NHS.

He also mooted the possibility of allowing local authorities to undertake work for each other subject to statutory constraints on the size of contracts, the manner in which bids are costed and the way risks are assessed.

The local authority associations and the Audit Commission are not alone in supporting new powers for councils. Anthony Scrivenor, QC, during his year as Chairman of the Bar Council, supported calls for a new power of general competence for local authorities, and PA Consulting Group, whose advice was commissioned by the government in relation to the practicalities of extending CCT to professional services, recommended that cross-boundary tendering be legalised and stimulated to create competition between authorities where no external market or service providers presently existed.

The Government's own position is changing towards a belief that councils can trade for profit and employ staff for such purposes but only a court ruling on local authority *vires* over-turning previous case law or new enabling legislation will really clarify the matter beyond doubt.

The position in Wales

The new Welsh Unitary Councils are in a different position in relation to cross-boundary tendering. Where CCT does not apply, councils are to be encouraged to establish agency agreements under which one discharges a function on behalf of another on a full cost-recovery basis.

Chapter 11

THE EXTENSION OF COMPETITION TO PROFESSIONAL SERVICES

Competition is now extended to a number of new professional disciplines, these being construction and property, legal, financial, personnel and information technology services. Each service is the subject of a specific chapter but this introductory chapter examines the extent to which the existing CCT regime under the LGA 1988 has had to be modified for professional services. It also considers the issues common to implementing competition in support activities, rather than functional services provided directly to the public with which until now market-testing was wholly concerned.

THE TENDERING REGIME

The mandatory tendering of professional services differs from the regime imposed for manual services in so far as the defined activity does not correspond with the service to be exposed to competition. Instead the defined activity includes the client functions and the competition requirement is expressed as a percentage of the value of the total service.

This fact places a requirement upon each local authority to ascertain the sum of the services comprising each defined activity (with the added difficulty of imprecise definitions set down by the legislators) and then to select sufficient services for tendering to meet the percentage target.

The upshot is the creation of two new areas of decision-making, which can in themselves be subject to complaint or challenge if an aggrieved potential tenderer chooses to allege that the purpose behind the stance taken by the council is to detract from the competition to be faced by in-house teams or has the consequence of doing so, whether intentional or not.

The selection process opens up the spectre of improper motivation. The clear expectation of the government is that selection will be as a result of criteria such as ease of specification, the degree of independence or linkage to the core or corporate activities of the council and the potential benefits achievable from competition. Choosing activities which are not duplicated in or available from the market will tend to be viewed as a decision with only one rationale: the aim of keeping services in-house at all costs. To be explicit, selections based wholly or primarily on the in-house team's ability to compete or the lack of external competition are liable to be viewed as unlawful. In such circumstances the Secretary of State might well be expected to intervene on the basis that competition has been frustrated by the council's decision.

Originally it seemed the government might modify the CCT framework more dramatically for professional services. At the end of the day, however, the cornerstones of the regime remain in place, in the shape of:

(i)   the criteria relating to advertising and specification,
(ii)   the need for written bids,
(iii) the prohibition of anti-competitive behaviour, and
(iv)   the ongoing requirement for DSOs to operate in conformity with the specification and the accounting provisions.

The changes materialising are minor. There are to be no minimum contract periods and constraints on the tendering timetable are modified. In particular the requirement to issue invitations to tender not less than three months nor more than six months from the date of advertisement is to be removed. Also being dropped are the minimum and maximum periods of 30 and 120 days respectively from the date of contract award for service commencement (the start-up period). These changes will undoubtedly increase flexibility for councils and assist in meeting the tight deadlines posed for the implementation of white-collar competition.

DE MINIMIS

As with manual services the *de minimis* concept applies. If the total cost of the service falls below the *de minimis* level stated in the relevant Statutory Instrument, the whole activity is exempt from competition. However, there is no single *de minimis* level—unlike the £100,000 level set for manual services. Each professional service has its own *de minimis* level for functional work and while £300,000 is the commonest, the level is different for construction and property services and housing management. All white-collar works contracts are permitted to take advantage of a separate *de minimis* level of £100,000.

THE COMPETITION REQUIREMENT AND THE SPECIFIED PROPORTION

As already stated, the competition requirement is a percentage of the total cost of the activity and the percentage is different for each of the professional services. However, each council will end up tendering a different value of work under CCT. This is so not only because the scale and cost of each service differs from authority to authority but because the competition requirement can be reduced by taking into account so-called credits (see below). The deduction of these credits from the competition requirement gives the specified proportion, which is the estimated value of the work that the individual council is obliged to market-test.

It will normally be the case that a local authority will select for CCT a value of work greater than the specified proportion for one very sound reason. Each year the authority will have to demonstrate that it is not carrying out more than the lawful value of the work in-house without competition. Selection of the bare minimum may mean that the competition requirement is satisfied in the first year but inflation of officer salaries and other in-house costs may mean that this is not the case in subsequent years. Furthermore, the tender accepted may be lower than the present in-house cost, in which case the new contract will not fulfil the competition requirement from the outset.

CREDITS

The competition requirement can be fulfilled not only by completing the CCT process but also by deducting work which is treated as having been exposed to competition. There are three categories of credit which can be deducted:

(i)   voluntary competitive tendering,
(ii) work for LMS schools, and
(iii) support for other local authority work which has itself been subject to CCT.

Work which has already been contracted out to the private sector but which falls within the defined activity is also credited as a final deduction

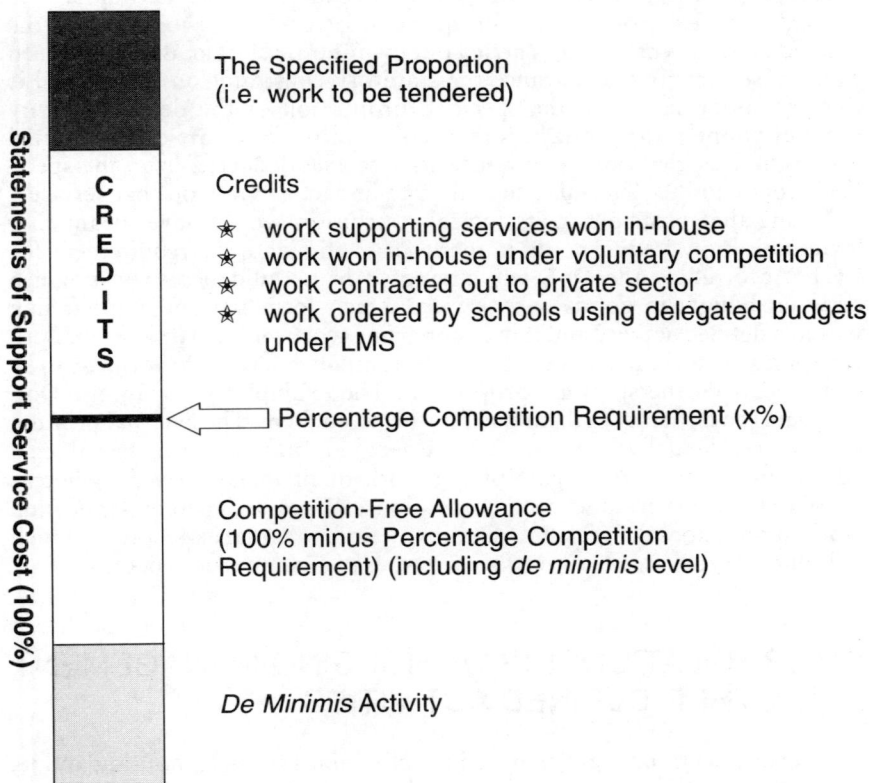

The Specified Proportion
(i.e. work to be tendered)

Credits

☆ work supporting services won in-house
☆ work won in-house under voluntary competition
☆ work contracted out to private sector
☆ work ordered by schools using delegated budgets under LMS

Percentage Competition Requirement (x%)

Competition-Free Allowance
(100% minus Percentage Competition Requirement) (including *de minimis* level)

De Minimis Activity

Statements of Support Service Cost (100%)

Figure 1   Calculating the value of professional services to be tendered

in calculating the residue, which is the specified proportion or the level of work to be exposed to market-testing.

Voluntary competitive tendering (VCT) relates to work awarded in-house before April 1994 in a tendering process involving the issue of invitations to tender to at least three external bodies. Although the tendering process may not have accorded in every detail with the CCT regime, such work qualifies as a credit against the CCT requirement for a maximum period of five years from the date of the award. After 1 April 1994 any in-house award must follow the LGA 1988 in every respect where a local authority does not wish to wait for the final date for CCT implementation set for that defined activity.

The second credit relates to work carried out in-house for a school with a delegated budget under the LMS initiative. Since such a school can choose with whom to spend that budget, the selection of the council takes place in an environment influenced by market pressures and therefore exclusion from further competition is justified. Interestingly the same thing applies where a school chooses to use its own directly employed staff to perform the defined activity. This counterbalances the inclusion of school-based staff in calculating the total value of each defined activity at the outset.

The third credit essentially covers support work to services won by a DSO in competition. Such support work forms an overhead taken into account in the original DSO tender for the service and thus has indirectly been exposed to competition and is included in the DSO's statutory annual accounts.

Finally there is, of course, the question of crediting work within the defined activity which is not carried out by in-house staff at all but has been externalised or bought in. Since the statutory constraint on the council is that it cannot carry out the specified proportion of the defined activity without winning the work in formal competition, any part of the defined activity not carried out by in-house staff can be deducted from the specified proportion to determine the ultimate impact of CCT on that service.

Taking that principle to its logical conclusion would have meant that 'externalisation credits' could in many cases eliminate the requirement for CCT. Accordingly the DoE has attempted in its guidance to distinguish between bought-in goods and services which form part of work falling within a defined activity and those supporting work within a definition. Both categories are included in the total defined activity but only the former can be deducted from the specified proportion. The examples given by the DoE illustrate the difficulty of distinguishing between them. The external printing of invoices, the delivery of council tax demands and fees for external legal advice are all said to be part of the work of financial services, whereas telephone, electricity and accommodation charges are merely supporting work. It does not take great imagination to find potential expenditure which falls into the grey area between the two types of examples used here.

INTER-RELATIONSHIP OF HOUSING MANAGEMENT AND OTHER DEFINED ACTIVITIES

The government, having recognised the close links between housing and its support services, is facilitating comprehensive housing management contracts where councils wish to achieve them by allowing postponements of the competition requirement for relevant support services which would otherwise be forced into compulsory competition prior to housing management.

WORK INCIDENTAL TO OTHER DUTIES

The competition requirement is based upon the total cost of the defined activity. There are two ways to reduce the competition requirement by removing activities from consideration when initially assessing the total cost of the service. The first and most obvious is to ensure that elements of work not expressly covered by the statutory definition are not included. The second is that work incidental to other duties does not fall within the defined activity and should be removed.

The costs of employing an officer whose duties do not fall entirely within the defined activity will be outside the total cost of the service if the percentage of his or her time spent on other work is great enough. For most professional services, any officer spending 50 per cent or less of his or her time on the defined activity is exempt. However, the percentage giving exemption is only 25 per cent for housing management.

OVERLAPS BETWEEN DEFINED ACTIVITIES

Many of the defined activities caught by the new competition requirements are activities supporting other services which are subject to competition. Thus computer costs are an overhead upon a legal service but both are a recharge to a front-line service such as housing management. The new defined activities subject to CCT generally require support service costs to be assessed as part of both the relevant specific defined activity and any other defined activities it supports. The element of double counting is then eliminated by permitting a council to net off from the competition requirement credits which include the value of any work for a DSO which has won its work in competition with external tenderers.

In any event the freedom already exists under the LGA 1988 to tender works falling into more than one defined activity in whichever is most operationally practical, provided the result is not anti-competitive.

CCT TIMETABLE

In setting timetables for the implementation of CCT for professional services, except housing management, the DoE has abandoned the approach afforded to manual services of allocating different implementation dates to individual bandings of authorities. Accordingly, common last dates for completing the CCT process are set, but these apply only to the London boroughs and metropolitan districts which were never affected by local government review and those shire counties and district councils which do not face reorganisation following review. A postponement from CCT until the elapse of a minimum period following the creation of a new authority is the outcome for the remainder.

The specific timetables applying to individual white-collar services are covered in Chapters 12–17.

CONTRACT PACKAGING

The government guidance on contract packaging (see Chapter 3) has a particular relevance to professional services where the overall scale of the activity is much smaller than in a typical manual service and thus local authorities are bound to be seeking to package work together to create viable contract sizes. The danger is that in doing so, the council will be subsequently ruled to have acted so as to prevent, distort or restrict competition if it has packaged unrelated work together, brought specialist work into a general contract, linked services which the private sector would not commonly do together or failed to so package the work as to appeal to a range of potential tenderers.

The only clarification of the DoE's position on contract packaging in white-collar services appears to be that local authorities will have freedom to package even across the boundaries of defined activities provided they do not act anti-competitively.

EVALUATION OF QUALITY

In relation to professional services, the quality of service provision is likely to be more important than the price of the service. Therefore evaluation processes are likely to be more complex than for the award of manual contracts. A separate section of Chapter 3 deals with these issues.

STATEMENTS OF SUPPORT SERVICE COSTS

The government has created a duty to publish annually the costs applicable to all council support services, covered by a defined activity. The resultant accounts will presumably be used by external auditors and the DoE as a simple means of checking whether the competition requirement for legal, financial, personnel and information technology services has been met in any given year.

The accounting requirement takes the form of a statement of support service costs (SSSC) covering the whole defined activity, not merely the elements subjected to CCT, but excluding work forming less than 50 per cent of an individual officer's duties. Such SSSCs must be produced for the financial year 1995/6 for all authorities not subject to local government review, that is to say London boroughs and metropolitan districts. Shire counties and districts that are unchanged following review are required to produce SSSCs for 1996/7. Councils still caught up in local government review will be exempt until the review is complete.

The relevant regulations prescribing the form of SSSCs are the Accounts and Audit (Amendment) Regulations 1994[1]. Broadly SSSCs for legal, financial, personnel, computer, and construction and property services must

1 SI 1994 No. 3018.

encompass the total direct costs and recharges from other specific activities and show

(i)   recharges out to other DSOs,

(ii) other support services,

(iii) capitalised costs,

(iv) charges to agency agreements under section 101 of the LGA 1972, and

(v) charges to front-line services (which are expressly categorised).

In effect, the production of SSSCs imposes a requirement to maintain an accurate time-recording system for support service staff and, in combination with the extension of CCT to professional services, renders it increasingly difficult for a local authority to load services not subject to market testing with an unfair share of overheads so as to subsidise DSOs with a view to assisting them to retain work in the face of competition.

OTHER FACTORS AFFECTING TENDERING

A study was carried out by PA Consulting Group for the government prior to the issue of the consultation paper 'Competing for Quality', which led to the application of CCT to white-collar services. It recognised a number of factors complicating or rendering difficult the tendering of professional activities. These are that the nature and scale of the services vary enormously between local authorities, they are organised in various ways with different degrees of devolution or decentralisation, there are complex links with council democratic processes and there is a lack of any track record of achievable savings from voluntary professional tendering.

It is also recognised that high tendering costs are a disincentive to the tendering of small-scale professional services; blurred boundaries to services create problems of contract packaging and specification; contracting-out imposes increased rigidity at a time of extensive local government change; and comparability between local authorities and fair competition can be undermined by switching costs out of the services subject to competition and into those that are not.

Chapter 12

TENDERING, CONSTRUCTION AND PROPERTY SERVICES

Local authorities generally have some limited experience in tendering the professional elements of construction and property services. Long-time holders of sewerage agency agreements have had to adapt to the fact that newly created water companies have chosen to place such arrangements on a contractual basis, requiring the submission of priced schedules of rates whether in direct competition with private-sector tenderers or not. In addition, the use of external valuers and estates management expertise has not been uncommon.

The implementation of competition for construction and property services, however, poses a major problem for local authorities almost unique among the other white-collar services affected by CCT. This is an issue of co-ordination given that the services included in the defined activity are usually split between technical, planning and housing disciplines at the very least, rather than concentrated in one lead department. This means that the implementation of market-testing requires first that the various factional interests, each fighting not to be selected to meet the overall percentage competition requirement, must be coerced into co-operation.

In addition, the types of activity included within construction and property services offer a great variety with few obvious links and do not lend themselves to inclusion in a single, mixed-disciplinary contract without considerable risk of challenge based on allegations of anti-competitive behaviour.

This chapter sets out the detailed requirements and implications of competitive tendering for this area of functional activity and the problems to be resolved.

THE DEFINED ACTIVITY

Construction and property services for CCT purposes are architecture (including landscape architecture), engineering, valuation, property management and surveying (including quantity and building surveying) and the detailed tasks included in the defined activity are set out in the Local Government Act 1988 (Competition) (Defined Activities) (Construction and Property Services) Order 1994[1].

1 SI 1994 No. 2888.

The work elements incorporated include:

(i)   giving advice,
(ii) establishment and management of capital and revenue programmes for development and maintenance of relevant land,
(iii) design and planning of development projects and maintenance work (including feasibility studies, investigatory work and the preparation of plans, costings and reports),
(iv) management of such projects (including financial and contract management),
(v)   the management of relevant land, and
(vi) procuring, monitoring or supervision of or arranging payment for any of the other services mentioned above.

Relevant land is that occupied by the council, or in which it has or is seeking to acquire an interest or which it maintains or manages by agreement and highways (or public roads). For the purpose only of management of relevant land, local authority housing is excluded from the defined activity.

The defined activity is thus all-embracing. It covers all services, including client activity and regulatory work, and it is for each local authority to determine which tasks are unsuitable for competition and to use the competition-free allowance to protect them from tendering. The principal difficulty with this is likely to be that professional construction and property officers have wide-ranging regulatory and enforcement actions (in particular in the interface between highways advice and town planning decisions) which, if preserved as the first call on the CFA, may impair the council's ability to provide a full professional client function for each aspect of the tenderable services.

CLIENT ROLE FOR MANUAL SERVICES CONTRACTS

The defined activity under the heading of construction and property services includes the management of maintenance work and of relevant land. This can be interpreted as incorporating the previously retained council responsibilities as client to supervise and monitor building, grounds and highway maintenance and street lighting. The Department of the Environment has written to Cambridge City Council stating its view that client management of manual work is not caught by the new defined activity. This gives comfort but as the Department of the Environment has been at pains to point out previously, it is for local authorities to take their own legal advice and for the courts to determine the interpretation of statute law. All that can safely be said is that councils remain at some risk of challenge if the total defined activity from which the competition requirement is taken does not include blue-collar client-side activity relating to land and buildings.

EXCLUSIONS

Agency work carried out under section 6 of the Highways Act 1980 (or section 4 of the Roads (Scotland) Act 1984) or on behalf of sewerage undertakers (the water companies) is exempt from CCT. In addition, work which would otherwise fall within the defined activity but which takes up less than 50 per cent of an officer's duties, is excluded.

COMPETITION REQUIREMENT AND
DE MINIMIS LEVEL

The statutory requirement is to subject 65 per cent of the defined activity to competition subject to the normal credits for services already competitively tested or externalised (see Chapter 11). This leaves a competition free allowance of 35 per cent within which all client activity for construction and property work and any regulatory work deemed unsuitable for competition must be reserved. The variety of services included in the defined activity and its traditional organisational separation between different departments mean that it may be impossible to secure a client-side presence that is as low as the figure of 5 per cent of the value of contracted work reported as the average for CCT by the Audit Commission[1].

The relevant *de minimis* level below which there is no competition requirement is £450,000.

INTER-RELATIONSHIP WITH
HOUSING MANAGEMENT

The management of local authority housing is expressly excluded from the definition of construction and property services. However, housing stock is relevant land for the elements relating to capital and revenue programmes and other elements of the defined activity may be carried out within a housing department as dedicated technical services.

Plainly this opens up a particular need for councils to determine whether technical support for housing management should be tendered as part of a housing management contract or separately as part of a construction and property contract. As originally stated by the Department of the Environment, the intention of the parallel definitions was to avoid the inclusion in construction and property services of any housing management tasks excluded from the housing management defined activity as being client-side tasks, but it is by no means certain that there are no more overlaps. The Local Government Act 1988 (Competition) (Defined Activities) (Housing Management) Order 1994[2] incorporates the planning and management of routine maintenance programmes for council housing (including the supporting construction or property services), excluding only construction and major repair work.

HIGHWAYS AGENCY WORK

Highways are relevant land for the purposes of the construction and property services defined activity. Engineering activity in relation to highways is

---

1 'Making Markets: a review of the audits of the client role for contractual services' (March 1995), Audit Commission.
2 SI 1994 No. 1671.

frequently the subject of agency agreements by which districts carry out the work on behalf of county councils. For the purposes of CCT such work forms part of the defined activity of the district council. A circular letter from the Department of the Environment dated 18 May 1995 clarifies that such agency work becomes functional work of the district council. The letter states as follows:

> Under the provisions of the 1988 Act defined activity work done by district Councils as agents of County Councils under highways agency agreements falls to be treated as part of the District Council's own work, a proportion of which must be exposed to competitive tender. The District may choose to tender agency work, and it may then be undertaken by a third party.

It then goes on to expand this and makes it clear that wherever:

> a local authority arranges for the discharge of a function by another authority . . . (for CCT purposes) the work is treated as the functional work of the executing authority and forms part of the defined activity of that authority.

ONGOING PROJECTS

Construction and property work of a project nature which is under way at the date when the CCT process must be completed can be set aside from the value of work which otherwise has to be won in competition by the in-house team. This temporary exemption from compulsory competition applies to ongoing work on design and planning, plus the management of the ensuing project. However, the exemption from CCT lasts only until the investigatory or feasibility work is concluded (leaving the detailed design to be subject to CCT) or, if the work is further advanced at the date of CCT's implementation, until the final certificate for the actual construction or project completion is issued.

In determining whether to utilise this power to postpone CCT for ongoing projects, local authorities will have to have regard to the consequences for the staff retained to complete them. If the contract for other related construction and property work is lost to an external provider, the staff retained pending project completion may lose their TUPE rights to secure a transfer of their contracts of employment (see Chapter 9) and ultimately become redundant.

TIMETABLE

London boroughs and English metropolitan districts are required to subject construction and property services to competition by April 1996. Local authorities which completed reorganisation by April 1995 have to complete CCT by April 1997, those subject to a structural change before April 1996 have until April 1998 and those changed before April 1997 have until April 1999. Essentially, therefore, English councils caught by local government review are given two years' grace to consider and implement CCT.

The timetable is set by the Local Government Act 1988 (Competition) (Construction and Property Services) (England) Regulations 1994[1] but as with the regulations covering legal services, the statutory instrument sets no

1 SI 1994 No. 3166

timescale by which county councils and non-metropolitan districts which are not subject to structural change are required to implement competition. The proposed date of October 1997, mooted by the Department of the Environment, has not yet therefore been given statutory effect. In Wales the newly created authorities will have to implement CCT for construction and property services by April 1998.

CONTRACT PACKAGING

The disparate nature of the block of activities making up construction and property services poses a considerable packaging problem for local authorities. There may be a real desire to entertain a single contract for any architectural, engineering, valuation, property and surveying services selected by the council for CCT. However, at this time there are few multi-disciplinary practices able to offer the range of services commonly undertaken in-house by councils. Conversely there exist any number of firms of architects, landscape architects, engineering consultants, planning specialists, chartered surveyors and valuers, all of whom would be precluded from tendering by requiring them to provide a range of services, including those outside their own specialist areas.

Even a decision to package together the operational management of buildings, management of commercial estates and valuation services (regarded by the Department of the Environment at the time of their Consultation Paper 'Competing for Quality' as readily capable of being tendered in a single contract) might be expected to be challenged, given the number of professional firms of valuers and estate agents who might handle certain aspects of this work but not the sheer scale of all of a council's property management requirements. Moreover, there is growing private-sector interest in separate facilities management contracts for administrative and operational buildings.

The Department of the Environment's own guidance on packaging, the aim of which is to appeal to a broad range of tenderers, maintains that specialist work is not to be included in general contracts. This guidance, in effect, precludes councils taking advantage of the inclusion within one defined activity of a number of different services by seeking a single contractor.

CONTRACTING EXAMPLES FOR CONSTRUCTION AND PROPERTY SERVICES

A number of local authorities have already privatised their architectural functions, which now operate at arm's length to a contractual specification. This includes Surrey County Council, the London Borough of Merton and the London Borough of Bromley's management buy-out. In addition, Westminster City Council considered tendering its building control services in the wake of the House of Lords' decision that released local authorities from liability in relation to economic loss resulting from breaches of building regulations[1].

1 *Murphy v Brentwood District Council* (1990) LGR 333.

Tendering of engineering services has been carried out by Sheffield City Council, the London Borough of Bromley, Birmingham City Council and Broadland District Council, the last of which now retains a single engineer to provide client management for external contractors.

Many councils already use external services and valuers on a contract-by-contract basis, but it is worth noting that Kent County Council and Lincolnshire County Council boast a history of internal trading-account management of their respective estates management functions as a means of obtaining effective cost comparisons with the private sector.

In addition, the London Borough of Ealing and Oxfordshire County Council have externalised their property services functions.

Chapter 13

TENDERING LEGAL SERVICES

Given that local authorities are already substantial purchasers of services from solicitors and barristers in private practice, the proposed introduction of CCT for legal services might not at first sight appear an overly onerous development. Difficulties arise, however, not from the necessity to test the cost of in-house provision against external competitors, but from the application of a tendering regime, with minimum contract periods, demanding much greater detail of specification and forecasting of future need for legal services than is required for the case-by-case basis and short-term or flexible arrangements under which work is presently placed with the private sector. Additionally, client–contractor separation poses problems in terms of the corporate advice, probity and monitoring officer functions, which are not found to the same degree in any of the other professional services liable to be subject to compulsory competition, with the possible exception of some elements of financial services.

This chapter examines the impact of competition on local authority legal services, the nature of and mechanisms for tendering elements of legal services suitable for competition, the preparation required in-house to run a legal department as a quasi-trading unit and the interface between such an entity and the staffing of corporate work.

LOCAL AUTHORITY LEGAL SERVICES

In-house legal services have arisen and grown within local authorities not only due to the specialist nature of some of the legal advice required but as a means of obtaining a competent and responsive service at reasonable cost. This approach is endorsed by its parallels with legal support for central government, the subject of Sir R Andrew's review of government legal services in 1989, in which he recommended that 'in the interests of effectiveness and economy the bulk of these services should continue to be provided on an in-house basis'. One of his principal reasons for so concluding was the need to call upon legal advisers on the instant who are familiar with the government's general policies and the procedures of Whitehall and Westminster, and who are available to be consulted for advice by their administrative colleagues at an early stage. His report stated: 'For most day-to-day legal business this sort of service can best be provided by in-house lawyers who have made a career in government dealing with public as well as private law.'

It is also instructive that the creation of the Crown Prosecution Service brought totally in-house a service formerly provided partly by local government but underpinned by the large-scale use of solicitors and barristers in private practice.

In-house services would be likely to be the continuing preference of most councils had CCT not materialised, its main virtues being the knowledge of the client business, ease of access, the scope for economies of scale, particularly in respect of preventive action and probity work, and specialisation. Any detrimental factors have readily been avoided in the past through a willingness to employ external advisers and representation where necessary, achieving a mixed economy offering all of the expertise available in the market-place in a flexible form. That said, the issue to be addressed is the manner in which in-house provision of legal services will have to change to face direct compulsory competition.

THE DEFINED ACTIVITY

Legal services constitute a defined activity under the Local Government Act 1988 (Competition) (Defined Activities) Order 1994[1]. The defined activity is limited to 'the provision of legal services by legal staff' and legal staff are defined as being solicitors, legal executives, barristers and advocates and licensed (in Scotland qualified) conveyancers.

Legal services include the provision of legal advice not only to the council, committees, members and officers, but also, where it relates to the discharge of the authority's functions, to any other person. The legislation incorporates:

(i)   legal work in connection with any criminal or civil proceedings before a court or tribunal or inquiry;

(ii) conveyancing in relation to property and in connection with contracts or agreements;

(iii) any property matters, insurance arrangements, statutory orders, notices and byelaws (and in Scotland management rules); and

(iv) local bills.

Finally legal work carried out other than by the authority's own staff is brought into the defined activity.

EXCLUSIONS

Assuming that the word advocate carries its Scottish legal significance, work carried out by unqualified staff is not within the defined activity even though legal in nature and incidental work forming less than 50 per cent of an officer's duties is excluded.

COMPETITION REQUIREMENT AND *DE MINIMIS* LEVEL

Compulsory competition applies to 45 per cent of the defined activity subject to credits for services already market tested or externalised (see Chapter

1 SI 1994 No. 2884.

11). This leaves a competition-free allowance of 55 per cent and the *de minimis* level is £300,000.

TIMETABLE

Legal services CCT must be implemented by London boroughs and English metropolitan districts no later than April 1996. Districts and counties reorganised or subject to substantial boundary changes on or prior to April 1995 have until April 1997 to complete the tendering process. April 1988 is the date for councils undergoing changes implemented not later than April 1996. Finally, those reorganised on or before April 1997 have until April 1999 in accordance with the provision set out in the Local Government Act 1988 (Competition) (Legal Services) (England) Regulations 1994[1]. These regulations are defective in one respect since they set no date by which county councils and non-metropolitan districts which are not subject to a structural change are required to implement competition. This omission contrasts, for example, with the regulations governing personnel services. The DoE proposal to make October 1997 the due date have therefore not been effected in regulations.

Welsh councils have until April 1998 to carry out legal services market testing.

CREDITS

Legal services budgets are invariably padded significantly by disbursements. These include counsel's fees, court fees and stamp duty which, being payment for specific services, ought to count as externalisation credits to be netted off the competition requirement. Whether all such disbursements will pass the DoE's stated test as services in their own right within the defined activity, rather than as support services, remains to be seen. The most unusual credit expressly mentioned relates to insurance-related legal work not carried out in-house. Where a council carries insurance and the insurers use solicitors to handle matters relating to claims, the cost of the legal service element is part of the defined activity and can then be claimed as an externalisation credit. This benefits the in-house team because every £100 added to the defined activity increases the competition requirement by £45 while the credit then given is £100 against the in-house work which would otherwise have to be tendered.

MEETING THE COMPETITION REQUIREMENT

Given the desire of most local authorities to protect corporate advice and support from competition, the probable options revolve around selection of work falling in the categories of civil and criminal litigation, conveyancing work and social services law and representation with planning support and public inquiries as a useful alternative.

1 SI 1994 No. 3164.

There will tend to be little point in tendering education-related legal work or employment law (including industrial tribunal representation) since these tasks will commonly be for schools with delegated budgets under LMS or Direct Service Organisations and therefore credits against the competition requirement can be claimed for them in any event.

CONFLICTS OF INTEREST

The Code of Conduct for solicitors precludes a firm from representing both parties in litigation, property transaction or any other situation where the interests of one may conflict with those of the other.

Accordingly it may well be a reasonable fetter on competition to require legal tenderers to refrain from representing other clients with whom the council is likely to be in litigation or dispute or any other situation where a conflict of interest might arise.

The Law Society's professional standards bulletin number 11 makes clear the importance of the issue and the scope for eliminating tenderers during evaluation on conflict of interest grounds:

> if a solicitor or firm of solicitors has acquired relevant knowledge concerning a client during the course of acting for that client, then that solicitor or firm must not subsequently accept instructions to act against that client. A local authority needs to consider this principle not only in the context of a firm seeking to tender for that authority's work but also in relation to a firm that has ceased to act for an authority in consequence of a subsequent retendering exercise or otherwise.

> At the tender stage both authority and tendering firm will need to ask themselves how frequently the range of work involved is likely to give rise to a situation where the firm will be unable to act for an existing client or the authority because of a clear conflict or where the firm will be unable to act for the authority on the basis of the relevant knowledge principle. If such situations are likely, in the opinion of either party, to arise frequently there would seem to be little point in the local authority awarding and the firm accepting a contract for that work. The wider the range of work, the smaller the geographical area and the fewer firms there are in that area the more likely it will be that a local firm will be unable to tender for the work of its own local authority or will be unacceptable to that authority.

> ... even where a breach of general principles would appear unlikely, it would not be unreasonable in some circumstances for the authority to make it a contract condition that the firm should not accept instructions to act against the authority for the duration of the contract; for example, where a firm is carrying out a wide range and volume of work for a particular authority which is thus a major client of the firm.

> The Law Society accepts that wider considerations arise ... such ... as the possible public impression of impropriety in circumstances where the solicitor is known to have a 'foot in more than one camp'. For example, the wrong impression could well be given by a firm that acted for a client in the assembly of land for future development if at the same time it was undertaking the planning work of the authority in whose area the land was situated.

> The wider the range of work and the larger its volume the more reasonable some form of general prohibition is likely to be.

RIGHTS OF AUDIENCE

An unresolved issue is the extent to which in-house legal services can compete on a level playing-field with private practice in respect of litigation. The Lord Chancellor's Advisory Committee on Legal Education and Conduct has recommended against granting rights of audience in the higher courts to employed solicitors as opposed to those in private practice. Lord Griffiths, as Chairman of the Committee, went so far as to propound the view that employed lawyers would find it difficult to demonstrate the degree of objectivity required to establish the necessary 'great trust between the judge and the advocate'. Notwithstanding pressure from the Law Society, whose president branded the argument that employed solicitors may lack detachment or impartiality as 'offensive to the employed solicitor' and one that 'does not measure up to the perceptions and experience of those who have worked for and with the employed sector', the recommendation of the committee presently stands. The result is that private-sector firms will be able to offer local authorities a completely integrated service in the field of litigation that will be achievable by in-house teams only if they are able to subcontract the element of higher-court advocacy.

AUDIT COMMISSION GUIDANCE

The Audit Commission has responded to the proposed introduction of CCT for legal services with a management paper[1] analysing the various roles, types of organisation and management techniques applicable to in-house local authority services. It distinguishes three roles within a local authority legal service: securing propriety in council affairs, providing corporate legal advice and direct legal services. This analysis is broadly similar to that made by PA Consulting Group for the government and is reflected in the DoE's 1991 consultation paper.

Corporate legal advice is required for elected members by virtue of the statutory nature of local authorities as to the lawful means of achieving their aims and the limitations on their ability to do so. This is linked by the Audit Commission with acceptance of the benefits for councils arising from the exercise of lawyers' professional skills in contributions toward sound management and administrative practice. Finally, there is the range of legal duties and powers exercised by local authorities that necessarily rely on access to legal expertise, often specialised in nature, in the shape of advice and action in the form of litigation, other forms of advocacy, draftsmanship and conveyancing.

The main issue posed is the extent to which it is possible to distinguish these roles, given that the propriety role, together with that of the statutory monitoring officer and corporate adviser, cannot be carried out without the support of legally qualified staff, and their costs are rendered viable mainly by ensuring a mix of service specific work to be exercised alongside the provision of advice and the monitoring of potential misconduct and maladministration. Then there is the need to review the organisation of legal services in the light of the changing demands placed upon them.

1 *Competitive Counsel? Using Lawyers In Local Government*, Audit Commission Management Paper No. 10, September 1991.

The provision of corporate advice sits comfortably alongside the client-officer function of commissioning, purchasing and monitoring legal services for the council. Its counterpart will be the in-house provider of legal services performing the contractor function.

The management paper goes on to suggest strongly that a local authority chief executive should not be the statutory monitoring officer or hold any lead role in terms of propriety. Instead, these functions are seen as suitable to be carried out by the senior lawyer responsible for corporate legal advice and, preferably, committee administration. This approach has already been taken by more than 50 per cent of local authorities in England and Wales, but in many smaller councils a legally qualified chief executive is seen as the appropriate alternative.

The nature of the organisational separation of client and contractor within legal services and the difficulties involved in securing staffing for the corporate and propriety roles are discussed below, taking into account the specific comments on these issues within the management paper. Similarly, the recommendation that proper systems of time recording and costing are necessary is examined elsewhere in this chapter against the practicalities of achieving them.

CATEGORIES OF LEGAL WORK

The three main categories of work identified by the Audit Commission are not of themselves sufficient to enable decisions to be taken on the manner of organising legal services in future or the extent to which client departments should be free to determine the level of service required (alongside those corporate and propriety services imposed upon them) and to examine the extent to which alternative means of provision could be considered. This section, therefore, attempts to break down the categories of work a little more while demonstrating the extent of the grey areas between them.

Corporate work will principally cover advice to the council and its policy committees, to the leading elected members, the chief executive and any executive management structures. The requirement for detailed and regularly updated knowledge of the organisation of the local authority, its policies and political dimensions favours in-house provision.

Advice and legal support to other service committees and departmental managers share many of the characteristics of corporate legal advice and it is highly desirable that this is provided by in-house staff also.

Legal support to service operations requires specialist knowledge and ought to be supplied by professionals who can offer a degree of continuity and build an ongoing relationship with officers of the client department. There is no reason why private practice professionals, if selected carefully and used regularly, should not perform such services as well as in-house staff, although convenience may dictate a preference for the latter.

Additionally, there are undoubtedly transactions and casework requiring less specialist knowledge that arise within local authorities for exactly the same reasons as they would for any other client in the public or private sector. Such services as debt recovery actions and commercial leases are examples. In this type of legal work there is no reason other than cost for preferring an in-house to an external service. Such work is suitable for tendering, provided that the costs of providing a client contact point for external solicitors are taken into account.

Finally, there is the provision of legally qualified staff to support the regulatory and propriety functions. While such staff could come from an external source, unless their firm is already carrying out substantial work for the local authority and thus already in possession of detailed knowledge of the council, its working and its staffing, the risk arises that they will be less effective at rooting out instances of *ultra vires*, maladministration, fraud and potential corruption than an in-house team.

ORGANISATIONAL OPTIONS FOR IN-HOUSE SERVICES

The organisational options for legal services are more diverse than any implicit requirement of client and contractor separation could indicate. The range of alternatives examined by the Audit Commission covers legal services as a business unit within an all-purpose legal or administrative department, the creation of a free-standing DSO and decentralisation with specialist staff seconded to the departments for whom they work.

Decentralisation may have some support from direct services in regular receipt of legal services, but is practical only where the volume of specialist work is sufficient to justify the transfer of a self-sustaining team of staff. Even where the bulk of a user's legal requirements is for specialist advice or representation the devolution of a team of lawyers and support staff will not render the recipient department self-supporting in terms of legal services. There will always be the need for general property, litigation and contract support, which cannot be economically provided other than centrally, however large the local authority.

An additional factor that militates against decentralisation of legal services is the loss of professional support and career development. One consequence is likely to be less stability in staff serving different parts of the council and potential recruitment difficulties.

Other options can work, but only a free-standing DSO avoids the consequence of staff subject to competition working directly alongside colleagues who are not. This is a problem only where DSO staff have been forced to negotiate changes to their salaries, terms and conditions to win a tender award.

The DSO model will necessitate careful examination of the means of securing legal support in the form of corporate advice and propriety work. The client side is unlikely to be able to sustain sufficient lawyers to handle all such work without risk of duplication and lost economies of scale. One solution is to purchase staff time at agreed hourly rates from the DSO for such legal work, irrespective of the fact that it is work not lending itself readily to competition or external provision. This is workable as long as a DSO is not threatened with dissolution because it has lost its warrant to provide general legal services through the operation of the formal tendering process. In that event the client must either accept the increased costs of direct employment of solicitors purely to perform this work (in the knowledge that recruitment of suitably qualified staff will become more problematic in the long run, since many lawyers will not wish to forgo involvement in purer legal practice for jobs that will appear increasingly managerial or administrative in scope) or negotiate terms for support work with the successful tenderer or a third party. Neither is likely to be totally satisfactory or other than a more costly solution.

Similar problems occur with initial specification since DSO staff are likely to hold the key skills for defining the type, level and standards of service currently received by the local authority. Unless such staff are seconded to work for the client side for a period and other mechanisms adopted to ensure the specification is not biased towards successful tendering by the DSO (see Chapters 4 and 8), the local authority's prospects of generating formal contract documentation to achieve the legal service required are greatly diminished.

Within a legal service DSO or business unit there may be room for consideration of less hierarchical models of management organisation. A partnership concept in particular may offer better chances of minimising the loss of chargeable professional time to managerial tasks. A well-supported managing partner may well cut the overheads for management within a legal service and the arrangement offers scope for increased remuneration and status for those experienced and ambitious staff who might otherwise consider leaving the organisation for the private sector only because steps up the internal career ladder appear blocked.

THE COMPARABLE COSTS OF IN-HOUSE AND EXTERNAL LEGAL SERVICES

Local government apparently places about 10 per cent of its total expenditure on legal services with the private sector, typically to cover staff shortages, to obtain specialist advice and for representation in courts in which solicitors have no right of audience or where obtaining a barrister is more cost-effective than in-house representation. Accordingly, most council legal departments will have access to information on the costs of external legal services, which can be supplemented by information as to the costs of other parties in property transactions or in litigation resulting in judgment against the local authority, where such costs are to be borne by the council.

The common feeling among in-house legal managers is that the hourly rates charged by the private sector greatly exceed the costs of directly employing solicitors, barristers and legal executives. Such untested confidence is in itself dangerous to services likely to be subjected to competition. Reliable comparisons of those hourly rates charged by external providers and the true cost of in-house provision, including all applicable overheads allocated across achievable chargeable hours, calculated in the manner outlined in Chapter 8, are required. Many legal managers may be basing existing comparisons on the salary budgets under their direct control rather than bringing fully into account all the costs that will fall to a legal DSO, once established on a trading-account basis.

The third such survey of cost comparables conducted by Chambers and Partners, a legal recruitment agency, in August 1991, provides interesting data for detailed comparison. Their overall findings were that external costs were three to four times greater than the costs of in-house provision. Although these findings must be tempered with an appreciation that the level of overheads attracted by fee-earners varied widely in Chambers' sample of legal practices, the raw data in their report is worthy of detailed examination.

The average fees charged for external legal services were £120 per hour for junior lawyers outside London (the lowest in the sample being £65 per hour) and £150–£175 in London. These were compared to average costs of £45 per hour for junior lawyers and £63 per hour for senior lawyers employed in local government and industry. Excluding all overheads, other than the direct costs of employment (salary, bonuses, national insurance contributions, cars and pension contributions), the average cost of employing a junior lawyer in private practice was £40,032 and of a senior lawyer, £71,324. The average overheads attributable were £13,442 per fee-earner for support staff and £25,136 for other general overheads.

Such figures demonstrate a basis upon which an in-house local authority legal department can be confident of winning work where required to tender on the basis of hourly rates. However, some elements of legal work lend themselves to other methods of costing. One approach is a fixed fee or retainer for a given level of work, hourly rates applying only when that work volume is exceeded; this could be used for advice services or litigation, for example. Another approach could be based on a percentage of the value of the work, which is common in property-based transactions. In neither case can an in-house team assume that the quoted costs from tenderers for volume work will remotely equate with the hourly rates chargeable for individual case work allocated *ad hoc* as need arises. After all, repetitive work, such as right-to-buy property sales or debt recovery actions, offers economies of scale, particularly where computerisation is a possibility, which will be worthy of private-sector investment if contracts running for several years are on offer and the local authority has not already produced in-house systems to reduce costs.

The present structures for legal services within London boroughs are the subject of a survey completed in 1991 by the London Borough of Southwark[1]. This demonstrates substantial differences in the size of legal services across the capital and offers interesting estimates of the administrative support required by them. Administrative support costs in the range of 10–50 per cent of the cost of employing a professional staff member were reported, the average cost being 29 per cent. While this takes no account of other overheads, it provides a useful comparison with the findings of Chambers and Partners.

TIME-RECORDING AND COSTING SYSTEMS

The issues of time-recording and accurate charging of clients for all work done are in few respects unique to legal services. The points raised below are therefore supplementary to the key tasks set out in Chapter 8.

The first step is setting up a legal-cost centre and organising the coding of clients or business units to whom charges fall to be made for legal services. Then hourly rates must be determined for each grade of staff employed based on chargeable hours not the total hours worked. The Law Society's Joint Practice Management Working Party has estimated that

---

1 *Legal and Administrative Services: A Survey of London Boroughs,* Internal Consultancy Services, London Borough of Southwark, December 1991.

billable hours equate to an average of 72 per cent of the hours worked by a legal professional.

The final phase is devising and operating a time-recording system, the results of which can be translated into invoices to client departments at regular intervals, using the hourly rates. Such systems can be manual or computerised but need not record all working hours, only those that are chargeable to clients. A cautionary note as to the reliability of manual time-recording systems is struck by an article in the *Law Society Gazette* reporting on a study in which solicitors consistently and wholly honestly misjudged the amount of lost or unproductive time and that spent on management and administration[1]. Such evidence provides a strong argument for fully computerised systems of the type used by the London Borough of Enfield (see Chapter 8).

CONTRACTING ISSUES FOR LEGAL SERVICES

Additional considerations for specification or inclusion in contract conditions in relation to legal services are care and diligence provisions and formal performance targets, in terms of response times for example; the points of client contact and the frequency thereof; the use of counsel and other technical experts (to avoid being charged for representation in addition to the contract price for services the client believed the legal contractor would perform personally); access to council files; methods of costing and verification, since hourly rates may not be an appropriate measure for all legal work; and conflicts of interest between the council and other private clients.

PRICING MECHANISMS

It has largely been assumed that the tendering of legal services will concentrate on hourly rates, with percentage fees or unit costs applicable only to limited areas of legal activity, such as commercial leases and routine conveyancing and debt collection. It is quite clear from recent developments in the United States that there are other means of pricing services even if contingency or results-based payments are largely inappropriate. These include retainers, volume discounts for bulk transactions, more generally applicable fixed-fee rates, averaged hourly rates under which all fee-earners bill at the same rate regardless of seniority, binding quotations with negotiating mechanisms for unforeseeable budgetary overspends and forms of performance incentive to reward successful outcomes. It remains to be seen whether local authorities will prove more innovative than the legal profession at large in fostering such alternatives.

MONITORING BILLS

Whatever pricing mechanism is chosen, the client responsibility extends to ensuring not only that the work is performed to the required standard but

---

1 'Solicitors Misjudge How They Spend Their Time', by Marion McKeone, *Law Society Gazette*, 26 June 1991, pp. 4–5.

that the cost of the services is correctly invoiced to the authority. Nowhere is this more important than in the field of legal services, if recent studies of the overbilling habits of American corporate lawyers have any relevance to the UK situation. Not least, this is particularly so wherever hourly rates are billed because budgetary compliance will rely upon control of the number of hours spent . There will be an additional complication where work can be carried out by different levels of staff since the council ought not to be paying for qualified expertise if the work is in fact carried out by trainees.

Plainly detailed descriptions of work completed will be required. Descriptions such as 'case management' or 'client administration' will be unacceptable and the tender documents should not admit 'uplifts for care and attention'.

Particular attention ought to be given to recovery of disbursements, although a wise authority will have carefully identified in the specification those expenses which are to be costed into the tender price and those which may be charged exclusively to the client. In any event, disbursements are liabilities incurred by a solicitor to a third party to enable him or her to provide services to the client. Thus, for example, travelling expenses (as opposed to fares) are not in fact disbursements. Nor are photocopies produced in a solicitor's own office since no cost is chargeable by a third party at the time of making them. Also those charged with verifying invoices should be aware that court fees, registry fees, stamp duty and search fees are not subject to Value Added Tax.

Finally, a warning as to the truly creative skills of solicitors in this field. If the production of documents is chargeable by the page beware of the use of double or even triple spacing, given the obvious impact on cost.

QUALITY ASSURANCE FOR SOLICITORS

While BS5750 and its applicability to professional services is discussed more fully in Chapter 20, it is worth noting here that the Law Society has produced a guide to obtaining quality assurance for legal services[1]. In addition, the Law Society and the British Standards Institution have developed a draft code of quality management for solicitors. This set of guidelines for managing the quality of legal work constitutes the main criteria for obtaining BS5750 certification. The 20 elements of the draft code are summarised below:

(i)   A solicitor's practice shall have a policy commitment to quality and clearly defined partner and staff responsibilities for implementing its quality system as well as verifying adherence and regular review.

(ii)   The quality system shall be documented.

(iii) There shall be a clear procedure for taking instructions from clients that records the nature of the business and the action to be taken and ensures that there are no conflicts of interest.

(iv)   There shall be a clear procedure for monitoring the progress of a case.

(v)   There shall be a clear procedure for document control.

(vi)   There shall be a policy for the selection of subcontractors, including technical experts and barristers.

1 *Quality: A Briefing for Solicitors*, rev. edn, The Law Society, 1992.

(vii) The practice shall be responsible for materials and documents provided by the client and shall catalogue, protect and store them properly.

(viii) There shall be a case reference system from which all information and correspondence relating to a case can be traced.

(ix) There shall be a case monitoring system and clients shall be regularly informed of progress and incoming correspondence prioritised immediately upon receipt.

(x) There shall be procedures for inspecting all work and supplies.

(xi) There shall be adequate training of, and updating of materials supplied to, personnel.

(xii) Inspections shall themselves be recorded.

(xiii) All identified problems shall be recorded and analysed.

(xiv) Prompt remedial action shall be taken wherever necessary.

(xv) The security and confidentiality of all documents and materials in transit shall be safeguarded.

(xvi) Verifications of the operation of the quality system shall be recorded.

(xvii) The quality system shall be audited by a systematic view of all its components and the reports of verification staff not less frequently than once a year.

(xviii) Partners and staff shall be trained to deliver legal services under the terms of this code.

(xix) Proper after-care and follow-up shall seek to ensure that the client remains satisfied.

(xx) Any analysis of business can be assisted by proper statistical procedures (following which will be compulsory for BS5750 registration).

A number of firms in private practice have now achieved BS5750. Whether enough of them yet hold certification to enable local authorities to seek it, without being held to be acting anti-competitively, is a moot point; the DoE's position is that there must be an adequate number of holders of BS5750 in the marketplace to specify it.

Council legal services are themselves securing certification. Braintree District Council was in 1993 one of the earliest, if not the first.

CONTRACTING EXAMPLES FOR LEGAL SERVICES

Voluntary competitive tendering in advance of statutory dates or outright privatisation has been as common within local authority services as any other defined activity as the examples below show.

The London Borough of Wandsworth elected to tender about two thirds of its legal work in four contracts, thus exceeding by some margin the statutory requirement. Its first contract for property work was awarded on a split basis to the in-house team and Gotelee and Goldsmith (of Ipswich) in 1994. Contracts for litigation, social services related work and a mixture of planning, highways and contract services are to follow.

The City of Westminster has followed a similarly vigorous line amid complaints from staff of a predetermination to award contracts externally. Its 1994 contract for civil litigation was split between Judge and Priestley and Bermans (of Liverpool), routine conveyancing went to Shindler and Co in 1993 and contracts formation work was awarded to Sharpe Pritchard. The in-house team, however, won a three-year award of criminal litigation and planning enforcement in 1993.

Prior to a change of political control in 1993, Lincolnshire County Council was publicly at the vanguard of voluntary tendering and awarded its first legal contract to Richmonds to commence in November 1992 for a four-year term in the face of stiff competition. All 63 firms applying for a place on the standing list were invited to tender and 31 bids including one from the in-house team were received. The three lowest tenderers included the DSO and the award was completed only following presentations. Accordingly, either the effectiveness of the external presentation or a predisposition against direct service provision carried the day.

The London Borough of Croydon has simply chosen to contract out its non-corporate legal work in a five-year contract commencing mid-1994 and awarded to Stoneham Langton and Passmore (based in Croydon, Piccadilly and Saffron Walden). Thirty staff transferred with the contract, leaving six people to monitor the contract and provide core advice.

The London Borough of Camden, at the other side of the political divide, contracted out its debt recovery and right-to-buy conveyancing to Parker Arrenberg (of Catford) and another private firm in 1992, the value of the contracts comprising some 15 per cent of the borough's legal work.

The London Borough of Bromley has awarded four-year contracts from mid-1994 to local firms: Judge and Priestley for conveyancing and Parker Arrenberg for litigation. The former company already held litigation contracts for Westminster.

The London Borough of Brent placed 70 per cent of its legal work externally in 1994, including a contract with Kingsford Stacey (of Lincoln's Inn) for conveyancing and commercial property work, another with the local firm of Hodders for private housing services and with a management buy-out firm Trivedy and Virdi (of Brent) for environmental services work, a broad mix of planning, highways and environmental health.

District councils have also shown unprecedented enthusiasm for VCT of legal services. Broadland District Council awarded all its legal work in 1994 to Steele and Co, an East Anglian firm, and Wansdyke District Council has also contracted out so that it no longer employs any in-house lawyers. Stirling has followed suit, awarding a three-year contract for its legal services to Harper Mcleod (of Glasgow) in 1993, a decision which has brought it to litigation over transfer of undertakings.

In contrast West Wiltshire District Council, having privatised its legal services, found itself re-establishing an in-house service from scratch within a two-year period.

Not all legal contracts have been lost through VCT, however. Hertfordshire County Council in 1993 awarded its conveyancing work to the in-house team after an evaluation of more than 70 rival bids in 1993.

Finally a warning must be placed on non-tendered privatisations. Where a council's whole legal service is the subject of a trade sale or management buy-out, the potential conflicts of interest between the council and the transferring staff require the authority to retain its own legal representation to oversee the process. The consequences of not doing so can at their worst include criminal investigation and termination of contract for undue influence as is the case with West Wiltshire District Council's solicitors and their formation of a private firm, Wilkie-Maslen, to buy out their own service.

Chapter 14

TENDERING FINANCIAL SERVICES

Traditionally a large range of functions appertaining to or only peripherally linked to finance have accrued to local authority treasurers. Making financial services a defined activity will necessarily cause much closer examination of the types of work which are core to the organisation or closely aligned with the statutory responsibilities of the treasurer. Moreover, it will focus consideration on tendering for the balance as a means of securing savings and efficiencies from which to some extent financial services have been better protected than other centrally provided services.

The economies of scale demonstrated for contracting-out financial services by a number of councils who have chosen to externalise, shows that the potential benefits from competition are greater than for most other professional services.

This chapter sets out the detail of the defined activity which is financial services, the contract packaging issues thrown up by the requirement to tender, and the examples of recent practice which may guide council decision-making in preparation for CCT.

THE DEFINED ACTIVITY

Financial services, as defined by the Local Government Act 1988 (Competition) (Defined Activities) Order 1995[1], comprise a long list of specific services commonly carried out by treasurers' divisions and departmentally based finance staff. The defined activity, as with other professional services, incorporates all the client tasks applicable to financial services and it is left to individual authorities to refrain from selecting for competition any tasks not suited for competition or vital to retain in-house.

The individual tasks within the defined activity are financial advice, accounting, administration of taxation, financial information and management systems, audit, administration, collection and recovery of rates, community charge and council tax, pay-roll, payments, income and debt recovery, pension management, investment, insurance and financial consultancy. Finally the procurement, monitoring or supervision of arranging

1 SI 1995 No. 1915.

payment for any services within the above categories (the client roles) are expressly included.

Financial advice covers the provision of guidance not only to the defined authority, its committees, its members and its officers but also to any other person if in connection with the discharge of the authority's functions.

The term accounting services expressly includes the completion of statutory accounts and the maintenance of appropriate financial records.

The administration of direct and indirect taxation and the administration, collection and recovery of non-domestic rates, council tax, water and sewerage charges or rates, community charges and general rates are included as two separate headings for no apparent reason. Together they tie in all of an authority's responsibilities for local taxation except the setting of council tax and rent levels, which are statutory responsibilities of the authority itself.

The development and maintenance of financial information and management systems create an obvious overlap with the defined activity of information technology services because in any authority the scale of financial information needs will require computerisation.

Audit services incorporate in particular liaison with external auditors and other bodies but not the statutory audit which is not the council's responsibility; it merely pays the District Audit Service or an external auditor to fulfil the role.

The provision of pay-roll facilities is self-explanatory but some mention must be made of the complexity of such services for a council. Monthly, weekly and cash paid employees must be catered for as well as car loan payments, mileage reimbursement, superannuation, pay awards and increments.

The determination, administration and making of payments, including arranging abatements and rebates, bring in all housing benefits and council tax benefits work, although these are not specifically mentioned. The difficulties of separating out the statutory elements of these services which cannot be contracted out are touched on elsewhere in this chapter.

The collection of income and recovery of debt require a careful interface with legal services if tendered, since civil litigation is a likely candidate for selection by local authorities as part of the requirement to tender legal work.

The administration of the authority's pension fund includes a specific reference to the management of investment and actuarial services. The requirement for actuarial services is itself likely to expand as local authorities endeavour to measure the comparability of pension schemes offered by tenderers for a range of local authority services (see 'Transfer of Undertakings' in Chapter 9).

The arrangement and management of borrowing and investment and the monitoring of cash flow essentially encompass all local authority treasury management.

The administration of a defined authority's insurance arrangements throws up two main issues. Much of the work on considering claims is carried out externally by insurers and this incorporates an element of legal work which could be claimed as a credit against the competition requirement for either financial services or legal services. Secondly, Zurich, as the insurer inheriting the majority of the local government insurance market on the demise of Municipal Mutual, has a firm policy that it will not deal with brokers but only directly with the council. Accordingly, however much councils may wish to subject the residual elements of insurance management to a third party by externalisation or CCT, they may be prevented from doing so.

Financial consultancy work, including research, may cause an overlap problem with personnel services in relation to training of staff on budget management and financial procedures and regulations for the authority.

Interestingly, no explicit reference is made in the defined activity to the preparation of the authority's proposed budget nor to its monitoring. It remains to be seen, therefore, whether some elements of this work can be said to escape inclusion in the accountancy and audit heads.

EXCLUSIONS

Finance work comprising less than 50 per cent of an officer's duties is excluded, as it is with other support services subject to CCT. This fulfils the DoE commitment to exclude financial tasks undertaken by managers and administrators whose primary responsibility is to a non-financial service.

In addition, education grants and payments administration are exempted notwithstanding that much of this work concerns financial evaluations and making payments. Housing benefit and council tax benefit administration are not similarly exempted.

COMPETITION REQUIREMENT AND
DE MINIMIS LEVEL

The statutory requirement is to tender 35 per cent of the defined activity subject to the normal credits for services already tested or externalised (see Chapter 11). This leaves a competition-free allowance of 65 per cent.

The relevant *de minimis* level below which there is no competition requirement is £300,000.

TIMETABLE

London boroughs and English metropolitan districts must complete CCT for financial services by April 1997. Local authorities having completed reorganisation or substantial boundary changes by April 1995 have to subject this defined activity to competition by October 1997; those subject to a structural change completed by April 1996 have until October 1998 and unchanged county councils and non-metropolitan districts have until April 1998. Those changed by April 1997 have until October 1999. This timetable is set by the Local Government Act 1988 (Competition) (Financial Services) (England) (Regulations) 1995[1].

In Wales the newly created authorities will have to implement CCT for financial services by October 1998.

1 SI 1995 No. 2916.

CONTRACTING EXAMPLES FOR FINANCIAL SERVICES

The financial services most obviously suitable for competition are accountancy services, exchequer services and cash collection, internal audit, investment management and pay-roll administration.

Financial planning and budget advice are commonly viewed as being too close to the corporate strategy elements of the local authority core and difficult to specify; potential benefits are therefore hard to identify. That is not to say that elements of this work cannot be tendered. In September 1991 Touche Ross won a contract from South Oxfordshire District Council, despite a cheaper internal bid, for budget preparation work. The council saw benefits of bringing in external expertise and simplified its budgetary process, departing from elements of internal recharge that would be required in strict adherence to CIPFA's code of practice in order to remove complexities that might have precluded interest from external tenderers.

Internal audit is a relatively self-contained function and there are a number of firms claiming the ability to offer such services. Such contracts can work well; for example, in 1991 the London Borough of Hackney entered a three-year contract with Price Waterhouse for the provision of internal audit services, a move occasioned by recruitment difficulties.

Exchequer services, cash collection and pay-roll services are, in the main, professionally supervised administrative and clerical operations. Competition could be expected for centralised service provision, but practitioners appear to doubt the availability of completely integrated services that could meet the whole of a local authority's requirements for services such as pay-roll, given that they incorporate tasks common to all employers alongside features unique to local government and its internal pension schemes.

East Cambridgeshire District Council is an example of contracted-out revenues (collection of community charge, business rates and future council tax) and benefits (council tax benefit and housing benefit) administration. Capita won a five-year contract, commencing in May 1992, from East Cambridgeshire to work from council accommodation and to use transferred local authority staff. Similarly, Oxfordshire County Council contracted out its exchequer services to CSL for a five-year period commencing in April 1993.

Subsequently a number of councils have externalised such services. In March 1995 the London Borough of Brent awarded a £50 million contract to EDS, a computer services firm, to run its revenues and benefits services. The deal involved the transfer of 240 staff and the size of the contract places EDS in a strong position to compete for other local authority financial services contracts. A number of other examples may be found in the list of externalisations included as Appendix VII.

Accountancy services may need to be split to enable tendering to occur. Operational work needs to be separated from corporate elements and this loss of economies of scale may in itself diminish the potential benefits of tendering the service.

Finally there remain investment management and responsibilities for insurance and pensions management. These may be well suited for contracting-out but they are small-scale activities, in terms of the number of staff employed in providing them: benefits to be obtained from competition could be minimal. In addition, a certain amount of use is already made of the private sector for investments and insurance broking.

It must be said that the appearance and growth of large-scale financial services companies means that some of the packaging problems predicted for other professional functions are unlikely to apply here. Indeed it may be those authorities that parcel up work into small individual service contracts who are accused of anti-competitive practices rather than those that choose to package all of their financial requirements into a single multi-disciplinary contract. This is speculative, however, because local firms of accountants and pay-roll specialists may still object if this work is not available separately from any other financial services to be tendered.

Tendering functions involving statutory duties

In considering CCT for financial services it is necessary to bring into consideration the issue of duties allocated by statute exercisable only by the council or its treasurer. Functions such as the determination of the budget and the setting of the council tax can only be carried out by the full council and cannot be delegated. Likewise the personal responsibilities placed on the treasurer by the LGA 1972 cannot be delegated. These responsibilities can give rise to tasks allocated to staff or contractors but since the treasurer is personally responsible for fulfilling the duty, he or she must monitor matters. Also, the treasurer can insist upon the provision of further resources if the justifiable fear of non-performance arises. Choosing to tender any elements of service this close to statutory responsibility requires careful evaluation before proceeding.

Then, in addition, there are duties which could technically be performed by contractors but which are precluded by the lack of any apparent authority to entertain arrangements other than direct performance by the council and its officers. Certain tasks in the collection of revenue and the allocation of benefits are obvious examples. To tackle this issue the government intends to lift some of the restraints, whether real or as a result of entrenched legal perception of the powers of councils, within its Deregulation and Contracting Out Bill.

In particular it is proposed to give the Secretary of State power to allow local authorities to employ contractors to carry out a range of prescribed functions. The main uses for this power are likely to be the use of a range of powers involving the exercise, in the government's eyes, of minimal discretion by council officers. One such power is the gathering of information to enable determinations to be made and the notification of such determinations. This information gathering could involve, for example, assessing the facts on the number of adult residents in a property since an abatement of council tax must be either given or withheld in accordance with the facts, once clear. Additionally in council tax enforcement the range of options once a liability order has been obtained is seen as so limited, depending upon the circumstances of the debtor, that the decision could be purportedly delegated to a contractor working for the authority. The only actions likely to be exempt from deregulation involve:

(i) the loss of an individual's liberty or the authorisation of entry into or seizure of property from premises,

(ii) the power to make subordinate legislation,

(iii) the imposition of civil penalties,
(iv) the rejection of appeals, and
 (v) allowing discretionary reliefs.

In addition, it is proposed that where council staff (other than solicitors or barristers) are currently authorised to represent the authority in the Magistrates' court, this representation could be extended to contractors' staff.

Contracting-out would carry certain mandatory requirements such as the reservation of access to all documentation held by the contractor.

Assuming the Bill becomes law and the Secretary of State issues the appropriate order, the outcome may be to enlarge further the range of financial functions that can be selected to tender to meet CCT obligations.

Chapter 15

TENDERING PERSONNEL SERVICES

As with most sizeable organisations that are large-scale employers, local authorities almost universally retain an in-house personnel function. Staffing accounts for the majority of council revenue expenditure and the quality of service provision to the public must inevitably suffer if effective policies are not maintained in the fields of recruitment, retention, disciplinary, grievance, equality of opportunity, redeployment and redundancy. It is unsurprising, perhaps, that local authorities should opt to control personnel issues, within the context of a detailed corporate strategy, by using directly employed staff to generate, monitor and revise policies and to give professional advice to members and chief officers. Furthermore, given an in-house personnel presence for corporate work, it may seem entirely logical for spare officer capacity to be used to perform or to supervise connected administrative or lower-grade functions such as job advertising or verification of time-sheets.

The requirement to subject personnel services to market-testing thus has an impact on functions close to the corporate heart of a local authority. Indeed, unless the scale of personnel operations itself employs a large number of persons, the requirement to tender part of the service may inevitably lead to the inclusion of corporate work in the specification, since a hard separation of client and contractor may prove impossible to achieve.

Nor do councils have much experience of purchasing personnel services, with the exception of recruitment advertising and consultancy and specialist training. Accordingly, the preparations for both ensuring the continuation of the quality of support needed by the council and for making the in-house team competitive necessitate a steeper leaving curve than for most other professional services.

Apart from setting down the statutory requirements, this chapter concentrates upon the task of selecting elements of personnel work to meet the percentage competition requirement. It also treats the practical problems posed by CCT in this area to the corporate health of any local authority that, despite CCT, continues directly to employ significant numbers of staff in future.

THE DEFINED ACTIVITY

Personnel services as defined by the Local Government Act 1988 (Competition)

(Defined Activities) Order 1995[1] cover all work connected with the provision of personnel services, including core client activity. The definition includes

   (i)   personnel advice and method studies,
  (ii) organisation,
 (iii) human resource management,
 (iv) training,
  (v) personnel research,
 (vi) managerial information systems,
 (vii) employee relations,
(viii) personnel work, and
 (ix) client-side role.

The sum of all these is the defined activity from which the percentage competition requirement must be met.

Personnel advice covers the provision of any advice and information to elected members and committees, and corporate policy and management advice to departments, officers or any other person in connection with the discharge of the authority's functions. Organisation and method studies cover management services reviews and work studies and business planning.

Human resource management includes recruitment, appointment, assessment and appraisal processes.

Training covers arranging, monitoring and evaluating training and development programmes (with the exception of operational police and fire officer training). There is, however, some qualification on the extent to which training and development is to be within the defined activity covered in a separate section below.

Personnel work covers pay and benefits (including superannuation), terms and conditions of employment, health and safety policies and procedures and redundancy arrangements and agreements.

Finally, the client-side role catches up advice on all aspects of procurement monitoring and supervision of personnel work.

The provision of all the above aspects of personnel services is the defined activity, except for personnel tasks undertaken by managers and administrative staff whose primary responsibility is to a service other than a personnel one. This activity is taken outside the ambit of CCT by the exclusion of personnel work constituting less than 50 per cent of an officer's total working hours.

TRAINING ELEMENTS OF PERSONNEL SERVICES

The word 'training' conjures up a broad range of activities, encompassing general management and skills training in the work environment, specialist and professional learning as well as initiatives of which the beneficiaries are not council staff but sections of the community at large. To define training more closely for CCT purposes, a distinction is drawn between

1 SI 1995 No. 1915.

job-based training provided by a line manager or supervisor and course-based training, whether provided in-house or by external contractors.

The defined activity for personnel services excludes the supervision of staff and, accordingly, job-based training is likely to be exempt unless performed by a person over 50 per cent of whose work is training others. A particular example of activity which is exempt is the practice placement supervision of those studying for Social Work Diplomas as it can only be carried out by the council's own qualified staff and is regarded as wholly supervision rather than training.

All course-based training potentially falls into the definition of personnel services but in practice such activity falls into one of two categories, depending upon the status of the person acting as tutor. If the course is led by a specialist within the council who has no formal training role but occasionally acts as a teacher for non-specialists or staff in other departments (in-house accountants and lawyers are good examples of this in practice), then the activity will be exempt because the training input will constitute less than 50 per cent of the tutor's normal work. Conversely, the work of staff employed as trainers or personnel professionals will form part of the defined activity.

The distinction between functional work and works contracts is also of particular relevance to training. Training undertaken for and funded by an external body, such as a TEC, will constitute a works contract and will not count in the defined activity since it can be set off against the individual *de minimis* level set for personnel services works contracts (see below).

THE PERCENTAGE COMPETITION REQUIREMENT AND *DE MINIMIS* LEVEL

The mandatory requirement is to be the tendering of 30 per cent of the total cost of the defined activity, subject to the deduction of the normal competition credit for work already won in competition and the like.

The *de minimis* level below which there is no requirement for market-testing is separated into two categories. Functional work, that is to say personnel services supporting functions directly carried out in performance of the council's own duties and powers, is to carry a *de minimis* exemption set at £400,000. In addition, councils will have a separate *de minimis* of £100,000 for personnel services performed as works contracts, essentially work performed for a third party.

Finally personnel work within the defined activity, forming less than 50 per cent of the duties of an individual officer, is not to be included within the total cost of the defined activity and so does not affect the competition requirement.

CCT TIMETABLE

October 1996 is the last date for new contracts for personnel services to commence for London boroughs and metropolitan districts and April 1998 for non-reorganised shire districts. Where local government reorganisation is completed by April 1995 the due date is October 1997, where completed by April 1996 the due date is October 1998 and where completed by April 1997 the due date is October 1999. The timetable is set down in the Local Government Act 1988 (Competition) (Personnel Services) (England) Regulations 1995[1].

The potential interaction of CCT for personnel services and for housing management is to be recognised and authorities with housing functions will benefit from a power to postpone personnel work in relation to housing staff until the relevant target dates for housing management CCT.

IMPLEMENTATION ISSUES

Much of the activity included within personnel services departments, such as human resource planning, industrial relations, health and safety monitoring and pay and benefits advice, is an integral part of line management or is corporate in nature and not well suited to competition. Conversely, organisational review and specialist training are achievable through external consultants (if at potentially higher cost) and are suitable for tendering on a project-by-project basis; Berkshire County Council, for example, contracted out its personnel training service. There are also market opportunities in the form of external agencies for recruitment (especially for senior and specialist staff selection) and for recruitment advertising.

Taking the above into account, it is likely that the majority of local authorities will select from management services, training, staff counselling, occupational health services and recruitment advertising to meet the percentage competition requirement.

The impact of competition in local authorities will differ, however, according to the extent to which personnel services are devolved between departments. Devolution may result in the allocation of personnel functions to officers whose primary responsibilities fall outside the defined activity and thus increase the level of exempt activity, especially if the work retained by a central team is below *de minimis*. For larger authorities, the consequence of past devolution may have been the dispersal of professional staff between departments and the creation of sizeable specialist teams such as education personnel units or social services training sections to meet specific departmental needs. This will pose additional problems in implementing CCT and may lead to pressure for re-aggregation and centralisation as a means of maximising economies of scale. Whatever the virtues of devolution, experience dictates that it tends to be more expensive, making the service more vulnerable to external competition. Even if centralisation does not result from CCT it will be difficult to avoid interdepartmental conflict over the selection of activity and sections to meet the percentage competition requirement and plans for performing the client role for the services to be tendered.

The final issue singular to personnel services relates to guidance on specification issued by the Institute of Personnel and Development under the title 'Guidance to the Evaluation of Quality', which suggests councils should ask tenderers for information on staff numbers and qualifications.

1 SI 1995 No. 2101.

This may prove difficult advice to follow given the general prohibition contained in the LGA 1988, which views workforce matters as a non-commercial consideration that councils cannot take into account in awarding contracts.

Chapter 16

TENDERING INFORMATION TECHNOLOGY SERVICES

No longer referred to simply as computer services (the original description in the government's CCT consultation papers), the functions under review are not only computer-orientated but also include voice applications and other technologically driven support to the processing and communication of information.

Given the ever-expanding incursion of information technology (IT) into all areas of council service, and the extent to which functional work is dependent upon it, it is not surprising that a full treatment of this area has been postponed, making it the last to see CCT. It does mean that there is a comparatively long lead-in to determine the level of client activity to be excluded from tendering and the strategy for introducing competition to the remainder. This will be particularly important for authorities now being forced to move away from mainframe computer reliance.

This chapter sets out the procedural CCT requirements for information technology services and outlines the key issues for future consideration.

THE DEFINED ACTIVITY

Information technology services as defined by the Local Government Act 1988 (Competition) (Defined Activities) Order 1995[1] are services which are designed to secure the availability or application of information technology. The definition goes on to detail services which are expressly included. They are giving advice, assessing IT requirements, arranging for IT requirements to be met, developing IT and monitoring equipment used in connection with IT. In this context IT advice covers not only guidance to the council, its committees, its members and its officers, but also to any person as to the application of IT.

In addition there is a provision delineating information technology as including any computer, telecommunications or other technology, the principal use of which is the recording, processing and communication of information by electronic means.

The extent to which the definition catches business analysis may be problematic but for most purposes the defined activity is reasonably clear-cut.

1 SI 1995 No. 1915.

148

EXCLUSIONS

Other than the application of the 50 per cent cut-off point, below which an IT element of an officer's duties becomes incidental and thus outside the defined activity, there are no specific exclusions. However, this definition should be sufficient to remove from competition tasks carried out using IT equipment as part of a person's normal duties for another service.

COMPETITION REQUIREMENT AND *DE MINIMIS* LEVEL

The statutory requirement is to put out to tender 70 per cent of the defined activity after deduction of the normal credits. This leaves a competition-free allowance of only 30 per cent against the relevant *de minimis* level of £300,000.

TIMETABLE

London boroughs and English metropolitan districts are to be required to implement CCT for information technology services by October 1997. Districts and counties reorganised or subject to substantial boundary changes on or prior to April 1995 will have until October 1998 to complete the tendering process. Shire counties and non-metropolitan districts emerging unchanged from local government review will have until April 1999. Authorities reorganised by April 1996 have until October 1999 and those reorganised by April 1997 have until October 2000. This timetable is set down in the Local Government Act 1988 (Competition) (Information Technology) (England) 1995[1].

Welsh local authorities will have until October 1998 to carry out IT tendering.

CONTRACTING EXAMPLES FOR INFORMATION TECHNOLOGY SERVICES

A number of concerns surround the compulsory tendering of computer contracts. The major computer systems used by local authorities emanate from a handful of suppliers and the number of potential tenderers capable of maintaining and supporting such systems is limited. Indeed, the original suppliers of mainframe systems may have an unfair advantage over all other external competitors in terms of any planned computer facilities management contract. Such a contract might lock the local authority into a monopoly situation for a period of years, after which contract renewal with the same company becomes the only practical option.

The other very real problem is that local authority information systems are being subjected to continuing demands for change at an unprecedented rate. For example, the moves from rates to community charge and then to council tax as a means of funding local authorities led to councils having

1 SI 1995 No. 2813.

to switch between three major computer applications within a period of five years, a situation that could not have been wholly predicted at the beginning of that period. The cost of such developments has been kept down by competition between different computer companies, each keen to exploit a new market opening. Once local authorities are locked into single-supplier contracts, it seems unlikely the companies will be motivated to offer reduced costings for unforeseen major changes requiring additional services or variations of the standing contract by consent. Particularly if the requirement arises by virtue of statutory developments affecting local government, councils may be seen as being over the proverbial barrel.

Despite these criticisms, over 30 computer facilities management contracts have already been voluntarily let by local authorities, although commonly these relate to selected parts rather than to the whole of the computer service supporting council activities. Hertfordshire County Council's approach, involving the retention in-house of 50 per cent of the services, is not untypical. East Cambridgeshire District Council offers an example of computer facilities management on the smaller scale appropriate to a shire district's functions. The list of externalisations set out in Appendix VII demonstrates the increasing acceptance that contracting out need not be the disaster predicted by so many.

Finally, telecommunications services are included in the defined activity. Examination of such services shows their principal elements to be equipment purchase or lease, line rentals and call charges, and switchboard staffing. Everything barring staffing will already be obtained from the private sector, leaving little by way of the service to be specified or from which gains in terms of reduced costs can be obtained through CCT.

ISSUES ARISING FROM TENDERING

The bulk of the costs associated with IT relate to the provision of equipment and software. Staffing costs form a much lower percentage of the recharges for support than in other centrally provided services. At first sight, even with a 70 per cent competition requirement, much of the staffing can be protected from CCT since the technology itself is purchased, upgraded and maintained by external providers and thus credited against the specified proportion of the work to be tendered. Care must be taken in forecasting the extent to which this will continue to be the case. Wage inflation can soon change the balance given that the ever-increasing level of competition among computer companies is dramatically slashing the costs of the technology itself.

Notwithstanding criticism in the trade press, as to the fairness of it, the government will permit local authorities to specify the software required providing this is done to meet genuine service needs rather than with the aim of deterring competition. It ought to be obvious to even the vested interests in the private sector that the ability to specify software is key to the council's interests. Nevertheless the impact of CCT may still be to drive small, specialist suppliers of both hardware and software to the wall and prevent new entrants to the market competing with existing multinational, large-scale firms.

Finally, given the fact that CCT across an ever-broadening range of council services must diminish the number of captive in-house customers for IT services, the economies of scale supporting old-style mainframe-based computer operations are declining. Even outsourcing may not solve the problem since maximising take-up of spare capacity will not turn around a situation in which low-cost Unix- or Personal Computer-based solutions may offer much reduced overheads to front-line services. And without these services they cannot expect to retain their work in-house in the face of competition.

Chapter 17

TENDERING HOUSING MANAGEMENT

The tendering of grounds maintenance for housing estates apart, the initial impact of CCT on housing functions was limited to housing maintenance and estate cleaning activity carried out in communal areas. The latter resulted in either small-scale tendering or restructuring of cleaning and litter clearance services to ensure that defined activities represented less than 50 per cent of the workload of caretaking and janitorial staff, rendering them exempt from compulsory competition. This could be legitimately achieved by emphasising the security aspects of such jobs and the monitoring of contractor activity on the states.

This should not be taken to mean that pressure for change has been absent from housing disciplines. Privatisation in England, Scotland and Wales has progressed since 1980 from the right to buy to the more recent grant of tenant rights to take over management of their own estates and to receive a transfer of freehold title to the affected properties or to choose a new landlord under the so-called tenants' choice provisions of the Housing Act 1988. All these developments have one element in common: they take effect only as a direct result of tenant choice, either of individuals opting to purchase their own homes or groups pressing for a change of landlord because of dissatisfaction with the quality or cost of services provided by the local authority.

Additionally, the potentially irresistible lure of achieving one-off capital receipts has persuaded a number of councils to consider voluntary transfer of the whole or large sections of their housing stock to other bodies, using powers contained in the Housing and Planning Act 1986. Most of such successful transfers have been to housing associations newly created by former council housing staff, an option that may be precluded in future if a requirement to use only existing organisations is imposed.

Housing initiatives taking advantage of these local authority powers and of tenants' rights to self-determination are now complicated by the extension of CCT to housing management.

The stated intention of competition for housing management is to improve services to tenants, reduce costs and achieve better service efficiency.

Debate is fuelled by examination of the current levels of rent arrears and unoccupied properties within some authorities and the considerable variations in the cost of housing management across the country, an issue highlighted by the ring-fencing of every local authority housing revenue account, a requirement of the Local Government and Housing Act 1989.

This prevents housing services to tenants and leaseholders being subsidised by council tax and business rates credited to the general fund. Henceforth housing must be funded entirely from housing income, primarily rents.

The introduction of competition comes as the culmination of a period of considerable change in both housing law and practice. Drives towards decentralisation of integrated housing services, with estate-based offices and decision-making delegated to local management, have accompanied increasing tenant involvement and consultation, much of it achieved voluntarily rather than by legislative means. Furthermore, central government encouragement of partnerships between local authorities and the private sector for the provision of affordable housing other than in the form of traditional council-managed housing stock has increased housing association activity, generating agreements under which local authorities act as enabling sources of funding, land and property in return for rights to nominate or refer potential tenants to the new units of accommodation created. It is against such a backdrop of innovation and change that the implementation of compulsory competition for housing management falls to be considered.

THE DEFINED ACTIVITY

Housing management is defined by the Local Government Act 1988 (Competition) (Defined Activities) (Housing Management) Order 1994[1]. It covers:

  (i)   dealing with applications for local authority housing once a property has been allocated to the applicant;
  (ii)   informing tenants of the terms of their tenancies and enforcing such terms;
  (iii) collecting rent, service charges and service charge loan payments;
  (iv) arranging vacating of local authority housing;
  (v)   work in relation to vacant property;
  (vi) taking steps to remove unlawful occupants;
  (vii) maintenance, repair and cleaning of common parts of local authority housing;
 (viii) handling repairs requests;
  (ix) carrying out inspections and surveys;
  (x)   assessing compensation claims and applications for payment from the council;
  (xi) operating reception and security services at the entrance to local authority housing;
  (xii) controlling disturbances; and
 (xiii) resolving disputes.

Handling applications up to the point where a specific property is allocated to a prospective tenant is outside the defined activity. Thus management of the waiting list remains exempt from competition. However, the handling of assignments and exchanges are part of the defined activity but giving or withholding consent are not.

Collecting payments is defined to include keeping records of sums collected, collecting arrears, negotiating on agreements for the payment of

1 SI 1994 No. 1671.

arrears and monitoring compliance with such agreements. In between negotiating agreements and monitoring compliance must rest an area of non-defined activity reserved to the council; that is approving or disapproving the agreements negotiated.

Several aspects of void property work form part of the defined activity. Once a tenancy or licence has been terminated, arranging for the vacating of the housing is a contractor function. So too is the inspection of vacant property, assessing whether works are needed, ensuring works are carried out and reporting progress to the landlord.

In relation to vacant property taking steps to prevent vandalism or squatting and taking steps to remove unlawful occupants from local authority housing are part of the defined activity.

Common part tasks included are:

- assessing condition;
- assessing maintenance, repair and cleaning requirements (including disinfection) and clearance;
- ensuring that any necessary works are carried out; and
- reporting on progress to the landlord.

Also covered are:

- assessing requests for repairs to local authority housing;
- ensuring that any necessary works are carried out and reporting on progress to the landlord; and
- carrying out inspections and surveys to ascertain physical conditions or state of repair or whether or not properties are occupied.

Assessing claims relates to compensation or reimbursement in relation to repairs, improvements and additions to council property. Together with making recommendations to the landlord, this also forms part of the defined activity.

All of the above-mentioned activities are housing management when performed in relation to local authority housing which is defined separately to include garages, parking spaces and out-houses provided in connection with housing and common parts of buildings containing two or more dwelling houses.

EXCLUSIONS

If the tenant of a property is not an individual then work in connection with the subject premises is not housing management (although it may fall into the defined activity for construction and property services).

The nature of the title to the accommodation may also give rise to an exemption if it is, for example, a long tenancy or within the meaning of section 115 of the Housing Act 1985. Hostel accommodation is expressly excluded from the housing management defined activity.

Housing management work forming less than 25 per cent of an officer's duties (50 per cent if the officer works for 30 hours or less per week) is exempted. In addition, the exemption contained in the LGA 1988 for staff required to live on site as part of their duties will apply so removing residential caretakers from the CCT arena.

Finally, the defined activity makes no attempt to cover a range of housing-related functions such as housing benefit administration and services for the homeless.

COMPETITION REQUIREMENT AND *DE MINIMIS* LEVEL

The percentage competition requirement for housing management is 95 per cent, leaving a competition-free allowance of only 5 per cent and the *de minimis* level is set at £500,000.

If councils choose to tender rent collection as a financial service and computer support as part of information technology services, housing management CCT may capture far fewer councils than the scale of the competition requirement would at first tender apparent. Some local authorities with up to 10,000 properties are already claiming to be exempt from housing management market-testing.

IMPLICATIONS OF THE DEFINED ACTIVITY

The complexity of the interface between the client and a housing management contractor is apparent from the wording chosen for the individual tasks comprising the defined activity. Many of them require the contractor to report progress back to the council as landlord or to investigate and advise the client, who will make the necessary decision. This in turn must be actioned by the contractor or the landlord's consent must be secured.

There are several areas of concern which demand careful specification as well as requiring regular monitoring audits. Void property, general repairs and maintenance orders may be issued by the council but there is room for collusion between a housing management contractor and a maintenance contractor. Having one contractor monitor another is seldom a satisfactory arrangement but it will arise in housing management, as the definition expressly states.

Equally disturbing is the risk of collusion between housing management contractor and tenant in relation to repairs requests, claims for compensation and applications for payment. Since the local authority will not have the ability to discipline, dismiss and remove (in cases of gross misconduct) members of a contractor's staff—the usual deterrents against in-house misconduct—it will be reliant upon well drafted default and damages clauses in the housing management contract. These may prove a lesser deterrent unless the contractor also enforces a rigid disciplinary code.

TIMETABLE FOR COMPETITION

Local authorities are required to expose housing management to competition over one, two or three years. Authorities with more than 15,000 properties may let contracts in tranches over two years, authorities with more than 30,000 properties may take three years.

The competition timetable requires housing management contracts (or the first tranche where relevant) to be let by April 1996 for some authorities and by April 1997 for others. The newly created Welsh authorities have until April 1998. For this purpose councils are distinguished in the Local Government Act 1988 (Competition) (Housing Management) (England) Regulations 1994[1].

It is not intended that council policy responsibilities be delegated, but particular emphasis is placed on the need to reflect in any specification for housing services the extent to which the successful contractor, be it an in-house team or an external tenderer, will be required to put such policies into effect and the manner of implementation. An obvious example would be determining the responsibility for allocations of void properties, since any contractor involvement in the process must be engineered to support the goal of fair prioritisation between the different levels of social need exhibited by individual applicants for housing.

Policy responsibilities are taken to include the setting of criteria for choosing tenants and for prioritising the housing waiting list (as distinct from the actual process of letting, which could be tendered), determining the basis on which the rights of tenants are to be safeguarded and their duties enforced (for example, the policies covering rent-arrears recovery and tenant nuisance), determining rent levels and setting budgets to avoid incurring housing revenue account deficits, carrying out periodic reviews of budget adherence, bidding for credit approvals from central government, settling the housing investment programme and dividing resources between estates and projects (even if the contractor is to have responsibility for managing the expenditure), laying down repairs policy and targets and fulfilling the duty to report annually to tenants on housing management performance.

STRATEGIC RESPONSIBILITIES

The impact of competition relates to the severable elements of the landlord activities of a local authority charged to its housing revenue account. There is some derogation from this position because of the excepted service elements (see below).

The approach to housing management CCT must thus endeavour to distinguish between setting policy and implementation, the latter being deemed capable of being performed through contractors. The only sting in the tail is the reminder that while service delivery may be delegated, the council, through its housing committee and client officers, will retain responsibility for any failure to translate policy into practice, as such failure will be attributable to ineffective contract enforcement or, indeed, to poor specification.

CONTRACT PACKAGING AND ANTI-COMPETITIVE BEHAVIOUR

Apart from setting a maximum contract size of 5,000 units, the government has laid particular emphasis on the need for a local authority to give proper consideration to contract packaging, emphasising the Secretary of State's powers to intervene where he believes that a council has devised a

1 SI 1994 No. 2297.

contract that is anti-competitive or obstructive. A single contract covering all the local authority's housing stock is viewed as potentially anti-competitive *per se* since few housing associations or other private-sector organisations could expand their capacities sufficiently to take on such a contract at this time. Such a large-scale contract would be likely to offer the in-house team a significantly increased prospect of winning the work and to limit genuine competition. Such a decision would therefore carry a very real prospect of ministerial intervention, but it is recognised that it may be appropriate for a small authority to consider this option. Accordingly councils with a maximum of 7,500 residential properties will be permitted to let their management in a single contract.

The only practical approach for most local authorities is to consider dividing up the stock into smaller units for tendering purposes or to consider functional separation. Administration of repairs and maintenance; special services on estates, including caretaking, lighting and lift maintenance; lettings, transfers and voids control; and the administration of grants to vacate are examples of functions that could be separately tendered. This option would undo much of the benefit achieved for tenants in the provision of integrated services for local offices and is unlikely to be in the tenants' best interests albeit that it might offer economies of scale.

Essentially, this leaves local authorities to divide their property holdings into geographically sensible parcels that may be similar in size or contain a range of numbers of units of accommodation. Such contracts for integrated services would cover all tenancy and leasehold management, rent and service charge collection, lettings, transfers and exchanges, voids processing, day-to-day repairs and maintenance.

Obviously, council housing is not necessarily concentrated entirely on purpose-built estates. Isolated acquired properties are held and there may be individual properties amid a sea of private owner-occupiers as a result of right-to-buy in areas of attractive or readily improvable houses. The management of such properties will also have to be tendered and in practical terms they must be grouped together or added to estate contracts to which they are sufficiently proximate to allay any argument that they have been added as a result of an anti-competitive consideration.

The government preference is that, so far as possible, each managerial area will have a fully delegated budget and run a comprehensive service, which may include monitoring responsibilities for local capital works. Thereafter decisions can be made to tender the whole service or create a small core management staff to win the work in competition and then operate a series of small estate-based subcontracts for particular activities or elements of the service.

Certain additional expectations of the contracting process have also been set. The normal tender price for any given group of properties, whether quoted on a per unit basis or not, will, in practice, be equated by central government to a fee per unit, allowing a direct correlation to be drawn between the cost of managing particular types of estates and the management and maintenance allowances for which housing subsidy payable to local authorities is calculated. Local authorities are also reminded in the housing consultation paper[1] that contracts will be expected to tie payments

1 Department of the Environment and the Welsh Office, *Competing for Quality in Housing— Competition in the Provision of Housing Management*, a consultation paper, HMSO June 1992.

closely to results in key areas such as reduction of rent arrears and void turn-around times between lettings.

MODEL DOCUMENTS

Housing management has attracted several bodies to consider model forms of documentation. First past the post are the Association of Metropolitan Authorities and the Association of District Councils, whose model for housing management (commissioned from Trowers and Hamlins Solicitors) is available from ADC Publications.

EXTERNAL SUPPLIERS

The most immediately obvious external tenderer for housing management services would appear to be housing associations, since they already share a philosophy of affordable housing with local authorities and largely operate on a non-profit-making basis. Early indications that housing associations might be reluctant to bid for such work were dispelled by a MORI poll conducted in 1994 for 'Inside Housing' (sponsored by the William Sutton Trust). The findings were that 70 per cent of England's biggest housing associations would actively bid or would respond if invited to tender for local authority contracts. The other side of the coin is that less than 20 per cent of associations have reserved resources for CCT bids or allocated staff for tendering preparations.

In a study completed in 1989 by Duncan MacLennan for the DoE, housing associations' total management and repair costs per property were found to be 25 per cent higher than in local government, with council officers averaging 128 properties managed in comparison to 72 for a housing association officer. This hardly indicates the possibility of major economies arising from compulsory competition. Less obvious but strong contenders may emerge from the rapid growth of large-scale, multi-specialism firms expanding into both blue- and white-collar CCT disciplines. Examples include Serco, who hold a contract for housing in Liverpool, and technical firms such as W S Atkins with existing property management interests in non-housing and engineering contracts already won.

The other probable tenderers are private-sector companies or consultancies. These include tenant co-operatives, existing major landowners or landlords, residential agents and providers of special services. Most of those presently focus on properties they own or on small-scale portfolios of properties managed for other people. Generally, such management covers less than 5,000 units in total per organisation, which may give rise to difficulties in expanding their capacity to meet local authority demands.

TENANT CONSULTATION

Section 105 of the Housing Act 1985 places a duty on local authorities to consult tenants on management matters that affect them, and this duty should embrace the key decisions involved in CCT. Tenants will need to be consulted on the level and type of services to be reflected in the specification for housing management and, indeed, on subsequent contract variations of particular significance once the contract has been let. Tenant groups should be represented in selecting the successful contractor and the contract specification should require contractors to recognise tenant groups and to liaise with them wherever practicable.

In organising tenant consultation regard should be had to draft guidance on the subject issued under cover of a DoE circular letter dated 22 March 1994[1].

THE RIGHT TO MANAGE

One of the key features of modern housing policy is a commitment to involve tenants in estate management. Tenant management organisations (TMOs) now manage their own properties, establish their own structures in negotiation with the council and take part in the process of competitive tendering, provided that they can demonstrate their competitiveness and cost-effectiveness.

As part of the local authority's tendering of housing management tenants will be given a short period to consider the options and, if they desire to do so, to indicate a wish to exercise their right to manage and to take over the management of the whole or part of the estate. That said, the role envisaged for TMOs relates to client responsibilities rather than the services to be tendered. They will be concerned with contract specification and monitoring through a management agreement entered into with the local authority, which will include targets and quality standards to be operated within a council-set strategic and financial framework.

If a TMO wishes to carry out operational work, then it may do so, subject to checks on its competitiveness, either using third parties or carrying out the work directly itself. Only if it plans to use seconded local authority staff will the work be subject to CCT.

THE POSITION OF HOUSING BENEFITS ADMINISTRATION

Local authorities are responsible for the payment of housing benefit to both council and private-sector tenants to defray rental costs for those on low incomes. The payment of housing benefit to council tenants creates a complete funding circle, with benefit monies returning to the council in the form of rent. This assists the prevention of serious rent arrears for those eligible for the benefit.

The only intrusion into this cycle is the element of central government funding of housing benefit, but this is now viewed as merely another element of housing subsidy payable to local authorities' housing revenue accounts. Given the ring-fencing arrangements, any short-fall of expenditure on housing benefit over subsidy must be met from rents and thus tenants ineligible for housing benefit may end up subsidising those receiving benefit.

1 The Housing (Right to Manage) Regulations 1994, SI 1994 No. 627.

The practical effect is that not only is the administration of housing benefit payments a crucial element of rent-arrears control, but the levels of housing benefits eligibility among tenants impact directly on rent levels and thus on a number of local authority policy decisions in relation to housing.

Notwithstanding the exclusion of benefits from the defined activity, its inter-relationship with rent collection and arrears may lead to consideration of some housing benefits administration, in particular the processing of payments, within CCT contracts. Such advantages need to be balanced by the statutory responsibilities for safeguarding public funds and detecting fraudulent claims, which militate against enforcing any delegation of responsibility to contractors supplying services at arm's length to the council.

CONTRACTING EXAMPLES FOR HOUSING MANAGEMENT

The experiences of a group of pilot authorities (comprising Newham, Brent, Westminster, Mid-Suffolk, Rochdale, Mansfield, Derby and East Staffordshire) contributed to nine consultants' reports published by the Department of the Environment (see Bibliography), which cover a broad range of housing management CCT issues.

Contracting-out is uncommon in housing but Kensington and Chelsea endeavoured to transfer their housing stock to a tenant management organisation covering virtually the whole borough during 1995, so side-stepping CCT. Nithsdale in Scotland has set up a housing association to manage stock as it becomes vacant for five years. Then there is Rutland, which in 1993 contracted the management of its 1,600 properties to CSL. Interestingly, the contract includes non-defined activity such as dealing with the homeless and the council retains only one housing officer as client. Finally, Waverley employs private consultants to run its Chantry's Estate.

Chapter 18

TENDERING IN EDUCATION

If the direct provision of tuition is not to be addressed by central government, education functions would appear at first sight to have been as affected by CCT as is likely in the foreseeable future. The extension of competition to significant support services such as personnel functions and home-to-school transport looms, but it was the inclusion of grounds maintenance, building cleaning and school catering as defined activities in the LGA 1988 that affected the broadest group of education employees. Those contracts, having been specified and let, would in the normal course of events have been retendered on expiry, with all of the benefits of the experience gained by both local authorities and contractors in the first round of tendering.

Potential problems arise, however, as a result of the changing nature of the relationship between schools and LEAs as a consequence of the Education Reform Act 1988, which established a process of delegating budgetary responsibilities and management control to school governing bodies. These responsibilities have a direct impact on client-side responsibilities and CCT processes, with the LEA having to build a new relationship with customer schools no longer constituting a captive market. These changes do at least recognise that schools, unless choosing to opt out of local authority control, remain attached to their local authorities, unlike further education colleges, whose new independent corporate status means that local authorities can provide services to them only to the extent permitted by the LAGSA 1970. It is necessary therefore to consider the effect of localised decision-making in schools on the arrangements for tendering and the management of services subjected to CCT.

LOCAL MANAGEMENT OF SCHOOLS

Local Management of Schools (LMS) describes the process of statutory delegation of budgets and management responsibility to school governing bodies and headteachers brought about by the Education Reform Act 1988. Essentially, all schools, secondary and primary, now have full delegated budgets.

Each local authority responsible for education functions has had to create an approved LMS scheme covering all expenditure associated with schools, including support services, other than certain minimal exceptional expenditure. The costs attributable to the cleaning of school buildings and

161

grounds maintenance were an exception to delegation only for a transitional period. Accordingly, schools have gained responsibilities in relation to those defined activities but will not be free to consider making their own arrangements, including tendering, until the existing contracts or arrangements expire, as they will do, given that the LGA 1988 laid down maximum contract periods for all defined activities.

APPLICABILITY OF CCT TO SCHOOLS

All defined activities are subject to CCT wherever a local authority employs or contemplates employing its own staff to perform the services. With effect from the date on which responsibility and resources for building, cleaning and grounds maintenance pass across as part of an aggregated schools budget, a governing body will hold certain client-side responsibilities for these services.

Under the LGA 1988 the local authority determines the manner in which work is specified and packaged for tendering and the manner in which it is put out to tender, but there is no clear dividing line between these duties and the responsibilities of the governing body. Consultation and co-operation must therefore bridge the gap, assuming the school chooses to remain part of the integrated contracting set-up after the existing arrangements expire. It is interesting in this regard that the onus to maintain DSO accounts for building cleaning and grounds maintenance and to achieve financial objectives on trading accounts remains on the council, notwithstanding that schools will have day-to-day responsibility for client functions that may well influence the results achieved by the DSO. The potential for increasing DSO costs or, indeed, those of any contractor, by unreasonable client expectation should be well understood.

Under LMS, school governors exercise many of the powers of an employer over non-teaching staff, but the council remains their formal employer. Accordingly, CCT applies to any work falling into the category of one or more defined activities carried out by such staff. The only general exception applicable to schools, as to other non-educational functions, is where defined activities account for less than 50 per cent of an employee's duties, and tendering of his or her responsibilities is not compulsory. This allows caretakers with significant functions other than defined activities, for example those spending less than half of their time on actual cleaning duties, to be exempted from CCT. Care needs to be exercised in relation to caretakers, since it may be argued that some part of their duties in relation to cleaning should relate to client responsibilities in terms of monitoring the work of other employees. This needs to be distinguished from the supervision of actual cleaning tasks, which should form part of an assessment of the proportion of his or her time spent on defined activities.

To simplify matters for smaller schools, exemption from CCT has now been granted for building cleaning and grounds maintenance work.

PRACTICAL PROBLEMS

Many of the initial problems facing schools in relation to CCT issues are similar to those faced with devolved budgetary management: lack of experience, training and expertise forces a continuing dependence on the parent LEA, whose officers, in turn, are frequently perceived as an impeding intermediary between the school and the professional services it might need to acquire from other council departments. Supportive advice on standing orders, tendering procedures, contract terms and specification, monitoring and the client role generally, as distinguished from that of the contractor, are all essential if schools are to have any chance of availing themselves of any option other than throwing in their lot with the particular council DSOs set up to provide those services to the local authority generally.

The separation of contracts for different defined activities and the differences in the timetabling and contract lengths may in themselves work against the best interests of schools, for whom monitoring and management effort could be saved if integrated contract packages were to be available. If schools allow the council to include the services they require in wider contracts, the effect may be overly restrictive. Once locked into such contracts with external tenderers or agreements with a DSO, there will be little room for variation, because section 7(8) of the LGA 1988 requires that the services be provided in accordance with the specification as tendered for the contract period. This is notwithstanding that the council could remove work from the DSO, there being no formal contract in existence, as even the then Department of Education and Science advised 'there is a strong presumption that the contract or agreement will remain binding on the school until it comes to an end'. Thus, if schools are serviced by a DSO that had to win the work in competition, they are no freer than if a formal contract existed with a private contractor, and will be tied to the agreed specification for the contract period stated at the time of tendering. Even a school opting out of local authority control will not have the freedom to cancel such an agreement.

In addition, schools may have little choice in seeking to personalise specifications prepared for a range of premises, since such departures from common standards and time periods are likely to have cost implications or disrupt service scheduling in ways that the local authority is not prepared to countenance. It ought not to be surprising when schools gain freedom of choice if they seek to obtain tenders for individual premises or for a self-created consortium made up of several schools.

This, in turn, poses another problem. The funding formula from which delegated budgets will be derived relates to average costs across the borough, and the actual cost of securing services for different schools may depart substantially from the average for all schools, a factor that militates strongly against the practicality of breaking down contracts into prices for individual sites.

EXEMPTIONS FOR GROUNDS MAINTENANCE AND BUILDING CLEANING

The Secretaries of State for the Environment and for Wales have, with effect from 1 August 1992, made an order bringing in a limited exemption from CCT in respect of grounds maintenance and building cleaning carried out in small schools holding delegated budgets. The qualifying requirements for claiming the benefit of the exemption are:

(i)   the school must have a fully delegated budget;
(ii) it must be covered by an approved scheme for LMS that delegates both the responsibility and the resources for grounds maintenance and building cleaning to the school;
(iii) the number of staff employed on the activities at the school must not exceed three full-time equivalent staff.

Where these requirements are satisfied, the school (irrespective of the local authority's views) will be able to carry out such work with its own school-based staff or have a local authority DSO station staff at the school to provide the services, without having to subject the work to CCT.

In determining whether there will be no more than three full-time equivalent staff employed in providing services, the actual number of staff employed does not matter, as long as the weekly number of hours worked (including overtime) on providing grounds maintenance and building cleaning does not exceed three times the standard working week of a full-time employee, currently 39 hours. If the caretaker at the school carries out defined activities as part of his duties, even if his workload is exempt from CCT because over 50 per cent of it relates to non-defined activities, the number of hours he or she spends on cleaning and grounds maintenance work must be included in the total to determine whether the three full-time-equivalents exemption also applies.

Schools that qualify cannot claim the exemption immediately, but must normally await the expiry of any contract with an external tenderer.

Theoretically, it ought to be possible for a DSO to surrender the part of its service and the relevant part of its income relating to a school's cleaning and grounds maintenance, but the notes of guidance issued in parallel with the order state: 'Where the DSO has won work, it would be open to the Local Authority, if it wished, to retender the work at any time excluding the schools which qualify for the exemption.' This seems to imply that only full retendering under the CCT regime of the residual service to be held by the DSO would enable the schools to be removed from the specification for service that was awarded to the DSO. Such a conclusion seems to make no sense and is arguably incorrect in law. If the local authority were contracted to an external supplier and would be free to renegotiate a variation to its contract, as the guidance notes accept as a possibility, an agreement with a DSO should be capable of being varied in an identical manner without retendering cleaning and grounds maintenance for all sites in respect of which the exemption is not claimed.

A practical difficulty arises due to the likelihood that in any given local authority cleaning and grounds maintenance contracts will have been let on different dates and will expire at different times. The only option offered by the then Department of Education and Science to a school faced with the situation is to claim the benefit of the exemption for each of the services in turn as the existing arrangements end. This may not provide the easiest of transitions.

Particular care must be taken by a school making use of the exemption not to allow grounds maintenance and cleaning activity to exceed the total of 117 work hours currently permitted in any one week. To do so will mean automatic loss of the entitlement to the exemption and a requirement to apply CCT with effect from the beginning of the next financial year. The ability to reclaim the exemption is lost until the resulting contract or agreement expires and the school again satisfies the three full-time equivalent criteria.

At its most draconian this provision could cause a school to lose its exemption in the spring term and have to retender with minimal preparation time. Indeed, the result may well be a hiatus period during which external contractors must be brought in because DSO staff cannot carry out the work unless won in competition. This potential financial burden could prove disastrous within a delegated, cash-limited budget.

CONTRACTING OPTIONS

Three alternative approaches were suggested by the then Department of Education and Science for schools with delegated budgets when existing contracts for grounds maintenance, catering and cleaning expire, whether or not the exemption for small-scale school operations applies:

(i)   to remain part of a centrally tendered service;

(ii) to form a school-based DSO organisation to bid for the work in competition with other external contractors;

(iii) for a group of schools to form an independent consortium and either create a DSO to serve them all or to contract out the service required by all participating schools.

Remaining part of the local authority's general CCT arrangements carries the benefits of economies of scale and permits the school to rely on the council's expertise in managing contracts. A uniform service and a clear relationship between client and contractor will be likely to result. From the school's viewpoint these advantages could well be offset to some degree by the slower responses of a central bureaucracy, communication problems between school and client officers and the lack of ability to vary services on site informally from time to time. The balance of these considerations will determine whether schools have any interest in contracting-out or in arranging tendering by themselves or in co-operation with neighbouring schools.

STAFFING ISSUES

Problems can arise from the fact that responsibilities in relation to non-teaching staff in schools are shared. The local authority may be the formal employer, but it is for the governors to appoint staff, including peripatetic staff working with the DSO if such staff work regularly in the school at specified times. Only staff working on an irregular basis are not within the limits of this responsibility. Likewise, it is for the governors to formally determine employment. In common parlance, the governors hold responsibility for both hiring and firing, whatever subsequent rights of appeal an employee may have in respect of dismissal.

One of the common issues arising in preparing for competition or retendering is whether staffing costs need to be reduced to maintain a DSO's competitiveness. Where DSO staff are employed in schools with delegated budgets, a termination of existing contracts of employment by the local authority and re-engagement on new terms is not possible without the involvement of the school. The governing body will have to make a formal determination that the staff should be removed from the school and then that they should be reappointed to what will in practice be new posts.

Governors also have certain powers over any member of the DSO working within a school. They may, for example, demand the removal of such an employee from the school. More vitally still, they have the power to determine the grading of staff holding posts in the school. This applies once again to DSO staff working specified hours on a regular basis at the school. The implications in terms of DSO viability and potential equal-pay-for-equal-work claims are obvious reasons why the local authority must maintain a good relationship with all its governing bodies and work in an open and co-operative way with them so long as they are using centrally organised DSOs to carry out defined activities in their schools.

THE IMPACT OF TENDERING ON OTHER EDUCATION SERVICES

It is common to assume that the functions of an LEA begin and end with services to parents, pupils and students in the form of direct educational provision and further-education grants. In fact, services provided to the public extend to youth and community work, adult education, careers services and special education needs assessment and placement, as well as the exercise of powers to provide joint facilities for schools and public use in relation to sports and leisure facilities. Additional support services in the form of contract evaluation and monitoring, management, personnel, financial and legal advice and specialist curriculum guidance are all provided to schools by or for an LEA.

The impact of the tendering of support services upon business units providing services to the general public has already been covered in earlier chapters. When schools and colleges hold their own budgets, they will be in the same position as a free agent, able to procure their support services from the local authority if they wish to do so or from the private sector. This leaves the issue of the extent to which CCT and LMS will affect the LEA's ability to provide services to the public for which schools and colleges have no responsibility and, conceivably, little interest.

The other primary problem relates to the use of school and college buildings outside normal hours for adult education, and of their sports and leisure facilities by the general public in pursuance of joint-use agreements. Such usage will now largely be controlled by governing bodies, but may give rise to a need for additional services that are themselves defined activities, such as grounds maintenance outside normal term time, catering other than school meals provision, or cleaning, all of which will have to be built into the service specification before the contract is awarded. Doing so may be very difficult even within the lengthy time-scales for competitive tendering, given the need to secure the consent of the governing bodies to such arrangements.

Chapter 19

TENDERING IN SOCIAL SERVICES

Compulsory competition directly impacts on social services only marginally; residential homes and day centres require grounds maintenance and in some cases cleaning, which are subject to CCT as is the preparation of meals for delivery to social services establishments. Tendering disciplines, however, are increasingly relevant even if the element of compulsion is less obviously present.

The Griffiths Report on community care[1] and the National Health Service and Community Care Act 1990 encourage a separation of service purchaser from service provider similar to the client–contractor split implicit in compulsory competition and developing the use of external suppliers. This, combined with devolved budgets and a changing relationship between social services and the voluntary sector, replacing ad hoc grants with formal contractual commitments, renders tendering an essential component of community care initiatives and general social work practice if the government's aim of a mixed economy of care is to be achieved.

THE GRIFFITHS REPORT

The Griffiths Report examines present social services organisation and makes a series of recommendations to change the nature of much of the work presently carried out. In particular, it postulates a gradual withdrawal from direct service provision towards an enabling role and argues for the in-house roles to become those of policy determination, assessment and purchasing, with direct services being supplied externally through the voluntary and private sector or by DSOs operating as quasi-contractors where the former is impractical in the short term. The trend would be towards a position where case managers assess need and specify the care package required, contract with direct service providers and hand over management to contract professionals and inspectors, who will monitor performance and client satisfaction.

The successful implementation of Griffiths' recommendations is dependent on the cultivation of specification and contracting skills not presently common among social services staff, the expansion of quality control and inspection functions, and market research into the availability and scale of alternative means of service provision already in existence or capable of

1 Griffiths Report, *Community Care: An Agenda for Action*, HMSO, 1988.

being nurtured over time. This last point is crucial, because in many areas unless support and training are provided, with a view to fostering workable long-term relationships with potential service providers, those suppliers will be unlikely to view the tailoring of their businesses to the exacting requirements of a major new purchaser, such as social services, to be either cost-effective or profitable. The end result could then be services offered on a 'take-it-or-leave-it' basis.

Contracting in social services is likely to run the broad gamut from fixed arrangements with a minimal number of suppliers to more flexible short-term or casual agreements from which small-scale organisations are not excluded but fostered. The Griffiths Report itself postulates a range of outcomes covering complete withdrawal of local authority involvement in direct service provision and active promotion of the private sector and voluntary agencies; a passive or reactive position, with tendering occurring where an external market demonstrates its strength but otherwise retaining direct service provision in-house; equal support for public and free-market-provided services; and, finally, continuing positive discrimination in favour of suppliers in the public sector or associated voluntary agencies.

THE ROLES OF PURCHASER AND PROVIDER

Distinction of purchaser from provider is a concept having an application across the whole range of social services, not one limited to the adult services to which community-care proposals apply.

The two presently intermixed aspects constituting social services are those of service delivery to specific clients and the direct rectification of justified complaints, as distinct from those of purchasing or commissioning services. The latter is the less focused role, covering the setting of policy, planning of service development and grants, assessment and prioritisation of need and allocation of resources within the context of overall budgeting control, resourcing of case management, monitoring access to services to be paid for by the council, ascertaining service availability, specifying and contracting for services, contract management, monitoring quality and providing the ultimate recourse for client complaints.

The benefits claimed for distinguishing the purchaser role from that of the provider are clarification of goals and objectives, opportunities to improve quality through explicit specification and setting of standards as well as by proper monitoring of results, extension of client choice alongside expanded private-sector participation in social services, clearer accountability alongside elimination of conflicts of interest and improved value for money.

It may not always be practicable or desirable to achieve complete separation in respect of in-house staff, as recognised by Department of Health guidance[1]. The need to retain social workers for the provision of direct advice to the public alongside the process of assessing the needs of the same clients is an obvious example of economies that arise from allowing staff to continue to

1 Department of Health, *Implementing Community Care—Purchaser, Commissioner and Provider Roles*, HMSO 1991 and Department of Health and Social Services Inspectorate, *Purchase of Service—Practice Guidance and Practice Material for Social Service Departments and Other Agencies*, HMSO 1991.

carry out tasks falling into each of the two distinct roles. Furthermore, the ease with which separation can be effected will be dependent on the extent to which services have been organised on the basis of geographical decentralisation and multidisciplinary teams or professional specialisms.

SERVICE CONTRACTING

This section examines problems peculiar to the specification and tendering of social services that arise by virtue of the nature of the services to be provided or the type of potential provider likely to be bidding for the work: in particular, the means of resolving difficulties in specifying the outcomes considered acceptable for clients in receipt of direct services and the exercise of restraint to avoid over-complication and thus the risk of alienating those voluntary agencies who might otherwise be prepared to provide cost-effective services to clients for whom councils continue to hold a legal duty of support and assistance.

Service philosophy

The type of service sought will frequently be dependent less on the definition of mechanical tasks than on the manner in which the client falls to be treated. Service philosophy and delivery of services in a manner calculated to preserve client dignity and independence are often as important as the service itself. Consideration has to be given therefore to tying service delivery to a series of principles against which the quality of provision will be judged. This can be achieved in part by annexing printed policies to the contract requirements for contractors to comply with. This will be a particularly effective step if the policies are nationally determined or can be related to commonly accepted standards of care, such as those laid down for residential care of the elderly.

Staffing

Social services contracting is more likely than most to throw up situations in which there is a desire on the part of the local authority to specify the number of staff required for particular functions or tasks. Bearing in mind the provisions of the LGA 1988 in relation to non-commercial considerations, there is a particular risk of a social service directorate attempting to use an overly restrictive specification. As far as possible other means of achieving suitable staffing levels should be used, such as reliance upon the enforcement of the Registered Homes Act 1984, which enables responsible officers to set minimum standards of care practice and staffing in the case of contracts for the placement of the elderly.

The other unique issue is the possibility of police checks as a means of vetting staff whose jobs will require them to work with children, and procedures to ensure no person is employed in providing relevant services for the council before vetting has been completed should be included in the contract conditions. Equally, there may be a need to require contractors not to employ persons with convictions for sexual offences or crimes of violence in the provision of services to vulnerable clients.

Detailed specification

One of the advantages of voluntarily tendering for services is that there is no applicable minimum contract period. This removes some of the pressure for an overly detailed specification, since short contracts can be let initially while a relationship is built up with particular tenderers. This is less applicable in respect of residential placements. Given the intention of establishing elderly persons in locations that will become their homes, the arrangements made will be so structured as to secure a longer-term sense of permanence for the benefit of the clients.

Tendering procedures

Subject to council standing orders, there is no reason why tendering for social services must be structured towards open invitations to tender or the creation of select lists of interested contractors, the normal process applicable to CCT. Direct negotiation with possible suppliers is a lawful, less formal alternative.

Since minimum-term or even fixed-term contracts need not be the end result of any tendering process, the potential flexibility of the supplier will be more important and consideration can be given to complete alternatives to contracting, such as the awarding of grants subject to conditions.

The possibility of the selection of contractors on the basis of known experience or standing with the local authority or the professional knowledge of council officers leads to a particular emphasis being placed on the need to document the reasons for all contracting decisions, since the possibility of less formal procedures and arrangements may increase the risk of disappointed tenderers requesting reasons for contracting decisions and challenging them. Reconsideration of the contents of Chapter 6 at this stage is recommended for officers charged with implementing social services contracting.

Problems for tenderers

A number of issues specific to the provision of services for social services clients may affect the willingness of contractors to tender or render it necessary to make concessions in the specification or contract conditions for the service. The obvious ones are dependency levels of different clients, which can dramatically affect the level and cost of the services required for them; geographical dispersal of clients and the resultant time lost travelling or the difficulty in finding employees to go out to them; and high set-up costs associated with services such as residential care, which may preclude interest in anything other than lengthy contracts.

Voluntary organisations

Special care is required in placing local authority relationships with voluntary organisations on a contractual basis. The agencies concerned will have become used to a consensual relationship or become dependent on grant aid. Attempts to change such arrangements are bound to be viewed initially as an unwarranted attack on their independence and professionalism. Whether attempts are being made to place services already provided or needed in future on a formal footing or to regulate the quality and quantity of operations to be completed in return for a grant, negotiations must tread a fine line between sensitivity and achieving explicit common understanding of the aims and objectives of the process. In particular, the danger of alienating unpaid volunteers working for such organisations must be recognised and no attempt made to impose arrangements with too much of the flavour of a commercial agreement for profit.

Additionally, voluntary organisations are likely to experience particular problems if certain contractual elements common in dealings with the private sector generally are proposed. These include payment in arrears, since this will cause obvious cash-flow problems; fixed term arrangements, given that most voluntary agencies have insufficient resources to commit themselves beyond the current year; and excessive administrative requirements (the simpler the payment, default and monitoring mechanisms, the better).

Chapter 20

ENSURING SERVICE QUALITY

Following analysis of the specific services to which tendering disciplines relate, it is necessary to supplement the earlier consideration of standards and performance measures in specifications by examining the available systems through which the possibility of sustaining quality can be improved once contracts are let.

Quality control is first and foremost dependent on the attitude of the contractor, which falls in turn to be monitored by the client. This chapter concentrates on systems that contractors may be encouraged to adopt as a demonstration of the extent of their commitment to quality. Essentially, there are two formal approaches: the first is a quality assurance process of the type necessary to achieve British Standard 5750 (BS5750); the second is a total quality management (TQM) package.

Coverage of the subject concludes with a review of Citizen's Charter rights as they impact on service quality (and hence on monitoring) and customer contracts as a means of demonstrating local authority commitment to achieving the provision of quality of service from its contractors.

DEFINING QUALITY

Fitness for purpose, conformity with pre-set requirements, reliability, uniformity and consistency have all been used as tests to determine whether quality is present. The British Standards Institution defines it as 'the totality of features and characteristics of a product or service that bear on its ability to satisfy stated or implied needs'. In the context of contracting the BSI definition is useful since it emphasises the satisfaction of specified requirements and does not make the mistake of confusing quality with excellence, as the latter may not always be the level of quality specified and demanded. The extent to which services achieve value for money may be a simpler restatement of the test of quality that contract-monitoring staff will utilise in building a relationship in which suppliers fully understand the client's needs and act promptly on expressed dissatisfaction.

QUALITY CONTROL

Assuming that it has been possible to build sufficient performance indicators and standards into the contract documentation in the first place, quality control is the process of monitoring by which services are checked against the specification with a view to rectifying shortfalls or mistakes after they have occurred or obtaining financial redress or compensation in some other form.

Monitoring is problematic wherever subjective judgements fall to be made due to the non-qualitative bias of a specification, arising from the nature of the service to which it relates. Given the difficulties posed once a difference has arisen between the client and the contractor as to the minimum requirement in terms of quality of the finished product, it makes sense to examine means by which such problems can be prevented rather than having to be the subject of retrospective cure.

QUALITY ASSURANCE

Quality assurance refers to processes constructed to ensure that quality is built into an organisation concerned with the provision of services. The systematic approach implicit in quality assurance requires policy and standards to be explicitly pre-set and comprehensive mechanisms designed to ensure that such statements of good practice are put into effect and can be readily verified and monitored. The assumption made is that if such systems are in place, whatever the service requirements demanded, the organisation will be incapable of achieving other than quality as its end product. If the theory can prove itself in practice, a contractor offering quality assurance certification ought to be able not only to show an in-built concern with quality but to offer potential savings on monitoring costs for clients.

Quality assurance is demonstrated by a complete commitment to the creation of quality working systems vouched for by a specialist independent agency, which will issue relevant certification of a contractor's processes, following detailed preparation and investigation.

Quality assurance systems require the generation of a logical overall policy on service delivery, stated values, appropriate systems of record-keeping, set methods for identifying and correcting problems, proper complaints procedures, a commitment to client involvement in the business accompanied by automatic rights of access to the contractor's management and service staff and, finally, policies for staff development and training. Nor should such procedures be regarded as static; they should be audited periodically and upgraded as potential improvements are identified.

In essence, quality assurance covers the planning of service delivery, conformity with such plans and proper documentation of the actions taken and the results achieved.

BRITISH STANDARD 5750

Established in 1979, BS5750 is the British standard for quality assurance systems. Achieving BS5750 certification demonstrates a commitment to a definable level of quality, which can be compared not only within the United Kingdom, but across the world, since BS5750 corresponds with EN29000, the European standard, and ISO9000, the international equivalent. The British Standards Institution and a number of other organisations are qualified through the National Accreditation Council for Certification Bodies to assess and award BS5750 under a process of the type illustrated below. NACCB authorisation is not mandatory and this loophole in the regulations means that anyone can set up in the business of awarding BS5750 certification. Local authorities planning to specify BS5750 (where it is not anti-competitive to do so) should also specify that the award be made by a NACCB approved body.

The process of certification under BS5750 requires the creation of a quality manual, covering all elements of the business and its controlling mechanisms, with advice from the accreditation body on its requirements. A period of months is then allowed for an assessment of the documented systems in practice. Only then is the manual accepted and a full assessment inspection arranged, usually involving inspectors visiting for two or more days. If no significant problems are identified, the certification will be awarded within weeks but may be subject to rectification requirements.

Assessment and certification are not the end of the process. To maintain BS5750, between two and four random checks will be made each year by the accreditation body, for which a fee is charged.

The principal benefit claimed for BS5750 is that it improves productivity and raises confidence and morale while providing an additional element of marketability to an organisation so certificated. The process is undoubtedly costly and complex, however, and has been described as demanding little more than a good firm will do already. Nor is it certain in all cases that quality of systems will automatically lead to a quality product, the precept upon which quality assurance through BS5750 is based.

The questions for individual companies and DSOs to address therefore are whether the process of certification will in itself force the organisation to significantly change its methods of working, whether any benefits would be cost-effective when measured against other possibilities, such as TQM initiatives and, finally, whether market forces dictate significant advantages for those achieving BS5750.

Main requirements

To achieve BS5750 a number of issues must be addressed in relation to everything from management to final output. Management responsibilities are to be defined and documented with operational policy. All responsibilities must be not only identified but assigned to staff. A quality system must be established and documented that covers both the preparation of quality control procedures and their effective implementation. Procedures for reviewing contracts regularly must be established and recorded alongside planning controls, input and output, verification material and modifications.

Control of documentation must be so organised as to ensure that pertinent material is always readily available, obsolete documents are removed, changes are reviewed and approved and a master list or index of documentation established.

Purchasing systems must be established to ensure conformity of all goods and services acquired, all subcontractors assessed and products verified. Procedures should cover storage and maintenance of materials, their identification and traceability.

Process control documentation must include all work instructions, suitability of equipment, the approval of processes and equipment and the criteria for judging workmanship. The handling, storage and prevention of damage to and deterioration of materials are specifically highlighted.

Inspection and testing, together with maintenance of accurate testing equipment, are to be properly documented, as are the procedures for handling instances of non-conformity with specification and the corrective action to be taken to investigate and analyse causation and prevent recurrence.

Quality records and systems for internal quality audits, staff training, servicing and maintaining proper statistical records are the final elements to be addressed in this lengthy list.

Costs

The obvious costs of achieving BS5750 are those of employing a certification agency to assess the organisation, consultancy to assist in guiding the process of documentation and improvement of records and the ongoing costs of annual assessment. This needs to be added to the hidden cost of diverting staff time into the exercise.

The first firm of solicitors to be granted a certificate under BS5750 calculated their costs in these respects as approaching £30,000. This estimate may be a reasonable benchmark for any moderately sized organisation. However, smaller firms, or those providing less complex services, may achieve BS5750 at a much lower cost if the preparatory work can be done mainly in-house, because the assessment and inspection account only for £5,000 or less of the initial cost.

Using BS5750

There is no obvious reason why quality assurance in the form of BS5750 accreditation should not be used by any service provider or, indeed, to underpin the exercise of client responsibilities (if no more appropriate or less costly means of achieving an efficiently functioning unit can be found). The range of local government services that have sought and achieved BS5750 seems to bear out its perceived benefits to organisations as diverse as fleet management and maintenance and refuse collection and street cleaning (London Borough of Lewisham), grounds maintenance and catering (London Borough of Enfield), sport and leisure facilities (Clydesdale District Council and Thamesdown Borough Council), refuse collection (Chester-le-Street District Council), multiple defined activities (Ashfield District Council), legal services and printing (Braintree District Council) and cleaning services (South Glamorgan County Council).

In the field of professional services use is presently more restricted. A Manchester firm, Pannone March Pearson (now reincarnated as Pannone and Partners), was the first in the country to pursue and obtain BS5750 in respect of legal services and it has been followed by a number of other requests to the BSI for registration. Other disciplines yielding examples of accreditation include environmental health and trading standards (Solihull District Council) and management consultancy (Leeds City Council).

Specifying BS5750 in competitively tendered contracts

Once DSOs have achieved BS5750, there will be a temptation for local authorities to specify that all tenderers must hold such certification or its European equivalent. At a time when achieving BS5750 has the type of cost implications outlined above and comparatively few firms in many industries hold such a qualification, an absolute requirement will be seen as an anti-competitive measure.

The solution may be for local authorities to require successful tenderers to achieve BS5750 within a period of two to three years from commencing to perform services for the council. If such a proviso were included in the specification, it would deter only cowboy operators with no ability to work towards quality assurance and forewarn all other tenderers to allow for the costs of compliance in setting the level of their ultimate bid to the local authority for the work.

It must be emphasised that a BS5750 certificate does not in itself guarantee quality. Putting aside the issue as to the credentials of the company issuing the certificate, a quality assurance system will deliver service only to the standards set as the minimum acceptable by the contractor holding the certificate. In a nutshell, BS5750 can be achieved by an organisation setting itself low standards as readily as by one setting itself the highest. The lesson to learn is not to take a certificate at its face value as a means of differentiating between service providers but to interrogate the performance standards and practices underpinning the BS5750 award.

Once a local authority is contracting with holders of BS5750 certification, it may wish to review its monitoring processes and consider substituting a form of monitoring of the contractor's self-auditing requirements through a system of the type advocated by BS7229 (Part 1), which covers the auditing of quality management systems.

NEW STANDARDS

BS5750 is not the only standard now available. New standards are in preparation and among the first to materialise are BS7750 for environmental management systems and BS7850 for total quality management.

TQM

Developed in the United States, TQM describes an approach to quality assurance that stresses the importance of creating a culture in which concern for quality is endemic to service delivery rather than one relying only on systems and documentation. In essence, it is more people-centred. Responsibility for quality of service is devolved to all staff at all levels in the organisation, together with clear and explicit quality objectives. TQM therefore goes beyond the systems necessary to achieve BS5750, in which supervision can, to some extent, offset the acceptance of responsibility for quality by more junior members of staff. TQM also stresses the need for continued improvement in systems, equipment, techniques and teamwork.

QUALITY WORK ASSURED (QWA) SERVICEMARK PROPOSALS

The Trades Union Congress has proposed QWA as a mark to be aspired to by organisations in respect of identifying the quality of working environments and of staffing generally. It is intended to cover training, career development, pay and conditions, equality of opportunity, health and safety measures, work-force consultation and staff contact with service users. It is hoped that the QWA initiative will promote best employment practice and relate quality of service provision to quality of treatment given to employees.

QWA is doomed to marginal significance in relation to CCT. Accreditation with the QWA servicemark could not legitimately be used as an evaluation factor in the selection of tenderers because the LGA 1988 regards most factors covered by the proposed standard as non-commercial considerations.

THE CITIZEN'S CHARTER

Published by the government in July 1991, the Citizen's Charter proposals[1] set out a series of quality standards for public services, including functions performed by or for local authorities. The LGA 1992 implemented the proposals. The principal element is a requirement for the Audit Commission and the Scottish Accounts Commission to determine specific services for which they will give directions to local authorities regarding the publication of performance information. This is allied to new duties placed on councils to consider auditors' resports and their recommendations and to publish them. The Audit Commission and the Scottish Accounts Commission may also publish local authority failure to meet performance standards or to comply with auditors' reports.

Similar provisions aimed at school governors relate to the mandatory release of inspectors' reports to the public and to the publication of proposals to remedy any criticisms of educational standards.

These developments are supported by a defined standard for the delivery of public services called the Charter standard. Its principles are openness in relation to the methods used and cost of public services, clarity of information about service provision and results, consultation with customers in setting standards and determining services to be provided, courtesy and efficiency towards customers (which includes the requirement for staff to identify themselves to the public), the establishment of an effective complaints procedure and independent validation of performance in the form of checks on the standards obtained and value for money. Those local authorities who meet the Charter standard will be entitled to apply for a Chartermark in respect of particular services, only 50 of which will be awarded in the public sector in the first year of the scheme.

Consultation with local authority organisations is expected to result in the eventual production by the Audit Commission of performance indicators for a broad range of services. Early indications are that the complexity

1 *The Citizen's Charter: Raising the Standard*, Cm 1599 (1991).

of the possible indicators and the extent to which they can be commonly applicable to all local authorities need to be the subject of careful consideration.

CUSTOMER CONTRACTS

A number of local authorities are pioneering initiatives aimed at harnessing the ability of the recipients of council services to monitor and report deficiencies in provision as well as exercise some degree of choice in relation to those services. Research into customer needs and expectations is a vital first step of such customer-care initiatives, with open publication of the standards set for the service and the measures of quality by which services are to be judged.

Local authorities like York City Council, Harlow District Council and the London Borough of Lewisham have gone further than this and launched customer contracts, offering guarantees of service quality, including response times, that surpass the rights set out in the Citizen's Charter and may yield spin-off benefits in the form of savings on monitoring costs if every citizen is encouraged to become an inspector of service quality.

Chapter 21

EUROPEAN LAW

One of the prime intentions of the European Community (EC) in recent years has been to ensure that the suppliers of goods and services across Europe obtain fair opportunities to tender for contracts let by public bodies and statutory undertakers without impediments imposed by national frontiers or restrictive practices. Accordingly, it has brought into being directives governing the public procurement of supplies and works, and a further directive covering public-sector services took effect in 1993.

The public procurement directive relating to the supply of goods has no direct relevance to local authority services subject to CCT or even to voluntary tendering and is therefore largely outside the remit of this work. However, material on the subject is included with a brief overview of the utilities directive towards the end of the chapter.

The works directives have a direct impact on services to which CCT applies by virtue of the LGPLA 1980 and to some mentioned in the DoE's 1991 consultation paper. The services directive affects some of the services caught by the LGA 1988 and some of the proposed areas for the extension of competition into professional services.

The effect of the directive is that advertising, following set time-scales, in the EC *Official Journal* and certain consequential aspects of the tendering process, including the evaluation of contractors and bids, are regulated, and the specifications to be utilised are the subject of attempts at standardisation. This raises the spectre of conflicts with the tendering regimes laid down by the LGPLA 1980 and LGA 1988, over which the directives take precedence, although legal arguments continue as to whether formal adoption by the British Parliament is necessary before this is so.

This chapter examines the detailed requirements of the directives and the modifications local authorities should make to the tendering processes developed to cope with the requirements of the domestic legislation.

THE APPLICABILITY OF THE PROCUREMENT DIRECTIVES

Common values

The procurement directives apply to work and services with an estimated value exceeding set thresholds. To achieve a common impact in all countries

179

in the EC, contract values are expressed in European Currency Units (ECUs). These are the subject of conversion rates into national currencies applying to the following two years. The latest rates were published in November 1995.

Works directives

The material relevant to the consideration of this subject comprises Directives 71/305 and 89/440 and draft works regulations. The directives apply to building, civil engineering and demolition work. Work in this context is defined as the 'outcome of works which is sufficient of itself to fulfil an economic and technical function' of a public body. The definition is phrased in the way it is so that contracts whose values fall below the thresholds set by the directives can be aggregated and treated as a single function where appropriate. This discourages the splitting of functional work into constituent elements to avoid the necessity of complying with the directives.

The work subject to the directives is general building and civil engineering and demolition work, construction of buildings, civil engineering construction, installation of fixtures and fittings and building completion work with an estimated value in excess of ECU 5 million (approximately £3.74 million) in any one of these categories. The principle of aggregation applies, so that only if the total value of all the work is below the threshold will there be total exemption from compliance with the directives.

In carrying out the required aggregation individual contracts with an estimated value of less than ECU 1 million (approximately £748,000) can be ignored, provided that the total value of such contracts is less than 20 per cent of the total value of all contracts for carrying out the work.

A statement of the aggregated contracts for each type of work must be published in the *Official Journal* as soon as expenditure is planned. The detailed advertising requirements are set out later in this chapter under the heading 'Contract advertising and deadlines'.

The services directive

Directive 92/50 impacts on a number of local authority services covered by CCT.

The affected services are divided into two categories: priority services, which are subject to all the requirements of the directive, and residual services, which receive a lesser level of regulation. In particular, residual services are subject to the same notice and specification requirements as priority services, but not to restrictions on the use of selective tendering or negotiated contract procedures, the requirements to publish prior notices (essentially preliminary or warning advertisements) or the rules covering contract awards.

Priority services include vehicle maintenance, building cleaning, refuse disposal (including the collection of waste), banking and investment services, insurance, accounting, auditing and bookkeeping, architectural services, computer services, telecommunications services, advertising, market research, management consultancy and housing management.

Catering, management of sport and leisure facilities, legal services, educational services, health and social services and corporate services are all listed as residual services.

Crossing financial thresholds again triggers the need for compliance with the directive's requirements. Any contract with a total value of ECU 200,000 (approximately £149,700) is caught, the only exceptions being insurance premiums, for which estimated expenditure of ECU 100,000 (approximately £74,900) is caught, and architectural services for complete design of projects, for which the threshold is total costs in excess of ECU 5 million (approximately £3.74 million). If a potential contract contains options affecting the estimated value, the highest figure is to be applied for the purpose of determining whether the procurement directive must be followed.

Subdividing the service into smaller contracts will not achieve avoidance of the EC requirements. Only individual contracts with a value over the contract period of less than ECU 80,000 (approximately £59,900) will escape aggregation, and then only if the sum total of all such contracts does not exceed 20 per cent of the total value of all contracts comprising a single service or function.

Figure 2   Priority services listed under the EC services directive

1. *Maintenance and repair services—includes vehicle maintenance but not exterior building maintenance*
2. *Land and air transport*
3. *Transport of mail by land and air*
4. *Telecommunications services*
5. *Financial services:*
    —insurance
    —banking and investment
6. *Accounting, auditing and bookkeeping*
7. *Computer and related services*
8. *Research and development services*
9. *Market research and opinion polling*
10. *Management consultancy and related services*
11. *Architecture, engineering, town planning, etc.*
12. *Advertising*
13. *Building cleaning*
14. *Property management—this will include housing management*
15. *Publishing and printing*
16. *Sewerage and refuse disposal; sanitation and similar services—this is expected to include refuse collection and street cleaning*

Residual services under the EC services directive

17. *Hotel and restaurant services*
18. *Rail and water transport services*
19. *Supporting and auxiliary transport services*
20. *Legal services*
21. *Personnel placement and supply services*
22. *Investigation and security services*
23. *Education and vocational education services*
24. *Health and social services*
25. *Recreational, cultural and sporting services*
26. *Other services*

The financial threshold relates to the total value of the services to be provided over the contract period and not to the annual value, as in the case of claimed *de minimis* activity exempted from the CCT provisions of the LGA 1988. The directive will therefore catch even small authorities choosing to contract for their services, which are otherwise exempt from regulation of their chosen tendering procedures. Additionally, since the LGA 1988 sets minimum contract periods, commonly three or four years, for services subject to CCT, the cumulative value of any contract tendered in consequence of domestic legislation will be likely to give rise to a need to comply at the same time with the EC services directive. For example, services costed at no more than £100,000 a year would be exempt from CCT, whereas a service contract valued at only £25,000 a year over five years would be subject to European procurement compliance, assuming the service is one to which the services directive applies.

Work undertaken in-house

The works and services directives do not apply unless a service is to be tendered with a view to awarding a contract. A decision not to put an activity out to tender and to retain a DSO to provide the service without competition, so far as it is lawful under domestic legislation to do so, is not precluded by the European rules. The rules apply only to procurement, the definition of which does not cover in-house provision, for which there is no possibility of the local authority entering into a contract. No legal entity, not even a public corporation, can contract with itself and a DSO remains part of the local authority, only its accounts having to be separated from those of the authority. This removes any threat of an obligation to tender services being imposed on a local authority by the procurement directives, where no obligation exists under the LGA 1988 or LGA 1992. The directives will apply, however, if the authority voluntarily decides to subject its services to competition.

CONTRACT ADVERTISING AND DEADLINES

The works directives and the services directive require two different forms of advertising in the *Official Journal* for any relevant contract to be let by a local authority. The first advertisement to be placed is a prior notice, warning potential tenderers of proposed large-scale works contracts or of the total value of likely service contracts to be awarded during the municipal year. The second is the publication of a notice. This is the advertisement proper, seeking tenderers for specific work or services. It offers the opportunity to tender, or to be registered as interested in tendering, for a contract.

Prior notices

An early warning must be published in the *Official Journal* as soon as a local authority has determined that it plans works with a potential contract value of at least ECU 5 million (approximately £3.74 million). This means a prior notice has to be published for any building, civil engineering and demolition work to which the works directives apply, other than aggregated contracts. It has to specify the essential characteristics of the work to be contracted and its format must substantially follow that set out in the draft works regulations.

Local authorities are required to prepare an estimate of the total value of their procurement of priority services during the forthcoming year, including contracts they intend to tender. The estimate must be prepared as soon as possible after 1 April each year; that is, immediately after the commencement of the municipal budgeting year. Residual services do not need to be included in the estimate.

If the total value of procurement for any single service to be procured in the financial year is ECU 750,000 (approximately £561,000) or more, that estimate must be published in the *Official Journal* in the form of a prior notice. The specific information to be included in the notice is set out in the services directive. Specimen notices are included in the appendices.

Prior notices cannot exceed 650 words in length and must include the date when it is forecast the notice proper will appear in the *Official Journal*. No charge is levied for prior notices.

Notices

Notices proper inform tenderers of the intention of a local authority to award a contract or contracts for relevant work or services, the estimated value of which exceeds the thresholds set by the procurement directives. Unless all interested parties are to be permitted to tender, notices must include the minimum and maximum numbers of tenderers to be invited. These must be predetermined; otherwise the directives require a minimum of 5 and a maximum of 20 to be invited. This contrasts with the position under the LGA 1988, whereby a minimum of three contractors other than a DSO are to be invited to tender, but the maximum is a matter for the unfettered discretion of the local authority.

The notices must also specify the information needed for financial and economic standing and technical capacity to be evaluated, which the tenderers must supply to the local authority as part of the qualifying process for tendering. Other matters that must be included are any permitted variations to the specification; whether deposits or guarantees, such as performance bonds, will be required; whether tenders for parts of the work or service will be considered; the criteria for awarding the contract and the last date for responding to the notice. As with prior notices, all the above information must be confined to 650 words, imposing the discipline of brevity and discouraging the imposition of unusual requirements.

The format of the notice for works contracts must broadly correspond to that set out in the draft regulations, and that for services must contain all the information in the directive, which gives greater detail than is possible in this text. Recommended standard form notices for publication in the *Official Journal* (compliant with Directive 91/561) are now available from HMSO.

Time periods

If an open procedure is to be utilised, whereby anyone can tender for the work or services, the period to the closing date for receipt of tenders must not be less than 52 days from the date on which the notice is dispatched to the *Official Journal*.

For restricted tendering, when contractors are selected to bid by the local authority, a minimum of 37 days following dispatch of notices to the *Official Journal* is required for tenderers to notify their interest in receiving an invitation to tender; the closing date for such responses must be specified in the notice. There is then a minimum period of 40 days from dispatch of the invitations to tender for submission of tenders.

An expedited procedure is permissible for urgent works or services. Provided a justification for using an accelerated timetable is included in the notice, the time period for expressing interest in tendering can be reduced from 37 days to 15.

In calculating time periods for the purposes of implementing the procurement directives the day from which time begins to run (in relation to notices, the date of dispatch of the advertisement) is not taken into account and the time period must include at least two working days and end on a working day, so must be extended in the event of intervening public holidays.

Advertising outside the *Official Journal*

The directives require that advertisements placed in publications other than the *Official Journal* may not be published prior to the date when the notices are dispatched to the *Official Journal*. Nor can any other advertisement include more information than that appearing in the *Official Journal*. This prevents companies based in the United Kingdom from obtaining any advantage over other European concerns in determining whether a particular contract should be pursued.

There is nothing in the directives precluding a local authority from making direct approaches to contractors to prompt them to tender for the work or services. This may be felt to undermine the effect of the previous proscription.

PROCEDURAL OPTIONS FOR CONTRACTING

The directives recognise three key methods for awarding any contract. The first is an open procedure, with all interested contractors permitted to tender. The directives assume this to be the normal practice. For British local authorities the need to ensure that they are not required to appraise and evaluate an impracticably large number of contractors and bids will militate against using the open procedure. The rest of this chapter is biased towards controlling the number of potential tenderers by an initial selection process and therefore less detailed consideration is accorded to the open procedure.

The second option is a restricted procedure, with contractors registering an interest in tendering and only those selected by the local authority able to submit tenders. This accords with the practices most authorities have evolved to cope with CCT under domestic legislation.

While there are no exclusions from, or conditions placed on, the use of the restricted procedure in respect of works or services contracts, the use of anything other than the open procedure for the procurement of supplies is heavily curtailed.

The final option is a negotiated contract, in which terms are negotiated with one or more chosen contractors, without any formal tendering, before a contract is awarded. Such a procedure is not open to local authorities having to comply with the LGPLA 1980 or LGA 1988 because a DSO is one of the parties that may be performing the works or services. It may be an option where a local authority is closing down an in-house service and wishes to secure a private contractor for future provision. Even in these circumstances there will be difficulties, given the Audit Commission's concern that negotiated contracts do not achieve demonstrable value for money, however administratively convenient they may be.

CONTRACTING DECISIONS

Under the procurement directives, contracts can be awarded either to the most economically advantageous tender or on the lowest price. If the former is chosen, this must be stated in the notice together with the specific criteria, preferably prioritised in order of importance, on which economic advantage will be judged.

In selecting companies to tender for local authority works or services discretion is given to exclude tenderers who are bankrupt or the subject of bankruptcy proceedings, who have been convicted of criminal offences or committed acts of grave misconduct in relation to their business, who have not paid social security contributions in any member state or failed to settle taxes due in the United Kingdom, who are not registered in the professional or trade registers of the member state in which they are established and, if tendering for services contracts, who are not members of an organisation of which membership is mandatory for the performance of the same services in their home country. Finally, tenderers who have provided information containing serious misrepresentations can be excluded.

Consortia may not be precluded from bidding, but can be required to form a legal entity for the purposes of effecting a binding contract with the procuring authority.

The extent to which contractors may be required to provide information about their companies and performance is addressed below.

Financial and economic standing

Bank statements, balance sheets compliant with the company law of the member state in which the contractor is based, statements of turnover covering the past three years and evidence of professional indemnity insurance (this last being applicable only to services, not to works) are generally deemed sufficient evidence of financial and economic standing.

Verification, in the form of judicial records or documents from relevant judicial or administrative authorities, that a company is not bankrupt or facing such proceedings or has not committed acts of misconduct, and certificates from competent authorities as to payment of social security contributions and taxes, where available, will be conclusive. If the member state in which the contractor is based does not issue such certification, declarations on oath must be accepted by the local authority.

Only if the tenderer is unable to produce the above-mentioned information or the information supplied is inappropriate or the notices in the *Official Journal* have specified requirements for additional financial information can further material be sought. One of the obvious things a local authority may have to seek additionally is confirmation of the contractor's ability to secure a performance bond or any other form of deposit or guarantee specified in the notice.

Technical capacity

Technical capacity is to be demonstrated by the contractor's educational and professional qualifications and those of the personnel and management who will be responsible for the works or services, statements of the technical services that the contractor can call upon, and statements of the available plant, equipment and tools and the average size of the workforce (including managerial staff) employed for each of the past three years.

References in respect of works contracts experience can be obtained in the form of a list of jobs carried out in the last five years, accompanied by certificates of satisfactory completion. The certification may be obtained directly from the persons certifying their satisfaction with the contractor if desired.

With respect to services, a list of principal contracts undertaken in the last three years, their values and the clients' identities can be requested. Additionally, indications of the share of the service to be subcontracted and the nature of the contractor's quality controls and study and research facilities can be required.

The notice placed in the *Official Journal* must specify the local authority's requirements for demonstrating technical capacity.

Following the directives to the letter in terms of the technical information that may be demanded of tenderers merits a degree of caution for a British local authority because of the potential conflict with the prohibitions on taking non-commercial considerations into account in contract decisions laid down by the LGA 1988. The references therein to the ineligibility of the composition of the contractor's workforce for consideration are particularly pertinent.

Ministerial guidance has already been given that the requirement of a tenderer to state whether an existing labour force will be used or if local recruitment is intended, on the face of it permissible information to be sought and acted on if the procurement directives are followed, implies that undertakings prepared to employ local workers will be regarded more favourably and is an anti-competitive practice[1]. Reliance should not be placed on the works directives as authority for such action according to the Secretary of State.

There is, in any event, a more obvious conflict, since the directives permit a local authority to specify matters appertaining to employment protection and working conditions and to require contractors to confirm they have taken such matters into account in their tenders. Other than the limited

1 DoE circular 21/89 and Welsh Office circular 50/89.

extent to which health and safety matters can be imported into contracts without breaching the LGA 1988, such considerations are unlawful in Britain. Even the extent to which it is possible to seek reassurances from tenderers that they are aware of the relevant national legal obligations is dubious.

Having established that the directives set firm limits on the information that may be requested of contractors, for complex services and those required for a special purpose (a phrase undefined in the services directive), checks may be made with competent official bodies in the countries in which the companies are based.

Inviting tenders

Except when the open tendering option is selected, at least five and no more than 20 tenderers can be invited to bid unless a different range is specified in the local authority's notice in the *Official Journal*. No guidance exists as to the situation appertaining if less than five tenderers meet the minimum eligibility standards to bid; there is nothing in the directives as clear cut as the position taken by the LGA 1988, which demands that if less than four tenderers other than the DSO register an interest in bidding, they must all be invited to submit tenders regardless of their standing and competence and thus of the willingness or sense in the local authority ever contracting with them, however keen their price.

The directives do state: 'The number of candidates invited to tender shall be sufficient to ensure genuine competition.' This may yet be interpreted as having a similar effect to the domestic legislation if five is now to be regarded as the lowest number of tenderers necessary to achieve competitive prices.

Time periods

A minimum of 40 days must be allowed for the submission of bids from the date of dispatch of invitations to tender. A longer period must be allowed if contractors are invited to inspect premises or documents in situ. This may persuade authorities to supply full contract clauses and specifications to all selected tenderers as a matter of course.

The minimum 40-day period can be reduced to 26 days where prior notices have been published in respect of the intended contract and to ten days where the accelerated procedure is being used for pre-stated reasons of urgency.

In the event that a contractor requires further information, it must be sent to him or her not later than six days before the last date for receipt of tenders (or four days if the accelerated procedure is being used). This places a local authority in an awkward position if requests for additional information are received so short a time before the closing date for tenders as to render compliance impossible. In any case, best contracting practice calls for the same information to be made available to every tenderer, so a request for better particulars or clarification should result in a circular response to all interested parties. In the context of tendering by foreign companies this may cause confusion as to the authority's requirements rather than minimise it.

Contractors not selected to tender may seek reasons for their rejection and a response to a request for reasons must be complied with in not more than 15 days. This corresponds neatly with section 20 of the LGA 1988. There is no date by which this right ceases to be exercisable.

Awarding contracts

Providing that the intention to award the contract to the most economically advantageous tender is stated, together with the specific criteria to be employed in judging economic advantage, in the notice in the *Official Journal* and the tender documents, local authorities are not proscribed from determining their own evaluation criteria. These must comply with the strictures of domestic legislation examined in Chapter 3.

The procurement directives accept that tenderers may be required to explain abnormally low bids or loss leaders, and a local authority may reject such a bid if dissatisfied with the explanation given. If in the notice in the *Official Journal* the local authority stated its intention to award the contract to the lowest tenderer, its failure to do so, because it is dissatisfied with the explanation for a suspiciously low price, requires the authority to inform the European Commission of the rejection of the lowest tender or tenders.

Post-tender negotiations

Fundamental contract terms, including price, are not permitted to be the subject of negotiation after tenders have been received. Only peripheral matters and details of contract implementation can be determined by agreement with the successful tenderer after potential contractors have submitted their bids.

Contract reports

Within 48 days of awarding a contract a notice must be sent to the *Official Journal* stating the number of tenders received and the range of prices (by stating the highest and lowest bids), the identity of the successful tenderer, whether the contract was awarded on the basis of lowest price or economic advantage and the proportion of work likely to be subcontracted. The report must also be supplied if no contractor is selected.

The report must not exceed 650 words in length and will be published automatically in the *Official Journal* if it relates to a works contract or one for priority services. Reports for residual services have to be made, but cannot be published without the consent of the local authority awarding the contract.

The European Commission may then demand a more detailed statement and, if it does, the full reasons for the award, the names of all tenderers and the individual justifications for their non-selection to tender or the rejection of their bids must be supplied.

Unsuccessful tenderers may request reasons and these must be supplied within 15 days of receiving the request. This applies equally to situations where the local authority decides not to award the contract to any of the tenderers.

SPECIFICATIONS

The procurement directives require local authorities to impose specifications that, so far as possible, replicate established standards and utilise European standards wherever possible. This builds on the existing case law to the effect that an insistence on national standards linked to refusal to accept broadly comparable European standards in the alternative is anti-competitive and unlawfully frustrates trade within the EC[1].

The directives define the following terms in respect to specifications:

(i)   technical specifications: 'defining the characteristics of a work, described objectively and in a manner such that it fulfills the use for which the authority intends it';

(ii) standard: 'a technical specification approved by a recognised standardising body' but not including mandatory national standards and their regulatory bodies;

(iii) European standards: those 'approved by the European Committee for Standardisation';

(iv) European technical approval: 'an approval of fitness for use of a product issued by a body designated for the purpose by a member state';

(v)   common technical specification: one that has been 'laid down in accordance with a procedure recognised by member states and has been published in the *Official Journal*';

(vi) essential requirements: those 'in the general interest, such as health and safety';

(vii) European specification: 'a common technical specification, a British standard implementing a European Standard, or a European Technical Approval'.

The directives require authorities to provide technical specifications defined by reference to relevant European specifications unless there is no set means of establishing conformity with such specifications, or it is impossible to satisfactorily establish the conformity or otherwise of the specific contract work or service with European specifications, or applying such specifications would be disproportionately costly or technically difficult or equipment already in use is incompatible with such specification, or the work or service is genuinely innovative and requires novel forms of specification. An additional exception for works contracts arises where different specifications are mandatory in the United Kingdom, provided that such requirements are compatible with EC obligations.

The reasons for any departure from using standards of the types outlined above in specifying contracts for work or services must be shown in the notice to be published in the *Official Journal*. The record of the reasons must also be supplied to the European Commission if requested. An additional requirement for works contracts that fail to use specifications based on European standards is that the local authority must have a clearly defined and recorded strategy for changing over to European specifications.

Where no applicable European standards exist, the directives allow

---

1 Case 45/87: *Commission v Ireland* [1988] ECR 4929 (the *Dundalk Pipeline* case).

technical matters to be defined by reference to British technical specifications recognised as complying with the basic requirements listed in the European directives on technical harmonisation. For works contracts, technical specifications may be defined by reference to British technical specifications for the design and method of calculation and execution of the work and the use of materials. For both works and services contracts, the preferred method of definition is by national standards implementing international standards and, only if these are unavoidable, by national standards alone, or if there are no national standards, by any other standards.

Definition of products by brand name or source is prohibited unless equivalents are expressly allowed. Any such requirement must be justified by reference to the subject of the contract and it must be the case that the use of any other description in the specification could not constitute a 'sufficiently precise and intelligible technical specification'.

OTHER EUROPEAN DIRECTIVES

While it is not possible in this text to deal with all the directives having an effect on local authority contracted services, the most significant attempts to regulate such activity, apart from the work and services procurement directives, are highlighted in this section.

The supplies directives

The supplies directives, 77/62, 80/767 and 88/295, apply to all local authority purchasing, or aggregated contracts for sufficiently similar or related products, with an estimated total value exceeding ECU 200,000 (approximately £150,000). Open tendering is required unless a procedure restricted to selected tenderers accords with national provisions compatible with EC law. Negotiated contracts are severely restricted. A minimum of 52 days from the dispatch of the notice to the *Official Journal* to the closing date for receipt of tenders is required under the open tendering procedure. Where restricted tendering is permitted, a minimum of 37 days must be allowed for companies to express interest in tendering with an additional minimum of 40 days from the issue of invitations to the closing date for receipt of tenders.

The utilities directive

The utilities directive, number 92/13, relates to agencies providing water, energy, transport and telecommunications. It affects local authorities, with railway functions, those managing airports and harbours and Scottish water and sewerage authorities. The directive applies to contracts for supplies valued at or in excess of the threshold of ECU 400,000 (approximately £299,000) and to works contracts of ECU 5 million (approximately £3.74 million) or more, involving the execution, design or realisation of civil engineering work.

In open tendering a minimum of 52 days is required from the dispatch of the notice to the *Official Journal* for submission of tenders, or 36 days if a prior notice has been published. Restricted and negotiated tenders require 35 days from the date of dispatch of the notice, and while the time limit for receipt of tenders may be agreed with the interested companies, the directive indicates it should not normally be less than 21 days as a rule and not less than ten days from invitation to tender to closing date in any event.

Prior notices are required in each procurement area whenever expenditure of ECU 750,000 (approximately £561,000) or more in respect of supplies is estimated for the forthcoming year or for works of not less than ECU 5 million (approximately £3.74 million).

In relation to supplies contracts, a local authority may reject a tender on the grounds that the proportion of the products manufactured outside the EC exceeds 50 per cent. Where tenders are separated by no more than three per cent, the lowest tender need not be accepted if the higher tender contains a greater proportion of parts manufactured in the EC even where non-EC manufactured parts is less than 50 per cent. These provisions of the directive clash with the LGA 1988, under which country of origin constitutes a non-commercial consideration and cannot be taken into account.

The unfair contract terms directive

A proposed directive that apparently will contain a list of outlawed standard conditions would have direct impact upon local authority contracts and specifications.

REMEDIES AND SANCTIONS FOR NON-COMPLIANCE WITH PROCUREMENT DIRECTIVES

The basic principle of European law is that it is applicable to the United Kingdom and must be enforced by British courts even if domestic law is inconsistent with it. This principle is not of direct application to EC directives. Under Article 189 of the EC Treaty a directive is binding as to the result to be achieved by each member state 'but shall leave to the national authority the choice of form and methods'.

A directive thus requires a member state to alter its own law to give effect to the directive, which usually specifies an implementation date by which the aims of the directive are to be achieved. Once the implementation date has passed, to the extent that the obligations laid down by the directive are clear, precise and unequivocal, an individual may rely on the directive in any action brought against the state or its 'organs' or 'emanations' in a British court. Local authorities are regarded in European law as manifestations of the state within the above-mentioned categories and may thus be the subject of court action to compel compliance with directives that the British government has not yet adopted by issuing an appropriate statutory instrument to regulate the matters covered by the directive.

The need for local authorities to determine for themselves the extent to which they are at risk if they do not follow the provisions of unadopted directives whose implementation dates have expired remains moot, but in any event Parliament has drafted regulations to give effect to the works directives and will in all probability do the same for the services directive.

An enforcement directive (89/665/EEC), the Compliance or Remedies Directive, requires member states to create an appeals procedure to deal with allegations by aggrieved contractors that local authorities have infringed the procurement directives. Such an appeals procedure is included in the Public Services Contracts Regulations 1993[1], which render a breach of the services directive actionable in the UK courts.

The Secretary of State already has powers under the LGA 1988 to intervene wherever anti-competitive behaviour occurs or a DSO is alleged to have been unlawfully favoured at the expense of an external tenderer. These powers cover most of the requirements of the enforcement directive, with the exception of awarding damages. Reference to the courts is likely to occur only if a contractor has suffered substantial loss, since recourse to the Secretary of State will normally produce a speedy and effective remedy at minimal cost to the contractor, in marked contrast to the costs incurred in pursuing legal action through the courts.

Finally, recourse to the European Court of Justice is not a practical or recommended recourse for most contractor grievances. Apart from the time taken for such actions to come to a hearing, the tendency of the court, when faced with allegations of discrimination against contractors based outside the member state, is to remit the matter back to the national courts with general guidance on its disposition. For example, a Dutch authority included a provision in its contracts that at least 70 per cent of the workforce must be recruited from local long-term unemployed persons. The aggrieved contractor's complaint to the European Court of Justice resulted in a referral back to the Dutch courts, with the finding that social conditions attached to contracts could be acceptable as long as all tenderers were treated fairly[2]. The general nature of the advice could be regarded as unhelpful in its failure to determine the specific grievance and this is a risk apparently common in proceedings brought before the European Court.

1 SI 1993 No. 3228.
2 Case 31/87: *Gebroeders Beentjes BV v Netherlands (Re Public Works Contract)* [1990] 1 CMLR 287.

Chapter 22

EXTERNALISATION

CCT applies only where defined work may be performed in-house. One legitimate response to the legislation is to sidestep the requirements to tender by privatisation in one form or another. The transfer of a DSO into the private sector with existing staff and assets and the benefit of guaranteed work for a period is a means by which known and trusted staff can be retained on council services without the application of CCT at regular intervals.

This chapter considers the practical difficulties in formulating a successful externalisation taking into account the views of the Audit Commission and the provisions relating to local authority companies to be found in the Local Government and Housing Act 1989, since to avoid CCT it is essential that the newly formed company cannot be viewed as an arm of the local authority.

ISSUES OF PRINCIPLE

Given a local authority's fiduciary duties, the decision to externalise must be based upon a proper and considered evaluation of the benefits and disadvantages involved in a specific proposal. Reasonable justification must also support the selection of a particular vehicle or a particular organisation for any externalisation.

Then there arise a series of interconnected issues in relation to value for money (and valuation) and conflicts of interest.

The council will be alienating itself from the profit stream from contracts already held by the in-house team and assets as well as relieving itself of potential liabilities such as future redundancy costs. A proper evaluation of both elements must be undertaken if value for money is to be demonstrated for the externalisation in question. Furthermore, the award of new contracts will also have to be subject to some form of competition if the district auditor is to be satisfied that the council is acting reasonably.

The risk of entering an unequal bargain in which the services are overpriced or the terms of disposal of the business and its assets are overgenerous is a normal financial issue for the council, but the complication is the risk that it will be persuaded into such a position by the vested interests of the staff who will transfer to the new company.

Accordingly, the information placed before the council to enable it to decide on externalisation and any recommendations must be made by officers who have no stake in the transfer. The dangers of allowing officers who will be transferring to advise the council were illustrated graphically in the externalisations of West Wiltshire's information technology and legal services, which have since resulted in criminal proceedings against former officers and surcharge consideration by the district auditor.

In respect of disposals of assets, the duty on the council to obtain the best price reasonably obtainable can be fulfilled by commissioning arm's length valuations. However, it is not the case that each element of the externalisation deal must provide value for money, as long as the undervalued elements are offset by other financial advantages such as the loss of redundancy liability. Alternatively, the equation could be balanced with a profit-sharing agreement by which the council participates for a period in the future success of the externalised service.

Finally, there are direct financial issues in relation to the costs of preparation for externalisation. The council should not have to meet costs which are the proper concern of others, in general costs which benefit the externalising organisation, unless there is a major collateral benefit to the council. The council and the externalisation team must bear their own costs of negotiations and drafting agreements and the council should not fund the costs of new company formation unless it is to retain a stake in it.

Then there is the hidden cost of lost staff time. Unless the council identifies significant benefits from externalisation, the starting point should be not to permit staff to effect preparations for a buy-out or the transfer of their own employment in council time or to use support services. The Audit Commission has gone as far as to express the view that allowing staff paid time off for these purposes could be *ultra vires*.

OPTIONS

A range of types of body are involved in externalisation; selection between them will be dependent upon the council's objectives in externalising. For example, if a capital sum is the prime aim, a trade sale or hosting is the best vehicle. If service protection for the community is the vital element, a trust or local authority company would be front-runners.

SELF-EMPLOYMENT

Staff can be made redundant and the residual need for services satisfied by buying back on a part-time basis from the former employees as self-employed persons or consultants.

To succeed there must be either a nominal future requirement for continuing services or the rehiring of former staff must satisfy certain tests if the Inland Revenue are not to regard them as continuing in local authority employment and thus subject to PAYE arrangements.

The service should be of a type commonly using self-employed persons or one which nationally will regularly do so in the future. The individual ex-council employee must not be a person tied to a single future employer, even if only part-time. Overlapping contracts for services to others and turnover of employers during the tax year will tend to persuade the Inland Revenue that the tax-payer is trading in his or her own right as a business rather than holding one or more contracts of employment.

Trusts

If profits are wholly subservient to the concept of community service then a potential vehicle for transfer may be a trust. Achieving charitable status may be unlikely since the Charity Commissioners are likely to regard a transfer to a trust as a simple divestment of council responsibilities. Nevertheless a bare trust may be effective in safeguarding assets and income from the services, may attract volunteer workers and safeguard service beneficiaries from cuts which may threaten from time to time due to financial exigencies within local authorities.

Local authority companies

Companies in which councils hold a significant stake are governed by the Local Government and Housing Act 1989. The Act defines four types of company in which a council may hold a stake:

(i)   controlled companies,
(ii) influenced companies,
(iii) arms length companies and
(iv) minority interest companies.

The first two are liable to strict regulation since they are regarded to some degree as extensions of the council.

Controlled companies are those in which the council holds the majority of voting rights at a general meeting or has the power to remove a majority of the company's directors.

Influenced companies are those in which at least 20 per cent of the total voting rights of all shareholders of the company will be held by persons associated with the council (or 20 per cent of the directors will be such persons) and a business relationship must exist in which the company is to some degree reliant upon the council. If over 50 per cent of the company's turnover relates to council business, for example, there could be little doubt that the company was local authority influenced.

Local authority-controlled and influenced companies are required by section 33 of the LGA 1988 to take 'reasonable steps for the purpose of securing competition' for work within a defined activity awarded to such a company.

The best course is therefore to ensure that companies have a less than 20 per cent council stake or are placed in the control of trusted ex-employees since former employees are not defined as persons associated with the council.

Management buy-outs

Management buy-out occurs when the in-house management purchase the existing operation setting up a new company or partnership to do so. The management buy-out would henceforth perform the services for less and usually buy or lease any required assets from the council and employ former council staff.

MBOs are more complicated in a council context than when an existing private-sector company is purchased. Valuing the operation for financing purposes may be problematic and one solution is to sell a block of shares in the new company to an existing organisation other than the council. Such a joint venture may well offer a greater chance of success for a management buy-out because the shareholding partner will have a particular incentive to assist in securing a broader base of customers and a long-term future for the new company.

Local authority management buy-outs start with significant disadvantages since they can, by virtue of their origins, possess few of the characteristics shared by successful buy-outs in commercial and industrial fields. They are unlikely to have a spread of products and services; they will have only one existing major customer; plant and equipment may well be less than ideal, let alone modern; a strong asset base will not exist or will not be transferable at an affordable cost; and working capital needs may be large, especially initially. Recognition of these obstacles in the business plan is almost as important as the evolution of a sound strategy to overcome them.

Research will need to be undertaken into funding alternatives, the potential for moving into new markets and company structures. Added to an analysis of existing assets and resources, these form the main planks upon which the business plan will be constructed.

The initial stages of a management buy-out thus comprise:

  (i)   reviewing the past;
 (ii)   determining options for future development;
(iii)   market research;
 (iv)   assessing financial feasibility;
  (v)   formulating business strategy;
 (vi)   structuring the new company; and, finally,
(vii)   writing the business plan.

Only then can concrete steps to arrange funding be taken, negotiations beyond the 'in principle' stage take place with the employing local authority and the proposed company's memorandum and articles of association be drafted.

It is vital, in preparing a successful management buy-out, for the buy-out team to secure the support of all the key staff who will be transferring to the new company. Without them the business will not be viable anyway.

The potential conflicts of interest in an MBO are perhaps more serious than in other forms of externalisation. In 1990, the Audit Commission issued guidance (now somewhat out of date) on the subject in their Management Paper No 6, entitled 'Management Buy-Outs, Public Interest or Private Gain?'.

Finally, it should be noted that an MBO may be thwarted or rendered yet more complicated if the transferring service is one covered by the European public procurement directives when open competition will be required for the resultant contract for services.

Trade sales and host transactions

Trade sales occur when an existing private-sector organisation purchases a council operation lock, stock and barrel. The transfer of the business, staff, assets, contracts and liabilities will be attractive if a DSO has a proved track record of past success in tendering and service delivery.

A host transaction is merely a trade sale in which the purchasing organisation is pre-selected, the choice normally being influenced by the affected staff and often involving staff consultation on all future service and organisational changes.

Host transactions cannot occur wherever open competition is required before a contract for services can be awarded. Accordingly, a function covered by the European public procurement directives will be advertised in the official journal of the European Community and the resultant transaction will have few of the elements of a pure host transaction. However, elements of staff consultation can be built into the evaluation process subject to the restrictions placed on non-commercial considerations set out in the LGA 1988.

PROCEDURES AND DOCUMENTATION

Externalisation is not a soft alternative to CCT in terms of the preparations required. To result in a successful private-sector organisation, properly providing the full range of services required without a serious risk of challenge, requires a full scrutiny of the options available and a process for selecting the best solution which is equitable and defendable.

Advertising

The starting point will almost inevitably be advertising for interested parties. Indeed advertising will be mandatory if the contract for services to be associated with the externalisation is covered by one or other of the European Community's public procurement directives.

It may be possible, notwithstanding Audit Commission concerns that negotiated contracts may not demonstrate value for money, to use a European option not usable in CCT under the negotiated procedure following advertisement. In this case the council selects parties with whom to treat as to the terms and conditions of the contract.

Specification

As with CCT, a full specification of the services required of the externalisation is essential if a satisfactory level and quality of service is to be maintained after the transfer of the staff.

Tendering documentation

In so far as an evaluation of the parties expressing interest will be required, forms of tender, instructions and questionnaires will need to be individualised to meet the complex requirements of externalisation.

Heads of agreement and conditions of contract

Whether heads of agreement or full draft conditions are produced at the outset, the range of issues to be covered is wide. They include service performance, staffing, assets, contractual assignments, leases of land and buildings, sale of goodwill, profit-sharing arrangements, performance bonds, warranties, guarantees, indemnities and option agreements should the council wish to require assets or re-engage staff if the venture fails.

Staff transfer arrangements

The initial step will be the production of a staffing profile to ascertain the employees to be transferred and the financial liability associated with them, including accumulated redundancy entitlements.

The terms of transfer will be relatively straightforward using the overarching provisions of the Transfer of Undertakings (Protection of Employment) Regulations 1981[1]. It is possible that redundancies will be a foreseeable risk for the contractor after the externalisation and that the council sees the shedding of that risk as a real benefit of externalisation. In this case the transferee organisation may seek a payment for acceptance of redundancy liability or an agreement that the council meet the whole or a proportion of redundancy cost if it proves necessary to make a former council worker redundant.

Sale of goodwill

The value of profits obtainable on third-party contracts held by the in-house team and any value placed on the continuing association with the council in the shape of the name used by the service when it operated as an in-house trading unit ought to be identified and realised in the terms of the externalisation.

Confidentiality agreements

Before providing confidential documentation, including the staffing profile, securing a confidentiality agreement may be important in case the transaction falls through leaving the tenderers as competitors with a continuing in-house service.

The agreement will make it clear that documentation is supplied only for externalisation purposes, must not be copied without consent, must be returned with all copies if the transaction does not proceed and must not be used by those formulating future bids for council services under CCT.

Confidentiality agreements with the relevant staff and trade unions may also be considered.

1 SI 1981 No. 1794.

Chapter 23

THE FUTURE OF
COMPETITIVE TENDERING

Compulsory competitive tendering is a politically motivated doctrine, but one alleged to serve the interests of the local taxpayer and the national exchequer to the extent that it motivates increased productivity, forces reconsideration of outdated working practices and tends to drive down costs whether the service is contracted out as the end result or remains in-house. The contribution it is said to make to increased economy, efficiency and effectiveness and to demonstrating value for money, is important in the context of the ever-growing pressure to limit the public sector borrowing requirement and to reduce the total expenditure on local government. In a nutshell, the realities of modern government are that there is little support in the electorate at large for higher taxation to sustain locally provided services generally, whatever goodwill and protectionism may be afforded to education and primary health care budgets by the major political parties.

If a government of whatever complexion must retain financial restraint, then in relation to market-testing, the only controversial element is likely to be the use of compulsion. This is the facet which might be expected to be a casualty in the event that the present Conservative government fails to secure re-election, an ever-looming possibility with a general election to be held no later than April 1997. It is by no means clear that compulsion will be completely removed, however. Even some prominent Labour strategists appear to believe that CCT should be retained, albeit with more flexible rules, while others would wish it to be available as a sanction of last resort for councils which fail to meet government-set targets. The noteworthy part of Labour Party policy as far as local government is concerned is that the proposed requirement of the production of annual community plans, setting out the type and level of services to be provided, may prove to be strikingly similar to the current discipline of specification and the proposed yearly audit of targets and performance indicators will be reliant upon client monitoring skills developed under compulsory competition. If failure to meet targets were to result in an instruction to subject the service to open competition with stipulations on conducting that competition, or led to the exercise of new powers to appoint interim managers to take over the services until they are brought up to scratch, the degree of interference with local democratic accountability could be worse than presently applicable.

Whatever happens, the timing of the next election will not save housing management and professional services from CCT in London and metro-politan boroughs and un-reorganised district and county councils in England (nor their opposite numbers in Wales and Scotland), nor the first cycle of manual trading in Northern Ireland. After that, reform is dependent upon the priority it receives from an incoming government. Given the pressures on parliamentary time, CCT and local government issues may not be anywhere near the top of the pile and an educated observer might hazard the guess that it will be 1999 before the duty, in its present form, to subject services to market-testing ceases.

And after 1999? Tendering will remain for at least two major reasons. Firstly financial pressures may persuade some authorities to continue with voluntary competitive tendering and secondly where contracts have been lost to the private sector, the costs and uncertainties associated with TUPE may prevent consideration of bringing services back in-house, particularly where the contract cost has been reduced by economies of scale reliant upon trading across broader geographical areas than a local authority lawfully can. Only if wider powers or a general presumption of competence were to be granted to local authorities might it be possible for them to compete with large national or multi-national concerns and it appears no political party in the UK relishes this prospect. As Paul Boateng MP made clear in an address to the Local Government Solicitors Group of the Law Society in March 1995, for budgetary reasons if for no other, even a Labour government supportive of the concept of increased local democracy and accountability would shy away from giving councils a power of general competence. Instead, the Labour Party's policy statement 'Renewing Democracy, Rebuilding Communities' issued in September 1995 proposed greater freedom to sell services to others but the proposal is hedged around with references to the need to safeguard public funds and prevent unfair competition. Accordingly the prospect of unfettered power to provide services, with a clear general power to charge as an authority sees fit, remains remote.

In fact freedom for local authorities to determine the nature of service provision may be yet further constrained in future, even without the strait-jacket of compulsory competitive tendering. For example, the Labour proposal to establish a service standards inspectorate under the Audit Commission could give rise to an enhanced level of intervention in benchmarking the cost and quality of individual council services. It might also recommend whether the Secretary of State should use sanctions to coerce improved quality or reduced cost. However good the relationship has been between many local authorities and the District Audit service or their external auditors, few inside the pale would welcome enhanced powers for the Commission as the parent body serving and directing individual auditors on the ground.

If a wish list were to be compiled for local authorities post-1997, the removal of compulsion to tender services would probably figure behind freedom to provide any service the community required on a commercial basis (a right given to health authorities by the Health and Medicines Act 1988) or to any other public body on an unconstrained basis (as to be enjoyed by the new unitary Welsh authorities), with clear general powers to charge as the authorities see fit. Neither appears an unfettered prospect.

Finally, it would be a considerable improvement to the current situation if a future government of whatever persuasion were to remove unfair competition, such as that generated by the Prison Services Agency in bidding for contracts. (Channing Wood Prison in Devon, using prisoners earning as little as £9 per week, won a school grounds maintenance contract in February 1995.) Instead, it could assess the true social costs of imposing competition on local services in accordance with the findings of the Equal Opportunities Commission, which in March 1995 published a report revealing the extent of the Exchequer's lost tax revenue and extra social security benefits in consequence of CCT.

APPENDICES

TYPICAL LOCAL AUTHORITY TENDERING TIMETABLE FOR COMPULSORY COMPETITION

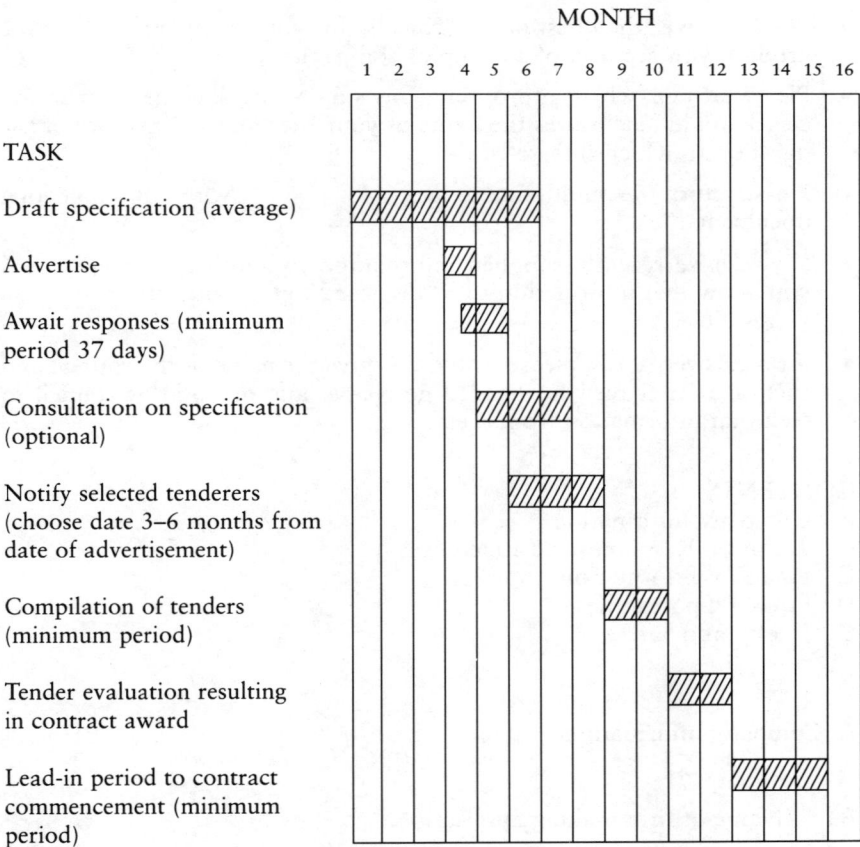

MONTH

1 2 3 4 5 6 7 8 9 10 11 12 13 14 15 16

TASK

Draft specification (average)

Advertise

Await responses (minimum period 37 days)

Consultation on specification (optional)

Notify selected tenderers (choose date 3–6 months from date of advertisement)

Compilation of tenders (minimum period)

Tender evaluation resulting in contract award

Lead-in period to contract commencement (minimum period)

Appendix II

SAMPLE QUESTIONNAIRE

Reproduced by kind permission of the London Borough of Enfield

PRIVATE AND CONFIDENTIAL

- Please answer the questions specifically for your company, *not* for the group if you are part of a group of companies.

- Please include, where appropriate, any supporting documents, marking clearly on all enclosures the name of your firm and the number of the question to which they refer.

- Please return the questionnaire by   with any supporting documents.

- If you have recently supplied information to another council, would you allow that information to be disclosed to this council?
  Yes/No.

- If the answer is Yes, please would you give the name of the council and enclose a letter on your headed notepaper authorising this council to seek that information from them.

CONTENTS
A   Company Information
B   Technical Resources and References
C   Financial Information
D   Equal Opportunities
E   Health and Safety

A   Company Information

A1   Name of firm making application.

A2   Main address for correspondence.

A3   Registered office (if different from above).

A4   Person applying on behalf of firm.

A5   Position in firm.

A6   Telephone number.

A7   Are you sole trader, partnership, private limited company, public limited company or other (please specify)?

A8   List the full names of every director, partner, associate and company secretary.

A9   Have any of the directors, partners or associates been involved in any firm which has been liquidated or gone into receivership?
      Yes/No
      If yes, please give details.

A10   Has any director, partner or associate been employed by this council?
      Yes/No
      If yes, please give details.

A11   Please state if any director, partner or associate has a relative(s) who is employed by the council or has a relative(s) who is a councillor.

A12   Please state the names of directors, partners or associates of your firm who have any involvement in other firms who provide or are offering services to the council.
      If a limited company, complete Questions A13–A16.

A13   Please state the firm's date of registration and registration number under Companies Act 1985.

A14   Date of registration and registration number under Industrial and Provident Societies Acts 1965 to 1978.

A15   If the company is a member of a group of companies, give the names and addresses of the ultimate holding company and all other subsidiaries.

A16   Would the group or the ultimate holding company be prepared to guarantee your contract performance as its subsidiary?
      Yes/No
      Any comments:

B Technical Resources and References

B1   Please indicate which contract you are applying for.

B2   Has your firm ever suffered a deduction for liquidated and ascertained damages in respect of any contract within the last 3 years?
Yes/No

B3   Has your firm ever had a contract terminated or its employment determined under the terms of the contract?
Yes/No
If the answer to Questions B2 or B3 is Yes, please enclose details.

B4   Has your firm ever declined to tender after receiving an invitation to tender?

B5   Has your firm ever withdrawn a tender post-submission?

B6   State the approximate number of employees in your company engaged in the specific type of work for which you are applying.
Type of work   Number of employees
Management
Professional/technical
Admin/clerical
Operative supervisor
Operative: plumbing
              carpentry
              joinery
              trowel/trades
              electrical
              painting & decorating
Other

B7   How does your firm assess the suitability and competence of potential workers? (Please indicate as appropriate.)
It uses assessment against:
Job description
Person specification
Application forms
References
Qualifications
Inspection of previous work
Trial period before confirmation of employment
Personal recommendations
Other (please specify)

B8   What qualifications do your key staff have that are relevant to the work that is the subject of this application? Please list.
Staff   Qualifications

B9   In the event the TUPE applies to this contract, does your company hold a certificate of pension scheme comparable with the local government superannuation scheme issued by the Government Actuary's Department?
Yes/No

B10   How does your company propose to satisfy the council and its actuaries that any pension scheme offered to former council employees transferring to your company is comparable, for the specific employees affected, with the local government superannuation scheme?

B11   Technical references

Please list below the full names, addresses and other details requested of organisations (preferably public sector) **other than this Authority** for which your firm has recently carried out work or supplied goods/materials. The information given should cover the whole range of work or supply of goods/materials for which your firm wishes to be considered.

Name and address of organisation & dept	Supervising officer	Contract title	Tender price (£)	Value to date (£)	Type of work	Date of contract
1.						
2.						
3.						
4.						
5.						
6.						
7.						

(NB: You may use additional sheets if necessary, but please mark clearly Question B11)

B12 Have you any previous experience in providing response to emergencies on a 24-hour basis?
Yes/No
If yes, please provide details.

C Financial Information

C1 Please state the name and position in the firm of the person responsible for financial matters.

C2 What is the name and address of the firm's banker? (Please give all if more than one.)

C3 Please enclose copies of audited accounts and annual reports for the last 3 years, to include:
Balance Sheet
Profit and Loss Account and Cost of Sales
Full Notes to the Accounts
Director's Report/Auditor's Report

C4 If the accounts you are submitting are for a year ended more than 10 months ago, can you confirm that the company as described in those accounts is still trading?
Yes/No

C5 If yes to C4, please enclose a statement of turnover since the last set of published accounts.

C6 Please provide details of any outstanding claims or litigation against the company.

Taxation

C7 VAT Registration Number.

Insurance

Please give details of insurance held.

C8   Employers Liability Insurance held.
       Insurer:
       Policy number:
       Extent of cover:
       Expiry date:

C9   Public Liability (Third Party) Insurance held.
       Insurer:
       Policy number:
       Extent of cover:
       Expiry date:

       N.B. Please enclose a copy of your policies in relation to C8 and C9.

C10 Please provide the name and address of any organisation which is prepared to issue a Performance Bond in the sum of £   .

D Equal Opportunities

D1   Is it your policy as an employer to comply with your statutory obligations under the Race Regulations Act 1976?
       Yes/No

D2   Is it your practice, in relation to decisions to recruit, train or promote employees, not to treat one group of people less favourably than others because of their colour, race, nationality or ethnic or national origin?
       Yes/No

D3   Has your firm in the last 3 years been taken to court or to an industrial tribunal or been the subject of formal investigation by the Commission for Racial Equality on grounds of alleged unlawful discrimination?
       Yes/No

       If yes, what was the finding of the court or tribunal or investigation, and if unlawful discrimination was found, what steps were taken to prevent a recurrence?

D4   Is your policy on race relations set out:
       (a) in instructions to those concerned with recruitment, training and promotion?
             Yes/No

(b) in documents available to employees, recognised trade unions or other representative groups of employees?
Yes/No

(c) in recruitment advertisements or other literature?
Yes/No

D5 Do you observe as far as is appropriate and reasonably practicable the Commission for Racial Equality's Code of Practice for Employment as approved by Parliament in 1983?
Yes/No

Health and Safety

E1 Name of director, partner or other person responsible for the implementation of this firm's safety policy.

E2 Please state the number of employees employed by your firm (including directors, apprentices/YTS trainees, etc.)

If you have five or more employees:

E3 Do you employ a person who has permanent responsibility for safety?
Yes/No
If yes, please state name and position.

E4 How are your health and safety policies and procedures conveyed to the workforce?

E5 Do employees receive induction and/or safety training before actually undertaking work tasks?
Yes/No
If yes, please enclose details of training/courses undertaken by staff and objectives.

E6 Please enclose a copy of your Health & Safety Policy (covering General Policy, Organisation and Arrangements) as required by Section 2(3) of the Health and Safety at Work Act 1974 and any codes of safe work practices issued to employees.

If you have less than five employees or if your company policy does not detail any of the following, please enclose written details of:

E7   Procedures to be followed in cases of emergency.
        Tick if enclosed.

E8   Procedures for the reporting and recording of accidents and dangerous occurrences.
        Tick if enclosed.

E9   First aid and welfare provisions.
        Tick if enclosed.

E10   Provision of appropriate protective clothing and equipment.
        Tick if enclosed.

E11   Please enclose details of prosecutions or notices served on your firm by the Health and Safety Executive.

E12   Would you agree to allow council officers access to your depot(s) for the purpose of inspecting depots, asbestos removal plant, protective equipment, shower units, etc?

        Yes/No

WHEN YOU HAVE COMPLETED THE QUESTIONNAIRE, PLEASE READ AND SIGN THE SECTION BELOW.

I/We certify that the information supplied is accurate to the best of my/our knowledge. I/We understand that false or misleading information could result in my/our exclusion from the List of Approved Contractors and Suppliers.

I/We understand that it is a criminal offence, punishable by imprisonment, to give or offer any gift or consideration whatsoever as an inducement or reward to any servant of a public body and that any such action will empower the council to cancel any contract currently in force and will result in my/our exclusion from the List of Approved Contractors and Suppliers and the Council will notify the appropriate authorities.

Signed   . . . .

For and on behalf of   . . . .

Date   . . . .

Please note, the term 'firm' refers to sole proprietor, partnership, incorporated, co-operative as appropriate. The undertaking should be signed by the applicant, a partner or authorised representative in her/his own name and on behalf of the firm.

BEFORE RETURNING THIS APPLICATION FORM, PLEASE ENSURE THAT YOU HAVE:

- answered all questions appropriate to your application;
- enclosed relevant documents;
- signed the above undertaking.

SAMPLE CONTRACT CLAUSES

Reproduced by kind permission of the London Borough of Enfield

This CONTRACT is made the   day of   199 between
          ('the Council') of the one part and   ('the Contractor')
of the other part

WHEREAS
(1) The Council may wish to have performed the Services as defined in the
    Conditions of this Contract ('the Services') and
(2) The Contractor is willing to perform the Services in accordance with
    the Conditions of this Contract
NOW IT IS AGREED between the Council and the Contractor as follows:
A   This Contract together with its Conditions ('the Conditions') and
     Schedules constitutes the sole contract or agreement between the
     Council and the Contractor for the performance by the Contractor of
     the Services
B   If required to do so the Contractor shall perform the Services in
     accordance with the Conditions and to the satisfaction of the Council
     for a period of years ('the contract period') from the   day of
              199 ('the commencement date')
C   So long as the Contractor shall continue to perform the Services in
     accordance with the Conditions and to the satisfaction of the Council
     the Council shall make to the Contractor the payments provided by
     this Contract
IN WITNESS whereof the parties hereto have caused their respective Com-
mon Seals to be hereunto affixed the day and year first before written

The Conditions

1 Definitions
In this Contract, save where the context otherwise requires, the following
expressions shall have the meanings hereby ascribed to them:

'Conditions' means these conditions and any modification thereof duly
made in accordance with their provisions

'Director' means the   for the time being of the Council and
save for Clause 2 hereof any persons duly appointed and notified to the

214

Contractor in writing by the Council to be a deputy assistant or representative of the said Director

'Other authorised officers of the Council' means the Borough Secretary and Solicitor the Borough Treasurer the Borough Architect the Borough Engineer and Surveyor the Borough Environmental Health Officer and the Chief Trading Standards Officer of the Council for the time being

'Services' means the services set out in Schedule I and any modifications thereof under Clause 8

'Supervising Officer' means any officer of the Director's staff notified to the contractor to be such for the purposes of monitoring the performance by the Contractor of Services

'Premises' means the premises described in the draft lease set out in Schedule III

'Annual Sum' means the annual sum payable by the Council to the Contractor in accordance with the contractor's tender appended as Schedule II hereto

or

'Schedule of Rates' means the Schedule of Rates in the contractor's tender appended as Schedule II hereto

2 Conditions
(a) No omission from addition to or variation of the Conditions shall be valid or of any effect unless it is agreed in writing and signed by the Director personally or such other officer as the Director or the Council's Chief Executive for the time being may in writing appoint and by a duly authorised representative of the Contractor
(b) Save for an omission addition or variation agreed pursuant to (a) any provision inconsistent with the Conditions contained in any other document or in any oral agreement is agreed to be void and of no effect

3 Assignment Sub-contracting and Agency
(a) The Contractor shall in no circumstances assign or sublet or purport to assign or sublet any part of this Contract to any person whatsoever
(b) The Contractor may not subcontract the performance of any part of the services save with the prior written consent of the Director the utilisation of self-employed staff to perform the services being the only exception
(c) The Contractor has not and shall in no circumstances hold himself out as having the power to make vary discharge or waive any by-law or regulation of any kind
(d) The employees of the Contractor are not and shall not hold themselves out to be and shall not be held out by the Contractor as being servants or agents of the Council for any purpose whatsoever
(e) The Contractor is not and shall in no circumstances hold himself out as being the servant or agent of the Council
(f) The Contractor is not and shall in no circumstances hold himself out as being authorised to enter into any contract on behalf of the Council or in any other way to bind the Council to the performance variation release or discharge of any obligation

4 The Director

Save as is provided in Clause 2 hereof the functions rights and powers conferred by this Contract upon the Council shall be exercised by the Director as defined in Clause 1 hereof. The Contractor shall in no circumstances question the existence or extent of the authority of any person notified to the Contractor in writing to be a deputy assistant or representative of the Director

5 Contract Period

With the agreement of both the Council and the Contractor the Contract period may be extended by a further period of one year/two years

6 Performance of Services

During the Contract Period and from the commencement date the Contractor shall perform the Services and any modifications thereof authorised under Clause 9 hereof in a safe proper skilful and workmanlike manner wholly in accordance with the specification contained in Schedule I hereto and to the entire satisfaction of the Director

7 Transfer of undertakings

[*Sub-clauses (a)–(c) below are for use in a contract to which TUPE does not apply.*]

(a) The parties hereto agree that the Transfer of Undertakings (Protection of Employment) Regulations 1981 ('the Regulations') are inapplicable to the staff previously performing the Services and as such the Contractor shall not seek from the Council any additional payment to the sums set out in Schedule II hereto whatever action may be taken by the said staff in the course of any endeavour to enforce rights under the Regulations or under the European Community Acquired Rights Directive 1977 ('the European Directive')

(b) Upon receipt of any request from the Council made to the Contractor during the contract period or 12 months following the expiry or earlier termination of the contract the Contractor shall supply to the Council such information in relation to the principal Terms and Conditions of Employment associated with the provision of the Services by the Contractor as the Council shall reasonably require for the purposes of satisfying any tenderer for the future provision of the Services as to the financial consequences of compliance with the Regulations and the European Directive

(c) The Contractor hereby indemnifies the Council its agents and servants against all claims made or to be made against it

  (i) by any Employee whose employment is transferred from the Council to the Contractor pursuant to the Regulations and/or the terms of this contract including reasonable legal costs and other related expenses in considering and/or defending any such claim and

  (ii) any claim by the Employee that either he or she has been unfairly dismissed by the Council or that the Council is in breach of contract and in either case it is alleged that one or both of the following applies namely:

    A that the pension scheme (including the provision of benefits arising from the pensions scheme) provided by the Contractor is not broadly comparable to that which had been provided by the Council immediately prior to the transfer of the Employee and/or

B   that the benefits due to the Employee on being made redundant are not the same as he or she would have received had he or she still been employed by the Council

or

[*Sub clauses (a)–(c) below are for use in a contract to which TUPE does apply.*]

(a)   The parties hereto agree that the Transfer of Undertakings (Protection of Employment) Regulations 1981 ('the Regulations') and the European Community Acquired Rights Directive 1977 ('the European Directive') apply to this contract

(b)   The Contractor further hereby acknowledges that all relevant information about the workforce undertaking the Services immediately prior to the commencement of this contract has been supplied to it subject however to the limitations imposed by the Data Protection Act 1984 where such information is recorded as described in Section 1 of the same Act

(c)   The Contractor hereby covenants

(i)   that upon receipt of any request from the Council made to the Contractor during the contract period or 12 months following the expiry or earlier termination of the contract that the Contractor shall supply to the Council such information in relation to the Principal Terms and Conditions of Employment associated with the provision of the Services by the Contractor as the Council shall reasonably require for the purposes of satisfying any tenderer for the future provision of the Services as to the financial consequences of compliance with the Regulations and the European Directive

(ii)   that during the subsistence of this contract the Contractor will provide the workforce engaged on undertaking the Services immediately prior to the date of commencement of this contract with comparable pensions or that the remuneration package as a whole will compensate each member of such workforce for the absence or shortfall of such provision

(iii)   that it will act upon or otherwise adhere to all statements given to the Council upon which the Council has relied and acted upon in entering into this contract

(iv)   to indemnify the Council its agents and servants against all claims made against it by an Employee whose employment is transferred from the Council to the Contractor pursuant to the Regulations and/or the terms of this contract including reasonable legal costs and other related expenses in considering and/or defending any such claim and any claim by the Employee which is either that he or she has been unfairly dismissed by the Council or that the Council is in breach of contract and in either case it is alleged that one or both of the following applies namely:

A   that the pension scheme (including the provision of benefits arising from the pensions scheme) provided by the Contractor is not broadly comparable to that which has been provided by the Council immediately prior to the transfer and the Employee and/or

B   that the benefits due to the Employee on being made redundant are not the same as he or she would have received had he or she still been employed by the Council

8 Access
(a) The Contractor shall at all times during the Contract Period allow such persons as may be nominated from time to time by the Director access for the purpose of
   (i) inspecting work being carried out pursuant to this Contract and
   (ii) inspecting records and documents in the possession of the Contractor in connection with the carrying out of such work or the supply of any goods or materials in connection therewith and
   (iii) interviewing at any time any member of the Contractor's staff in connection with the carrying out of all or any of the Council's services and
   (iv) as required for any purpose connected with the Contract
(b) The Contractor shall at all times allow the other authorised officers of the Council the same right of access as are reserved herein for the Director

9 Modifications
The Director shall be entitled to issue to the Contractor oral instructions provided that the said instructions shall be confirmed in writing within twenty-four hours requiring the Contractor to do all or any of the following:
(a) to omit and to cease to perform any part of the services for such period as the Director may fix
(b) to perform such additional services outside the scope of the Services as the Director may require provided that such additional services shall be the same as or similar to the Services under the Contract in which case the Schedule of Rates if such a schedule shall have been agreed between the Council and the Contractor shall apply to such additional Services and the Contractor shall be bound by and shall forthwith carry out all such instructions

10 Payment
[*Sub-clauses (a)–(b) below are intended for use in a contract for a pre-specified volume of work with payment claimed by the contractor in equal instalments. The requirement for pre-notification of the programmed work is not essential for payment purposes, but is worth retaining to assist contract monitoring.*]
(a) Not less than fourteen days before the week in which the Contractor proposes to carry out work forming part of the Services the Contractor shall complete a detailed work-sheet ('the work-sheet') in respect of such work in such form as shall be approved by the Director and shall submit the same to the Director
(b) On the fifth Friday following the commencement date and on every fourth Friday thereafter the Contractor shall submit to the Director an invoice ('the invoice') in respect of work forming part of the Services which has been completed by the Contractor during the previous four

weeks and the invoice shall be in a form to be agreed by the Director and shall claim payment of one thirteenth of the annual sum exclusive of Value Added Tax subject to any additions and deductions in respect of modification to the services made in accordance with Clause 8 hereof

or

[Sub-clauses (a)–(b) below are intended for use in a contract for variable volumes of work with monies payable to the contractor determinable from a schedule of rates or prices.]

(a) Not less than fourteen days before the week is which the Contractor proposes to carry out work forming part of the Services the Contractor shall complete a detailed work-sheet ('the work-sheet') in respect of such work in such form as shall be approved by the Director and shall submit the same to the Director

(b) On the fifth Friday following the commencement date and on every fourth Friday thereafter the Contractor shall submit to the Director an invoice ('the invoice') in respect of work forming part of the Services which has been completed by the Contractor during the previous four weeks and the invoice shall be in a form to be agreed by the Director and shall show an amount exclusive of Value Added Tax calculated in accordance with the Schedule of Rates

[Sub-clauses (c)–(f) below cover council certification and payment, together with variations to the sum payable to the contractor.]

(c) Within seven days of the receipt of an invoice the Director shall issue a certificate certifying the amount due in respect of that invoice having regard to any adjustments pursuant to these Conditions and the sum (if any) to be added by way of Value Added Tax and within twenty-eight days of the issue of such certificate the Contractor shall be entitled to payment by the Council of the sum so certified

(d) The Council shall be entitled to deduct from the invoice any sum certified by the Director as being deductible by reason of any omission by the Contractor (whether pursuant to an instruction under Clause 8(a) hereof or otherwise) or defective performance by the Contractor or any variation in the Services (whether pursuant to an instruction under Clause 9(a) hereof or otherwise)

(e) The Council shall add to the invoice any sum certified by the Director as being due to the Contractor in that period by reason of any additional works performed by the Contractor or any variation in the Services performed by the Contractor pursuant to an instruction under Clause 9(b) hereof

(f) In making any deduction from or addition to the invoice in respect of any variation in the Services the Director shall have proper regard to the Contractor's tender price or schedule of rates contained as Schedule II hereto but if any additional or increased services are not the same as or similar to any parts of the Services for which the Contractor has supplied a detailed breakdown of the tender price or a schedule of rates then the Director shall certify for payment such sum as may be agreed between the Director and the Contractor or in default of such agreement, such sum as the Director may in his entire discretion fix as being a fair and reasonable sum for the performance of the said additional or increased services

11 Value Added Tax

(a) Sums payable to the Contractor pursuant to this Contract are exclusive of any Value Added Tax ('VAT')

(b) The Council shall pay to the Contractor in the manner hereinafter set out any VAT properly chargeable on the supply by the Contractor of the services

(c) The Contractor shall in connection with each invoice inform the Director in writing in respect of the services performed during that period

    (i)   which part or parts of such services are exempt from VAT

    (ii) which part or parts of such services bear a zero rate of VAT

    (iii) which part or parts of such services bear a rate of VAT greater than zero in each case specifying the exact rate chargeable

(d) Upon receipt of the Contractor's written notice under sub-clause (c) above unless the Council objects to any part of such notice the Director shall calculate the amount of VAT due in accordance with the contents of such notice and shall so certify pursuant to Clause 10(c) hereof

(e) Upon receipt by the Contractor of any payment made by the Council pursuant to Clause 10(c) hereof being a payment including VAT the Contractor shall forthwith issue to the Council an authenticated receipt in such form as may be required by the Finance Act 1982 ('the Act') or any amendment or re-enactment thereof or by any Regulations made thereunder

(f) If the Council objects to any part of the Contractor's written notice under sub-clause (c) above and such objection cannot be resolved by the parties by agreement the Council may require the Contractor to refer to the Commissioners of Customs and Excise ('the Commissioners') any dispute difference or question in relation to any of the matters specified in section 40(1) of the Act

(g) If the Contractor refers the matter to the Commissioners (whether or not under sub-clause (f) above) and the Council is dissatisfied with their decision on the matter the Contractor shall at the Council's request refer the matter to a Value Added Tax Tribunal by way of appeal under section 40 of the Act whether the Contractor is so dissatisfied or not. Should the Contractor be required to deposit a sum of money equal to all or part of the tax claimed under section 40(2)(a) of the Act the Council shall pay an equivalent sum to the Contractor. The Council shall further reimburse the Contractor any costs or expenses reasonably or properly incurred in making the reference (less any costs awarded to the Contractor by the Tribunal)

(h) Upon the final adjudication by the Commissioners or (in the event of a reference to the Tribunal) by the Tribunal the Council shall pay the amount of VAT adjudged due to the Contractor. Should the amounts already paid by the Council either by way of payment of VAT or by way of reimbursement of any money required to be deposited by the Contractor with the Commissioners under sub-clause (g) above exceed the VAT adjudged to be due the Contractor shall forthwith repay such excess to the Council

(i) Notwithstanding any provision to the contrary in the Conditions the Council shall not be obliged to make any further payment to the Contractor if the Contractor is in default in providing the receipt referred to in sub-clause (e) above provided that this sub-clause shall only apply where the Council can show that it requires such receipt to validate any claim for credit for VAT paid or payable which the Council is entitled to make to the Commissioners

12 Liability of Contractor
The Contractor shall be liable for and shall indemnify the Council against any expense liability less claim or proceedings whatsoever arising under any statute or at common law in respect of personal injury to or the death of any person whomsoever or damage whatsoever to any property real or personal in so far as such injury death or damage arises out of or in the course of or by the carrying out of the Contract by the Contractor unless due to the act or neglect of the Council or its servants or agents

13 Insurance
(a) Without prejudice to his liability to indemnify the Council under Clause 7 the Contractor shall maintain such insurances as are necessary to cover the liability of the Contractor in respect of personal injury death or damage to property real or personal arising out of or in the course of or caused by the carrying out of the Contract by the Contractor his servants or agents

(b) The insurance in respect of claims for personal injury to or the death of any person under a Contract of Service or apprenticeship with the Contractor and arising out of and in the course of such person's employment with the Contractor shall comply with the Employers' Liability (Compulsory Insurance) Act 1969 and any statutory orders made thereunder or any amendment or re-enactment thereof

(c) For all other claims to which sub-clause (b) above applies the insurance cover shall be for a sum not less than £..... in respect of any one incident

(d) Prior to the commencement of the Contract the Contractor shall produce to the Director of Finance for approval all such policies of insurance together with such other documents as the Director of Finance may require such approval being prerequisite to commencement of the Contract

(e) As and when he is reasonably required so to do by the Director of Finnance the Contractor shall produce for inspection documentary evidence that the necessary insurance is being properly maintained

(f) Should the Contractor or any subcontractor default in insuring or in continuing or in causing to insure as required the Council may themselves insure against any risk in default and may deduct the cost of such insurance from any monies due to the Contractor

14 Liability of Council
Save only in respect of liability for death or personal injury resulting from the negligence of the Council or its servants above the Council shall not be liable for any loss or damage whether caused by the negligence of the Council its servants or agents or in any other way whatsoever and the Council shall in no circumstances be liable to the Contractor for any loss of profit business or production or any similar loss or damage whether direct indirect or consequential howsoever caused

15 Recovery of Sums Due to the Council
(a) Whenever under the Contract any sum of money shall be recoverable

from or payable by the Contractor to the Council the same may be deducted from any sum then due or which at any time thereafter may become due to the Contractor under the Contract or under any other contract between the Contractor and the Council

(b) In the event of any failure by the Contractor to pay the Council any sum due under the Contract or under any other contract between the Contractor and the Council the Contractor shall further pay to the Council interest at the rate of 2 per cent per month on any such sum and such interest shall run from day to day and shall accrue before and after any judgment and shall from time to time be compounded monthly on the amount overdue until payment thereof

16 Inducements

(a) The Contractor shall not offer or give or agree to give to any person any fee or consideration of any kind as an inducement or reward for doing or forbearing to do or for having done or forborne to do any action in relation to the obtaining or execution of this Contract or any other contract with the Council or for showing or forbearing to show favour or disfavour to any person in relation to this Contract or any other contract with the Council nor shall any like act be done by any person employed by the Contractor or acting on their behalf (whether with or without the knowledge of the Contractor) nor in relation to this Contract or any other contract with the Council shall the Contractor or any other person employed by him or acting on his behalf commit any offence under the Prevention of Corruption Acts, or give any fee or reward the receipt of which is an offence under subsection (2) of section 117 of the Local Government Act 1972

(b) No employee of the Contractor shall solicit or accept any gratuity from any person nor accept any legacy whatsoever in connection with his employment in the performance of the Services whether from a client or any other person

17 Staff

(a) The Contractor shall employ in and about the provision of the Service only such persons as are careful skilled honest experienced and suitably qualified in the work which they are to perform

(b) The Contractor shall employ sufficient persons to ensure that the Services are provided at all times and in all respects to the Contract Specification

(c) The Contractor shall be and shall ensure that every person employed by him/her in and about the provision of the Services is at all times properly and sufficiently qualified experienced and instructed with regard to the Services and in particular:
  (i) the task or tasks such person has to perform
  (ii) all relevant provisions of the Contract
  (iii) all relevant policies rules procedures and standards of the Council
  (iv) fire risks and fire precautions
  (v) the need to maintain the highest standards of hygiene courtesy and consideration
  (vi) the need to recognise situations which may involve any actual or potential danger of personal injury without personal risk to make

safe such situations and forthwith to report such situations to the Director

(d) The Contractor shall not in employing persons for the purpose of performing the Services or of supervising such performance unlawfully exercise discrimination in the matter of colour race creed or sex

(e) The Contractor shall at all times take all such precautions as are necessary to protect the health and safety of all persons employed by him/her and shall comply with the requirements of the Health and Safety at Work etc. Act 1974 (and any amendment or re-enactment thereof) and of any other Acts Regulations or Orders pertaining to the health and safety of employed persons

(f) The Contractor shall at all times be fully responsible for the payment of all income or other taxes national insurance contributions or levies of any kind relating to or arising out of the employment of any persons employed by the Contractor and shall fully and promptly indemnify the Council in respect of any liability of the Council in respect thereof

(g) The Director shall be entitled to instruct the Contractor to remove from the performance of the Services any employee of the Contractor providing that the Director shall within seven days confirm such instruction by a notice in writing

(h) At any time prior to the expiry of seven days after the service of any notice served under sub-clause (g) above the Contractor shall have the right to make representations to the Director concerning such employee and the Director shall take such representations into account (while being under no obligation in any way to accept them as valid)

(i) After taking any representations made under sub-clause (h) above into account the Director shall be entitled at his/her entire discretion to withdraw such notice to suspend its operation upon such conditions as he/she shall think fit or to confirm it and if the Director confirms such notice then the Contractor shall permanently remove such employee from the performance of the Services and the Council shall in no circumstances be liable either to the Contractor or to the employee in respect of any liability loss or damage occasioned by such removal and the Contractor shall fully and promptly indemnify the Council against any claim made by such employee

(j) The Contractor shall appoint a Contract Manager empowered to act on behalf of the Contractor for all purposes connected with the Contract and any notice information instruction or other communication given or made to the Contract Manager shall be deemed to have been given or made to the Contractor

(k) The Contractor shall forthwith give notice in writing to the Director of the identity address and telephone numbers of the person appointed as Contract Manager and of any subsequent appointment

(l) The Contractor shall forthwith give notice in writing to the Director of the identity address and telephone numbers of any person authorized to act for any period as deputy for the Contract Manager

(m) The Contractor shall provide a sufficient number of supervisory employees, in addition to the Contract Manager to ensure that the Contractor's employees engaged in and about the provision of the Services are at all times adequately supervised and properly perform their duties to the Contract Specification

(n) The Contractor shall ensure that his employees perform their duties in an orderly manner and in as quiet a manner as may reasonably be practicable having regard to the nature of the duties being performed by them and the Contractor shall further ensure that his employees do not in particular:

(i) unlawfully remove any article or thing from any location whether the property of the Council or of its employees agents or subcontractors or of any other persons or

(ii) sell to any person any plants or materials used or to be used in connection with the Services

(o) The Contractor shall ensure that his employees observe the security of all secured areas of the Council's premises and grounds

(p) The Contractor shall ensure that his staff carry out their duties and behave in such a way as to cause no unreasonable or unnecessary disruption to the work of any of the Council's own staff or any member of the public and perform the Services without closing any premises or grounds to which the public have access without the prior written approval of the Director and if the Contractor feels that it is desirable to close any such premises or grounds he shall request such written approval at least five working days prior to closure unless closure is urgently required for any health or safety reason

(q) When requested to do so or when communicating with other persons as a representative of the Contractor in the performance of the Services any employee representative or agent of the Contractor shall disclose his identity and shall not attempt to avoid so doing

(r) The Contractor shall maintain current and accurate records of the employees who are employed in providing the Services and these records shall include employee attendances and shall differentiate between those engaged as operatives and those exercising supervision and these records shall be open for inspection by the Director and any Supervising Officer at all reasonable times

(s) The Contractor shall maintain current and accurate records of all work carried out in the provision of the Services and these records shall be open for inspection by the Director or any Supervising Officer at all reasonable times

(t) The Contractor shall not employ any staff in the direct provision of the services who are either below the age of sixteen or above the age of sixty-five

[*Sub-clause (u) below is to be used only for contracts in which staff are required to or are likely to come into contact with children or other vulnerable persons. The reference to dishonesty is relevant only where staff will handle money or are placed in some other position of trust.*]

(u) The Contractor shall take all reasonable steps to ensure that any person employed in the pursuance of the contract shall not have been convicted of a sexual offence [or an offence involving dishonesty]

(v) The Contractor shall require his/her staff at all times to be properly and presentably dressed in appropriate uniforms or workwear to the satisfaction of the Council and all such uniforms and workwear and any special protective clothing to be worn by the Contractor's employees shall be supplied by the Contractor

(w) The Contractor shall provide and require his/her employees to wear at all times when employed in the provision of the services such identification (including photographic identification) as may be specified by the Director

(x) The Contractor shall use his/her best endeavours to make available to the Council any employee who is required to give evidence on behalf of the Council in any Civil Proceedings whatsoever whether brought by or against the Council

(y) at the expiry of the contract period or upon the determination of the Contract in accordance with the Conditions whichever shall first occur the Council shall be entitled to offer employment to any person employed by the Contractor in the performance or supervision of the Services and in the event of such person accepting employment with the Council the Contractor shall forthwith release such person from all contracts of Service without any payment being made to the Contractor by either the Council or the employee

18 Premises

(a) Prior to the commencement date the Council shall grant and the Contractor shall take a lease ('the lease') of the Premises described in the form of lease set out in Schedule III for a term of   years from the commencement date upon the terms and subject to the yearly rents and other covenants in the said form of lease provided that the grant of the lease shall be conditional upon the grant of a Court Order excluding the provisions of sections 24 to 28 of the Landlord and Tenant Act 1954 (as amended) and the parties hereto shall use their best endeavours to obtain such Order and comply with any formalities in relation thereto and if the said Court Order has not been granted within three months from the commencement date the Agreement to grant the lease comprised in this contract shall be rescinded without further act on the part of either party and thereupon the Agreement to grant the lease shall become null and void and neither party shall have any claim against the other (apart from any accrued right) and the Contractor hereby confirms and warrants to the Council that it has no interest in the Premises or any part thereof except and to the extent to which such interest arises under this Agreement

(b) The Contractor shall at all times during the contract period provide and maintain such additional premises as are necessary for the proper performance of the Services

(c) The Contractor may be required to hold access keys and padlocks in respect of certain premises or grounds and in such circumstances the Contractor will be responsible for the security of such premises or grounds and shall ensure in particular that such premises or grounds are properly locked (where appropriate) both while the Services are being carried on and at the end of each working day

(d) The Contractor shall be responsible for the safekeeping of any keys padlocks and access passes provided to him by the Council and shall only permit such keys and padlocks to be given to those members of its staff whose names and addresses have been supplied to the Council and then only to the extent strictly required for the purposes of performing the Services and the Contractor shall ensure that the Council is informed immediately of the loss of any such keys padlocks or access passes and the Contractor shall at his own cost replace any such lost keys or padlocks if so required by the Director

19 Vehicles, Plant and Machinery

(a) The Contractor shall at all times during the contract period provide and maintain all such vehicles plant equipment and machinery (hereinafter together referred to as 'plant') as are necessary for the proper performance of the services

(b) For the duration of the contract only the Contractor shall at no cost take from the Council a licence of Council plant as set out in Schedule IV ('the licensed plant')

(c) All other plant employed by the Contractor in the performance of the Services at any time must be either owned by the Contractor or hired by the Contractor pursuant to a contract of simple hire (and not hire-purchase) which contract must contain a clause permitting the Contractor to assign the benefit of the contract to the Council

(d) The Contractor shall put and keep all plant employed in the performance of the Services including the licensed plant at all times in good and serviceable repair and in such condition as is commensurate with the proper performance by the Contractor of his obligations under this Contract

(e) The Contractor shall at all times permit the Director access to all plant and equipment employed for the purposes of this Contract and the Director shall be entitled to serve upon the Contractor a notice in writing requiring the Contractor to put any item of plant/equipment into such condition as is required by sub-clause (d) above and the Contractor shall forthwith upon receipt of such notice cause all necessary works to be carried out to comply with such notices and in the event of the Contractor failing so to carry out such works the Council shall be at liberty to have such works carried out by such persons as it may choose and that any sums expended by the Council in so doing may be charged to the contractor and deducted from monies payable to the contractor under the contract

(f) At the expiry of the contract period or upon the determination of the Contract in accordance with the Conditions whichever shall first occur the licence referred to in sub-clause (b) above shall determine and the Council shall be entitled to serve upon the Contractor a notice requiring the Contractor to transfer to the Council the benefit of all contracts relating to the hire of such plant as may be specified in such notice

(g) Upon receipt of a notice under sub-clause (f) above requiring the Contractor to assign to the Council the benefit of any agreement for the hiring of any item of plant the Contractor shall forthwith and without any payment from the Council execute all documents necessary to effect such assignment and shall deliver such items to the Council in such condition as it may be in at the date of the notice and the Council shall thereafter indemnify the Contractor in respect of any liability arising under such hiring contract after the date of such assignment save where such liability arose from or was contributed to by any breach of the hiring contract by the Contractor prior to such assignment

20 Performance Bond

Not later than the commencement date the Contractor shall at his own expense provide two good and sufficient sureties approved by the Council or the guarantee of a Bank or Insurance Company approved by the

Council to be jointly and severally bound with the Contractor in the sum of £.... for the due performance by the Contractor of his obligations under this Contract and for the payment by the Contractor to the Council of all sums due hereunder in the terms of a Bond to be approved by the Council and the Contractor shall ensure that such Bond remains in force throughout the Contract period

21 Confidentiality

(a) The Contractor is aware that of necessity for the performance of the Services the Contractor will have access to and be entrusted with information in respect of the commercial interests of the Council all of which information is or may be confidential

(b) The Contractor shall not during or after the period of this Contract divulge to any person whatever or otherwise make use of any confidential information concerning the commercial interests of the Council and in particular the names and details of any paying customers of the Council's Services performed by the Contractor

(c) All notes and memoranda concerning the commercial interests of the Council which shall be acquired received or made by the Contractor during the period of this Contract shall be the property of the Council and shall be surrendered to the Director at the termination of this Contract

22 Data Protection

[*This clause is for use where the contractor acts as the Council's agent for data protection purposes.*]

(a) The Contractor hereby confirms and covenants that data as defined by Section 1 of the Data Protection Act 1984

  (i) Has been received by it from the Council for the purposes of enabling the Contractor to complete the Services as agent for the Council as required by this Agreement is the property of the Council and that upon termination of this Agreement will be returned to the Council

  (ii) Will not be amended or altered by the Contractor its Agents or employees in any way whatsoever unless required by the Council

  (iii) Will be used only for the purposes specified in Schedule 1 of this Agreement or for other purposes communicated to the Contractor in writing by the Council including a certificate that such purposes have been disclosed to the registered recipients

  (iv) Will be kept secure and treated as confidential commercial data as provided by Clause 21 of this Agreement

or

[*This clause is for use where the contractor is required to register as a Data User in its own right.*]

(a) The Contractor hereby confirms and covenants that

  (i) Data as defined by Section 1 of the Data Protection Act 1984 is or may be required to be kept by the Contractor to enable it to complete the Services as required by this Agreement

  (ii) The Contractor will do all things necessary to register itself as data user as defined in Sub-Section 1(5) of the Data Protection Act 1984

  (iii) Data collected to which the Data Protection Act 1984 applies shall comply with the data protection principles set out in the same Act

(iv) Data collected by or on behalf of the Contractor pursuant to the terms of this Agreement shall be the property of the Council and shall be used for no purpose whatsoever other than for the purposes specified in Schedule 1 of this Agreement and upon termination of this Agreement will be lodged with the Council. No copies of such data will be retained by the Contractor after termination of this agreement other than for taxation or accounting purposes.

23 Special Conditions
[Special conditions may be required to cover any number of service-specific issues that may otherwise be lost within the specification. The following are common examples.]

Handling of Lost Property
All monies or other items of value found by the Contractor's employees at any place other than the premises of the Contractor shall be handed to the Director or his/her representative as soon as possible and a written receipt obtained therefor

Collection of Fees
The Contractor shall collect and where required account for any fees for the use by the public of the Council's facilities in accordance with the specification contained in Schedule I hereto

Advertising
The Contractor shall ensure that the clothing of staff engaged in or any plant equipment machinery or materials used in connection with the performance of the services shall bear any advertising material without the prior written consent of the Director

Food Handling
The Contractor shall ensure that all statutory requirements in relation to the handling of food are met wherever the services to be provided include the preparation of meals

Non-solicitation and Non-competition
[In this example for trade refuse operations.]
The Contractor covenants with the Council that the Contractor will not for a period of two years after the termination of this Contract without the prior written consent of the Council in connection with the carrying on of any business in competition with the Council seek to procure orders from or do business with any person firm or company who has at any time during the period of this Contract or in the two years immediately preceding it been a customer for the Council's fee paid sack collections regular weekly special collections or contract bulk waste storage container hire as herein before defined provided that nothing in this Clause shall prohibit the seeking or procuring of orders or the doing of business other than the business described above

24 Due Performance and Default Provisions

(a) The Contractor shall carry out all work forming part of the Services strictly in accordance with the specification with all statutory requirements and with any special requirements notified to the Contractor by the Director

(b) The Contractor shall comply strictly with any target times and dates and start and completion times and dates specified by the Director

(c) If the Contractor fails to comply with sub-clause (b) above then unless the failure is due to events beyond the Contractor's control the Council shall be entitled to deduct from the payments referred to in Clause 5 hereof the actual amount of any costs or damages occasioned by any breach of this Contract by the Contractor together with the Council's administrative costs reasonably incurred in connection therewith

(d) If in the opinion of the Director or Supervising Officer the Contractor has omitted to perform any part of the Services satisfactorily the Director shall be entitled to issue a written notice (hereinafter called an 'omission notice') which shall give full details of the failure to perform the services and the rectification if any which is required of the Contractor

(e) Upon receipt of an omission notice containing rectification requirements the Contractor shall undertake that part of the Services the subject of the omission notice on the same day if the omission notice is issued before 12 noon or by 12 noon on the next working day otherwise

(f) In the event that the Contractor complies with the omission notice to the reasonable satisfaction of the Director no deduction from the payment to the Contractor shall be made

(g) In the event the Contractor fails to comply with the rectification requirements of an omissions notice to the reasonable satisfaction of the Director or if rectification is not requested by the Director within an omissions notice then the Council shall be entitled to deduct from the payment to the Contractor such sum or sums as shall appear reasonable to the Director having reference to Schedule II hereto together with an administrative charge of £.... in respect of each omission notice issued

(h) In the event that the Contractor fails to comply with the omission notice to the reasonable satisfaction of the Director the Council shall be additionally entitled to issue a further omissions notice in respect of the same default or without further reference to the Contractor to secure another party to rectify the default the subject of the omissions notice and to deduct from the relevant payment to the Contractor the cost of the said rectification together with an administrative charge of £.... and the Council shall in taking such a course of action be under no obligation to the Contractor to secure the lowest price for the said rectification of the default

(i) If any deduction from a payment falls to be made the Council shall be entitled to retain an additional sum not greater than 10 per cent of the total sum due to the contractor as shall seem to the Director a prudent retention against any additional cost which may be incurred in consequence of the Contractor's default out of such payment and also from any consequent payments for a period not exceeding six months from the date of the initial payment from which a deduction fell to be made

25 Termination
(a) The Council shall be entitled forwith upon the happening of any of the following to exercise the rights contained in sub-clause (b) below:
  (i) the events referred to in Clause 24(d) hereof
  (ii) any breach by the Contractor of any condition of this Contract
  (iii) at any time when the payment to the Contractor is reduced by 5 per cent or more on more than two occasions in any twelve-month period or by 10 per cent or more on more than one occasion in any six-month period or by more than 20 per cent at any time (any retention made under Clause 24(d) hereof excepted)
  (iv) the Contractor suffering an execution to be levied on his/her goods or if the Contractor consists of one or more individuals any such individual dying entering into a composition or arrangement for the benefit of his/her creditors or having a receiving order in bankruptcy made against him/her or if the Contractor consists of a body corporate the Contractor having a receiver or a receiver and manager appointed or being the subject of a resolution or order for winding up
  (v) Any change in control of the Contractor (or where the Contractor is a subsidiary company) its ultimate holding company
(b) In any of the circumstances referred to in sub-clause (a) above the Council may at its option and without prejudice to any of its remedies under this Contract and without prejudice to any rights of action which shall accrue or shall have already accrued to the Council do any or all of the following:
  (i) require the Contractor to remedy any default within such time as may be specified by the Director without further charge to the Council
  (ii) suspend payment to the Contractor
  (iii) retain any amount due to the Contractor howsoever arising from the Council
  (iv) without determining the whole of the Contract determine the Contract in respect of part of the Services only by notice in writing having immediate effect and thereafter itself provide or procure a third party to provide such part of the Services
  (v) terminate the Contract by notice in writing having immediate effect
(c) In the event of the termination or expiration of the Contract:
  (i) the Contractor shall unless requested otherwise by the Director forthwith cease to perform any of the Services and
  (ii) the Contractor shall fully and promptly indemnify the Council against all loss and damage suffered by the Council by reason of such termination and without prejudice to the generality of this Condition shall fully and promptly indemnify the Council in respect of the cost of causing to be performed such Services as would have been performed by the Contractor during the remainder of the contract period to the extent that such cost exceeds such sums as would have been lawfully payable to the Contractor for performing such Services and the Council shall be at liberty to have such Services performed by any persons (whether or not servants of the Council) as the Council shall in its absolute discretion think fit and shall be under no obligation to employ the least expensive method of having such Services performed and

(iii) the Contractor shall deliver to the Council a schedule detailing the state and condition of each item of licensed machinery and the location thereof and

(iv) the Council may retake possession of any of the Council's materials equipment or other goods loaned or hired to the Contractor and exercise a lien over any of the equipment clothing materials or other goods belonging to the Contractor and upon any of the Council's premises at the date of such termination or expiration for any amounts due hereunder or otherwise from the Contractor to the Council

(d) The rights of the Council under this Condition are in addition and without prejudice to any other right the Council may have to claim the amount of any loss or damage suffered by the Council on account of the acts or omissions of the Contractor whether pursuant to the bond or guarantee and indemnity given in accordance with the Bond Undertaking or Guarantee Undertaking or otherwise

(e) Termination or expiration of the Contract shall be without prejudice to the rights and remedies of the Contractor and the Council accrued before such termination or expiration and nothing in the Contract shall prejudice the right of either such party to recover any amount outstanding at the termination or expiration

26 Notices

(a) No notice to be served upon the Council shall be valid or effective unless it is sent prepaid post or delivered by hand to the Borough Secretary and Solicitor at the [address]

(b) Any notice served upon the Contractor shall be valid and effective if it is sent by prepaid post or delivered by hand to the registered office principal place of business or to the Premises or is delivered by hand to a director proprietor or other responsible representative of the Contractor

Arbitration

All disputes between the parties arising out of or connected with this Contract or the performance of the Services by the Contractor shall be referred to an arbitrator to be agreed upon by the parties or in default of such agreement to be nominated by the Chairman for the time being of the Chartered Institute of Arbitrators or in the case of his incapacity by the Vice-Chairman thereof and the finding of such arbitrator shall be final and binding upon the parties

Schedule I: The Specification of the Services

Schedule II: The Tender and Schedule of Rates

Schedule III: The Form of Lease in Respect of Council Premises

Schedule IV: The Form of Licence for Use of Council Plant by the Contractor

SAMPLE PERSONAL SERVICES CONTRACT DOCUMENTS

Reproduced by kind permission of the London Borough of Enfield

The two extracts that follow are extracts from schedules for contract for provision of, first, group homes for clients with severe learning difficulties and, second, home-care services. Used in conjunction with contract conditions of the type set out in Appendix III, they illustrate ways of specifying services by reference to published policy documents where detailed specification of tasks is either inappropriate or particularly onerous.

Extracts from Schedules for Contract for Provision of Group Homes for Clients with Severe Learning Difficulties

Schedule I: The Specification of the Services

Part One: The Detailed Service Requirements

1 Introduction
1.1 The Council is desirous to produce within a community a number of group homes, each capable of providing living accommodation and the necessary support services for 4, 5 or 6 of the 48 clients with severe learning difficulties who presently reside at the [*name*] hostel and for such similar clients as shall be referred to the Council in future.
1.2 The Council wishes these clients to enjoy the same levels of support, assistance and care as they presently enjoy, together with the advantage of living in smaller properties within the community.
1.3 To this end the Council has devised the following detailed specification of the services to be provided within each group home supplied and maintained by a private contractor, be that contractor an individual or an organisation.

2 The Service Specification
2.1 This Service Specification relates to the management of group homes for people with severe learning difficulties.
2.2 The Specification defines:

(a) the services that the Contractor will provide for clients;
(b) the manner in which such services will be provided and the manner in which the Council's policy will be observed by the Company, so as to further the interests of the clients;
(c) particular arrangements that the Contractor shall make for the management and control of its staff in pursuit of the service objectives as defined in the Part Two of the Schedule;
(d) the arrangements between the Contractor and the Council for the co-ordination of their respective services;
(e) the mechanisms by which the Council shall ensure the adherence by the Contractor to the terms of the Specification.

3 Operational Policy

3.1 The Contractor will provide an operational policy in respect of each home under this control and such policy will include a statement of:
(a) the objectives of the services provided within each group home;
(b) the Contractor's expectations of his staff in respect of the amount and quality of service to be provided and the general philosophy upon which support to the client is to be based;
(c) the resources in terms of staffing, training, management support and equipment which the Contractor will provide;
(d) operational details essential to the function of each group home;
(e) the arrangements for buying food and preparing meals; for undertaking the domestic cleaning; for storing service-user records; and for storing medicines.
3.2 The operational policy for each group home and any amendments thereto will be drawn up in consultation with the Council.
3.3 The Contractor will produce in consultation with the Council an annual report in respect of each home that will review the implementation of the operational policy the extent to which the objectives of the home are being achieved and particular achievements or difficulties
3.4 The Contractor will provide an annual report in respect of each client, which will include a review of:
(a) the long-term and short-term goals for the client;
(b) the responsibilities for ensuring the said goals are met;
(c) the methods to be used;
(d) the criteria for judging success;
(e) the time-scales within which progress towards the said goals are to be measured and assessed;
(f) the date of the next such review and report.

4 Nomination of Clients

4.1 A formal nomination procedure to enable vacancies occurring within a group home to be filled shall be agreed between the Council and the Contractor.
4.2 The said nomination procedure shall reflect the rights of the Council to nominate clients directly or through other bodies approved for this purpose by the Council.
4.3 In nominating a replacement client to fill a vacancy in a group home the Council shall have regard to the relative dependency of the former client at the time of his or her admission to the group home and

shall not nominate any client of a substantially greater dependency level.

5 Services to Clients

5.1   The Services required are those necessary to ensure compliance with the Registered Homes Act 1984 and the Residential Care Homes Regulations 1984 and in particular Regulations 9 and 10 thereof.

5.2   The Services include the property requirements and staff cover ascertainable by reference to Schedule 2 hereof.

6 Fire Precautions

6.1   While the Contractor shall endeavour to maintain the highest standard for fire safety measures, it will also attempt to minimise the effects of such precautions upon ordinary domestic living in order that the clients' sense of homeliness is not compromised.

6.2   The Contractor and the persons in charge of each group home shall:

   (a)   take adequate precautions against the risk of fire, including the provision of adequate means of escape in the event of fire, and make adequate arrangements for detecting, containing and extinguishing fires, for the giving of warnings and for the evacuation of all persons in the home in the event of fire and for the maintenance of fire precautions and fire fighting equipment;

   (b)   make arrangements to secure by means of fire drills and practices that the staff in the home and, so far as practicable, the clients know the procedure to be followed in the case of fire;

   (c)   keep a record in respect of each home of every fire practice, drill, fire-alarm test and inspection by the Fire Prevention Authority and of any action taken to remedy defects in fire alarm equipment;

   (d)   consult with the Council in respect of the frequency of fire drills and practices;

   (e)   comply with the advice and recommendation of the Local Fire Authority;

   (f)   ensure that the group home contains no furniture and furnishings that are easily ignited or demonstrate rapid spread of surface flame characteristics.

7 Client Rights

7.1   The Contractor shall provide every client with a written contract outlining the rights and obligations of the said client and the contract shall expressly state the name of the person to whom any request or complaint relating to the group home can be made and the Contractor shall ensure that any complaint so made by a client or person acting on a client's behalf is fully investigated and the Contractor shall notify the Council of any complaints received.

7.2   The Contractor shall also inform every client in writing of the name and address of the Director of Social Services, to whom complaints in respect of the group home may be made by clients or persons acting on their behalf.

7.3   The Contractor shall use its best endeavours to enable clients to achieve their full potential in respect of their physical, intellectual, emotional and social capacity and shall support and encourage clients when it is in their best interests to move into more appropriate surroundings.

7.4   The Contractor shall use its best endeavours to ensure that the self-respect of clients is fostered by staff, who shall treat clients with courtesy.

7.5   The Contractor shall ensure that clients are accorded every right to their privacy and to determine so far as possible their own routines and lifestyles.

7.6   The Contractor shall ensure that religious, ethnic and cultural observance, whether dietary or religious, is provided for wherever the Contractor has agreed to accept the nomination of clients from religious or ethnic minorities.

7.7   The Contractor shall use its best endeavours to ensure that provision for leisure and recreation activities in the neighbourhood of the group home is made to such extent as shall match the tastes and capabilities of individual clients.

7.8   The Contractor shall permit and encourage clients to enjoy the ownership and use of their own personal possessions and the Contractor shall ensure that such possessions are adequately insured within the Contractor's policies of insurance for the group home.

7.9   The Contractor shall permit clients the normal opportunities for emotional expression and the freedom to enjoy personal relationships outside and within the group home.

7.10 The Contractor shall permit clients to manage their own affairs and take their own risks so far as they are competent to do so without threat to the safety of others.

7.11 The Contractor shall ensure clients have access to a social worker or other suitable persons to provide support and advocacy.

7.12 The Contractor shall encourage and use its best endeavours to assist clients in the use of education facilities and in the seeking and taking-up of employment opportunities.

7.13 The Contractor shall not use physical methods and seclusion or medication to control clients.

7.14 The Contractor shall normally permit clients to have access to their own records.

7.15 The Contractor shall use its best endeavours to encourage and permit residents to wear their own clothes and to properly clean and maintain the said clothes.

7.16 The Contractor shall encourage visitors and ensure flexible arrangements for visiting the group home.

8 Records

8.1   The Contractor shall ensure that effective systems for record-keeping are devised and properly maintained in order to safeguard the interests of service users and the Contractor will specify such arrangements in the operational policy for each group home.

8.2   The person in charge of each group home shall compile the records specified in Schedule 2 of the Residential Care Homes Regulations 1984 and shall keep them at all times available for inspection by any person authorised by the Council.

8.3   The person in charge will keep records in a safe place and ensure their confidentiality.

8.4   Every record compiled in accordance with this clause shall be retained for a minimum of five years from the date of the last entry in it.

8.5   The Contractor shall devise a procedure, to be agreed with the Council, that will set out the clients' entitlement to have access to personal information about themselves held in the records.

9 Clients' Finances

9.1   The Contractor, in accordance with clients' wishes and individual care plans, will encourage and assist clients to manage their own money.

9.2   The Contractor shall, in consultation with the Council, devise procedures to govern its handling of clients' money, including any personal allowance payable by the Department of Social Security, when this is deemed necessary for specific clients and the person in charge shall keep a record showing for each individual client any money or other valuables received on his or her behalf and how it has been spent.

10 Medication

10.1 The Contractor shall ensure that clients are registered with a local General Practitioner of their choice.

10.2 The Contractor shall devise a policy and procedure in consultation with the Council in respect of the storage and administration of medicines and for the keeping of appropriate records.

10.3 The operational policy for each group home will detail the arrangement for storing medicines.

10.4 The person in charge of each group home will encourage clients to participate and become as independent as possible in managing their own medication.

10.5 The Contractor shall have reference to the Guidance Note for Medication referred to in Part Two below.

Part Two: Policy Considerations

1 Introduction

1.1   Each Contractor providing a group home for the Council's clients under this contract must organise the services to be contractually provided so as to fulfil so far as is reasonably possible the Council's operational policy as it relates to the lives of clients with severe learning difficulties within its accommodation.

1.2   The Council's operational policy for the running of its own home (now to be replaced by group homes) is therefore reproduced below to such extent as it is intended to bind each Contractor.

1.3   Each Contractor is additionally referred for information to the appendices to this part of Schedule I, which contain the following documents for further guidance:

(a) *A Handbook for People in London Who Run Residential Homes*, London Borough of Croydon, 1987, and the Council's Homes Registration Package;

(b) *Joint Philosophy of Care in the Community for People with Learning Difficulties*, London Borough of Enfield, 1989;
(c) *General Manual for Homes in the Community*, Mencap, 1988;
(d) 'Medication' Guidance Note, London Borough of Enfield, 1990.

2 Operational Policy
2.1 *General*
The Local Authority is guided by the general belief that residential services for people who have severe learning difficulties should:
(a) affirm and enhance the dignity, self-respect and individuality of the residents, who are people first and should not be influenced by any form of discrimination by virtue of race, ethnic origin, creed, sex or disability;
(b) be developed on a basis that all people with severe learning difficulties have a right of access to a range of housing for them to live in which is as near the range of housing offered to non-handicapped people as possible;
(c) enable people to:
  (i) remain in their own home as long as they would wish;
  (ii) move from hospital, hostel/voluntary home or family home into an ordinary dwelling in their local neighbourhood or wider community, either individually or in small groups;
(d) ensure that people are not subjected to repeated moves, but place emphasis upon the type and degree of support any individual might require at a given point in time, and that support is subject to review;
(e) pay due regard to the residents' wishes and preferences;
(f) enable the residents to share in and contribute to the community.

2.2 *Basic principles and objectives*
The aim is to provide a permanent home and a homelife for four, five or six adults with a mental handicap in each group home. This objective will be pursued in accordance with the following principles:
(a) People with severe learning difficulties have the same human value as anyone else, and the same rights as all other members of the community.
(b) As much as possible should be done to diminish the barriers that separate them from other people.
(c) Their own abilities, preferences and needs must be individually recognised in providing the service.
(d) Each group home will be run on the principles of normalisation as interpreted into five service principles by the Jay Committee report of 1979:
  (i) Mentally handicapped people should use normal services wherever possible.
  (ii) Existing networks of community support should be strengthened by professional services and not supplanted by them.
  (iii) Specialised services should be provided only where their needs cannot be met by general services.
  (iv) There should be Individual Programme Planning for every individual to provide continuity and co-ordination of care.

(v) There should be someone to intercede on behalf of mentally handicapped people to enable them to obtain appropriate services.

(e) Each resident will be given the opportunity to experience and participate in the normal community activities, eg shopping, swimming, library, clubs, etc.

(f) It is expected that the residents will be encouraged to integrate themselves into the community-based activities with help from the staff and volunteers.

(g) The staff will take into account the individual needs of the residents and their capabilities when planning and offering residents support.

2.3   *The client group*

(a) There will be a maximum of six people living in each group home.

(b) The residents living in each group home will be adults who have severe learning difficulties, of both sexes, who will benefit from the facilities and opportunities offered by the group home.

(c) Potential residents will be assessed for suitability by the Council and, once accepted, will be kept under review. In the initial stages of a placement the reviews will be more intensive, involve staff, social workers, the resident and relatives if appropriate, and be aimed at ensuring the validity of the initial assessment. The last care-giver will be asked to keep a place open for up to six months against the eventuality of the placement being unsuccessful (if appropriate).

(d) The residents will be of mixed-level dependency. They will be selected for compatibility and the potential to develop further their self-help and social skills within the stimulating environment of each group home.

(e) All residents will come from the Council's area or have links with the authority (as defined in the AMA Social Services Circular No 9/1988).

(f) A group home is not intended to provide accommodation for *severely* behaviourally disturbed people.

(g) It is envisaged that for residents this will be their permanent home as long as it continues to be suitable and meet their needs.

2.4   *Referral procedure*

If for any reason someone should have a group home, then the following procedure should be implemented.

(a) Referrals suggested by current residents, relatives, carers, social workers, and voluntary agencies to the Council, via PSW (Mental Handicap), OIC, or Adult Services, will be assessed for suitability and then nominated on to the Contractor for placement in a selected group home.

(b) Joint assessments will be done by the Contractor's staff of the group home and a field social worker in conjunction with the departmental form MH/ADULT/7.

(c) Key staff together with the PSW (Mental Handicap) under the umbrella of the department's 'Residential Placement Panel' would have the responsibility for making the final decision re filling any vacancies in conjunction with the guidelines/procedures as outlined by Adult Services.

(d) It is envisaged that when future vacancies arise priority will be given to those in greatest need.

2.5   *Accommodation charges*

No additional charges will be levied by the Contractor.

2.6   *Health Care*

Whenever possible residents will remain with or choose their own individual GP and use any appropriate community service available (eg, dentist, optician, family planning clinic, etc). When a resident falls sick, and in case of minor ailments, the care provided at the hostel will be the kind of attention someone would receive in his/her own home from a caring relative under guidance of the consultant, GP, or nurse member of the primary health care team. However, the staff of the home will not be expected to provide the professional kind of health care that is properly the function of the primary health care services.

2.7   *Client concerns*

(a) Clients will have access to a telephone and the privacy to use it both for outgoing and incoming calls.

(b) Clients will be encouraged and given every available assistance to take holidays individually or in small groups as appropriate.

(c) It is anticipated that each client will have his/her own allocated Key Worker.

(d) Where appropriate, individual residents will be encouraged to administer as much of their own financial affairs as possible.

2.8   *Conduct of the group home*

(a) The conduct of each group home will be based upon the guidelines contained in the publication *Home Life: a code of practice for residential care*. It suffices to say that while the Officer in Charge has overall responsibility for the general welfare of the residents, every effort will be made towards achieving the normal family home atmosphere, with a high degree of individual freedom and mutual helpfulness. The normal resident routine ought to be based on daily attendance at the local authority Social Education Centre, or another suitable occupation. Weekends will provide for participation in personal interests as well as sharing in domestic chores, shopping excursions, etc. The residents will be encouraged to participate in the running of the group home and in making decisions concerning social or other activities.

(b) There will be a significant element of 'learning through doing' in the normal conduct of the group home aimed at developing independence in self-care, domestic competence and daily living skills. Residents will participate, under guidance, in the planning and preparation of meals as well as sharing other domestic tasks. Residents will also be expected to maintain the tidiness of their own rooms and to do their laundry and share the work of cleaning the common rooms and gardening where appropriate.

2.9   *Privacy*

(a) The privacy of each resident's room will be respected at all times. Except in an emergency, nobody shall enter a resident's room without that resident's express permission. Knocking on doors should be encouraged as correct procedure.

(b) Residents will be encouraged to 'personalise' their rooms with the use of their own ornaments, pictures, plants, etc, and, as far as possible, furniture.

2.10 *Visitors*

(a) Residents may invite their relatives and friends to visit at any reasonable time.

(b) Visitors, except those with statutory authority, concerned with the theory, principles or operation of the home shall not be permitted to visit except in the most exceptional circumstances without first seeking the agreement of the residents and in consultation with staff.

2.11 *Council monitoring*

(a) Designated officers will undertake regular monitoring of the service provision within each group home and will in particular evaluate the following:

   (i) unit organisation;
   (ii) philosophy, attitudes, client–staff relations;
   (iii) programming;
   (iv) support and counselling;
   (v) support from other professional services;
   (vi) links and interchange with the wider community;
   (vii) staffing and client levels;
   (viii) physical features/resources;
   (ix) catering and domestic services;
   (x) clerical support/client information records;
   (xi) fire precautions;
   (xii) individual client development.

(b) Unit organisation is taken to incorporate the following:

   (i) operational policy;
   (ii) unit plans;
   (iii) formal staff meetings;
   (iv) management/staff communication;
   (v) staff/staff communication;
   (vi) identified staff team roles;
   (vii) identified instructor supervisor/social care assistant roles;
   (viii) availability of information to management;
   (ix) availability of information to staff;
   (x) management support and appraisal;
   (xi) staff support and appraisal;
   (xii) systems (records, files, planning, monitoring, etc);
   (xiii) communication (unit/line management/HQ);
   (xiv) staff morale/identification.

Schedule II: The Tender and Schedule of Rates

Total tender price Option A

Total tender price Option B

Total tender price Option C

Total tender price Option D

Total tender price Option E

Total tender price Option F

Total tender price Option G

Total tender price Option H

Total tender price Option J

TOTAL TENDER PRICE	

Additional Tendering Information

A full price tender is required for each and every option on the attached sheets.

The Council would wish to know the maximum and/or the minimum number of homes you are prepared to operate. Please specify:

Maximum

Minimum

Do you have a preference in terms of the options to be operated by you if a contract were to be awarded to you? Please specify.

Staffed Group Homes

	DATE COMPLETED	
OPTION		
SOCIAL SERVICES AREA (if identified)		
NO. OF WEEKS BUDGET IS BASED ON		
NO. OF RESIDENTS		
RESIDENTS' BEDSPACES		
STAFF BEDSPACES		
HOUSING ASSOCIATION (if applicable)		

TOTAL WEEKLY CHARGE PER RESIDENT	

STAFFING DETAILS

Post	No. Staff	Annual salary, or otherwise	Total
Principal residential social worker (if applicable)	x	–	
Head of home senior residential social worker (if applicable)	x	–	
Deputy senior residential social worker (if applicable)	x	–	
Residential social worker	x	–	
Assistant residential social worker	x	–	
Waking night staff	x	–	
Subtotal I			
Emergency cover/relief staff	x	–	
Sleep-in allowance	x	–	
Subtotal II (excluding National Insurance and Pensions)			
Estimated % increase			
Subtotal III			
National Insurance @ %			
Pension			
Total Salaries including National Insurance and Pensions			
Manual Workers (if applicable). Please specify below			
Total Wages			
Total Staffing Costs			

SERVICE COSTS

Community charge	
Water rates	
Subtotal rates	
Electricity	
Gas	
Other fuel	
Subtotal heat and light	
Catering/Food and Provisions (**subtotal**)	
Cleaning	
Laundry	
Subtotal	
Equipment rental	
Servicing of equipment	
Replace household goods	
Subtotal Replacement/service	
Garden maintenance (**subtotal**)	
Total Service Costs	
MAINTENANCE: Properties	
Day-to-day (**subtotal**)	
Provision for internal decoration (**subtotal**)	
Provision for cyclical maintenance	
Subtotal decoration	
Total Maintenance Costs	
RENT AND MORTGAGE COSTS	
Rent payable	
Mortgage payable and interest on property loans	
Subtotal rent and mortgage	
Registration (First Year)	
MANAGEMENT AND WELFARE COSTS	
Printing and stationery (**subtotal**)	
Telephones and postage (**subtotal**)	
Travel and petrol for staff	
Vehicle leasing for staff/clients, including car tax, insurance, maintenance	
Subtotal travel and fuel	
Recreation/holidays	
Medical	
Other professional fees	
Residents' welfare	
Staff training	
Advertising	
Subtotal training and recruitment	
Insurance—organisation	
Insurance—housing association (if applicable)	
Subtotal insurance	
Audit (**subtotal**)	
Management fees administration	
Other management costs (**subtotal**)	
Total Management and Welfare Costs	
FURNITURE AND EQUIPMENT	
Initial purchase of furniture	

MANAGEMENT AND WELFARE COSTS (CONTD),

Fixtures and fittings loan	
Furniture and equipment provision	
Furniture replacements (**subtotal**)	
Subtotal	
Total Furniture and Equipment Costs	
Total Expenses/Costs	
Other Additional Costs, if any (please specify)	

TOTAL TENDER PRICE

Extracts from Schedules for Contract for Provision of Home Care Services

Schedule I: The Specification of the Services

Part One: Service Requirements

1 The Contractor shall provide Home-Care Service to such clients as are nominated by the Council at such times and dates as the Council shall specify using the Council's Model Works order

2 The Contractor shall ensure that the Services are provided as reasonably required by the client in accordance with the Council's Code of Practice for Home Care staff included as Appendix One to this Schedule

3 For the purposes of defining the Services Home Care shall include the tasks set out below and any other task similar in requirement specified by the Council
   (a) Assisting a client to get up, dress and wash in the morning
   (b) Preparing breakfast, a hot drink, a hot lunch, tea and supper for a client
   (c) Making a fire or regulating heating appliances
   (d) Assisting a client to use a WC or commode and emptying and cleaning the latter
   (e) Assisting a client to wash shower or bathe
   (f) Assisting a client to prepare for and get into bed
   (g) Securing the client's house
   (h) Assisting client with his/her medication
   (i) Carrying out a client's shopping and collection of a pension
   (j) Paying a client's bills
   (k) Washing a client's clothes using the client's washing machine or a launderette and handwashing small quantities of clothing
   (l) Washing linen or other household fabrics using the client's washing machine or a launderette
   (m) General household work including cleaning and ironing

4 In carrying out the Services the Contractor shall have regard to the Council's policy for Home Care (and in particular to any relevant Monitoring Criteria within the said document) included as Appendix Three to this Schedule

5 The Contractor shall have regard to the reasonable expectations of the client in performing the Services but shall not be required to perform the Services unless the client has provided the necessary equipment and materials to enable the Services to be performed without risking the health or safety of the Contractor's employees

6 In providing the Services the Contractor shall employ only such persons as are careful skilled honest and suitably trained and so far as possible shall use his best endeavours to enable that such persons are able to comply with the model person specification included as Appendix Two to this Schedule

7 The Contractor shall employ sufficient persons to ensure that the Services are provided at all times and in all respects to the Contract Specification

8 The Contractor shall take all reasonable steps to ensure that any persons employed in the pursuance of the contract shall not have been convicted of a sexual offence or an offence involving dishonesty

9 The Contractor shall explicitly require each person to be employed in providing Services to the Council's clients to state whether he/she has any convictions and shall not employ him/her in providing the said Services until the declaration of convictions has been given

10 The names and particulars of any employee who will be required to work in the home of a Council client which contains children must be supplied by the Contractor to the Council for the purpose of carrying out a check for relevant convictions with the Police and the employee shall not be allocated duties in a home containing children until such a Police check has been completed and the Contractor notified of a favourable result by the Council

11 The Contractor shall not seek any payments in addition to invoices served in accordance with Clause 4 of the conditions and the Contractor shall fully indemnify the Council against any other claims in respect of income or other taxes national insurance contributions or levies of any kind relating to or arising out of the employment of any persons employed by the Contractor

Schedule I: Appendix One

Code of Practice for Home-Care Staff

This code of practice includes the following:
1 Introduction and General Aims of Home-Care Service
2 Code of Practice when Working with Clients
3 Health and Safety
4 Abuse at Work
5 Confidentiality
6 Dealing with Abnormal Situations
7 Other General Conditions of Service
8 Charges for Home-Care Service
9 Hypothermia
10 Elsans/Commodes

1 Introduction and General Aims of the Home-Care Service
1.1   *Introduction*
      The purpose of these guidelines is to give guidance and general information that, it is hoped, will be helpful to you when carrying out your responsibilities as a Home Carer.
      The Home-Care Service is a vitally important service provided by the Social Services Department and is considered to be the cornerstone of community care. It is the first point of contact with Social Services for many people.
1.2   *General Aims of the Home-Care Service*
      It is important for you to be aware of and understand the general aims of the Home-Care Service as defined by the Social Services Committee.
      1.2.1 To provide for people who have lost, either temporarily or

permanently, the ability to carry out, or the means whereby others carry out on their behalf, key tasks and responsibilities necessary for independent living. Such people must have a home to live in or the promise of one. This service should be available for all client groups.

1.2.2 To encourage and assist clients to achieve an optimum level of independence.

1.2.3 To enable people who wish to remain in their own homes to do so and to enable people living in institutions to move into more appropriate accommodation.

1.2.4 To respond to clients' personal needs as well as their practical ones.

1.2.5 To provide a service that is sensitive to the client's culture, disability, race or religion.

1.2.6 To provide a consistent high-quality service across the Borough that responds flexibly to local needs and changing demands.

1.2.7 The Home-Care Service, although helping predominantly elderly people, will need to assist younger disabled people, those with infectious diseases, families in crisis, people with mental health problems and people with learning difficulties. It also needs to be aware of and give a high priority to the needs of carers.

2 Code of Practice when Working with Clients

The conditions below must be observed in the interests of both clients and staff.

2.1 *Your duties*

The duties you undertake in each client's home will be those considered most urgent by the Home-Care Manager following his/her assessment. Although you will usually be working alone in clients' homes, there will be regular contact with your manager.

2.2 *Working with other people*

It is important when working with other professionals/family members, you work effectively and as part of a team. If you experience any difficulties, consult your manager.

2.3 *Client's rights*

Always respect your client's rights. If you are concerned about any aspect of these, eg where you feel a client is taking a dangerous risk, then consult your manager.

2.4 *Changes in client's circumstances*

Any deterioration in your client must be reported. This includes physical and mental health. If your manager is not available, ask to speak to someone else in authority. If it helps, write the problem down. Your feedback is vital. Unless you keep your manager informed at all times, clients may well be at risk. If you call a GP, let the office know.

2.5 *Independence*

Your role is to maintain the independence of your clients. The emphasis is on working with them rather than doing for them. Please remember, helping clients to maintain their independence or regain lost skills requires sensitivity and patience.

2.6   *Client's dignity*
Remember that some of the tasks you undertake with your clients would normally be done by them in private. Their dignity is of paramount importance at all times.

2.7   *Ethnic minority clients*
It is important not to make assumptions when attending clients from ethnic minority groups. Be aware of cultural differences, eg religion, and be sensitive to the client's needs/wishes.

2.8   *Punctuality*
Always try to be punctual. Your clients depend upon you arriving regularly and on time.

2.9   *Your relationship with clients*
Try to maintain a caring but professional relationship with clients. Always remember the danger of becoming over involved. Never give your home telephone number or address to a client or family member. If anyone should ask for details, give the office telephone number. This rule is for your own protection.

2.10   *Work programme*
The clients that you go to may be changed from time to time for a variety of reasons. Your manager will discuss the need to do this with you.

2.11   *Working with clients on a temporary basis*
If covering a client on a temporary basis, always prioritise the tasks that need to be done with the client. Be clear about how much time you have available. Please remember to update your records.

2.12   *Unable to gain access*
If you arrive at a client's home and you cannot get a reply, never just walk away. Some clients may take a long time to answer the door. If you are sure no one is there, try to find out where the client is. Report all information to the office immediately. Leave a card to say you have called.

2.13   *Securing a client's home*
If a client is taken to hospital, please make sure the house is secure before leaving. Try to attend to any rubbish, perishable food in the fridge, turn off lights and fires, close windows and doors. Make sure the client takes the front-door key and any money/purse. You must not take responsibility for these things. Always advise the office.

2.14   *Emergencies*
If you find a client on the floor, do not try to move him/her. Make him/her comfortable and call the Emergency Services straight away.

2.15   *Lifting and transferring clients*
Many of the clients we help need assistance with transfers or lifting. It is therefore important to be clear about the distinction between lifting a client and assisting a client to transfer.
Lifting
Where the client is unable to support their own body weight. In these cases you must not try to lift alone. Home-Care Staff are expected to lift in pairs.
Transfers
Where the client can support their own body weight but needs assistance when carrying out daily tasks eg transferring from bed to commode. In these cases Home-Care Staff are expected to assist clients alone.

If at any time you feel you are placing either you or your client at risk by lifting or transferring them you must contact your manager immediately and ask for assistance.

The above duties must only be undertaken in consultation with your manager.

In the interests of health and safety of both clients and staff you must have attended the necessary training before lifting or transferring clients.

2.16 *Escorting clients*
Never escort/take your clients out without first discussing the need to do this with your manager.

2.17 *Keys*
Never accept a key for one of your clients without discussing it first with your manager. This is very important, as Home-Care staff are often the first to be accused if something goes missing. In the interests of security your client's keys should never have name and address tags attached.

2.18 *Clients' responsibilities*
Clients are expected to provide you with the correct materials/equipment. If you have any problem, consult your manager.

If asked to go shopping or to the launderette by a client, then the client must pay any bus fares or parking fees.

2.19 *Finances*
If you are asked by your manager to become involved in dealing with a client's finances, keep accurate records at all times and keep your manager informed. (See section on General Conditions of Service.)

2.20 *Bathing*
Where clients are in need of assistance to get in or out of the bath, normal practice is to encourage clients to accept a wash as an alternative; in these cases it may be appropriate for your manager to make a referral back for an assessment for the provision of aids or adaptation works. Where appropriate, clients may be escorted to have a bath in a safe environment, eg a Day-Care Unit. This task should be undertaken only after consultation with your manager.

2.21 *Medication*
It is important to remember that all medication is the property of your client. Where possible all clients are responsible for their own medication. It is permissible for all Home-Care Staff to assist with medication under instruction from the client's GP and always in consultation with your manager. This must be undertaken as specified in the 'Policy Guide for Medicines in Home-Care'.

2.22 *Emotional and social needs of clients*
These are as important as the practical needs of your clients. Try to make some time to talk and listen to your clients, encourage them to maintain interests/hobbies and keep social contact, eg relatives/friends, etc.

2.23 *Nursing duties for clients*
You are not expected to undertake the duties of a trained nurse, such as enemas, injections, stitches, complicated dressings, but you will need to work closely with the District Nursing Section in providing effective care for your clients. (See also Health and Safety guidance and HIV/AIDS Policy.)

2.24　*Incontinent clients*

Many clients who become incontinent are often acutely distressed by this. Check that your client has been seen by the Continence Adviser who is employed by the Health Authority. Check he/she has the right continence aids to use. Above all, treat clients with respect and try to maintain their dignity.

2.25　*Aids and adaptations*

Many of your clients may have difficulty in coping around their homes because of disability. An Occupational Therapist may be able to help and would need to visit to assess for aids that may make your client's life easier, eg helping hands, grab rails, zimmer frames, raised toilet seats.

2.26　*Other services*

There may be times when a client needs assistance from other sources/departments to help with short-term or longer-term needs. Ask your manager if you feel this is the case. Social Workers can become involved if there is a need for Respite Care, Sheltered Housing, Residential Care, Day Care or Counselling. These services may further enhance the quality of your client's life, give relief to carers and help people to remain in their own homes longer.

3 Health and Safety

Please read these guidelines in conjunction with the more detailed *Home-Care Safety* booklet. This section is very important.

3.1　You are required by law to work in a responsible and safe manner at all times.

3.2　People run their homes in different ways. While making every endeavour to encourage and maintain standards of health and welfare in clients' homes, you must make allowances for these differences and try to overcome them to the best of your ability.

3.3　Try to be aware of hazards in your clients' home and report them at once.

3.4　If you are concerned about the safety of an appliance a client has asked you to use, report this to your manager.

3.5　Always use the correct equipment. Clients are expected to provide you with this. Any problems, see your manager.

3.6　Protective clothing must be worn at all times.

3.7　If you are attending a client who is incontinent, check with your manager that they are using the incontinent waste collection service and, if appropriate, the incontinent laundry service. You must tell your manager if you feel conditions are becoming unsafe or difficult for you to cope with.

3.8　If you are concerned about any aspect of your client's environment, discuss it with your manager. You have the right to ask for professional advice from another department, eg Environmental Health or Occupational Health.

3.9　*Infectious diseases/control*

The Department will, wherever possible, discuss any special circumstances relating to your clients if these will affect your work with them. As with other aspects of normal daily living and work, it is possible for any individual to unknowingly come into contact with infectious conditions. Please be aware of your responsibilities to clients. Some clients may be particularly susceptible to infection from you. (Please refer to HIV/AIDS policy.)

3.10   *Accidents*

If you have an accident while working, you must report it straight away, however small. This will enable your manager to record the information.

4 Abuse at Work

4.1   It is acknowledged that, because of the nature of the work, staff who work for Social Services Departments are sometimes the subject of abuse.

4.2   The vast majority of Home-Care staff work alone in clients' homes, often sustaining high levels of individual contact with clients. It is also recognised that Home-Care staff have to work at night or week-ends when limited support is available. This can potentially place them in a vulnerable position.

4.3   As a member of staff you are not expected to suffer or endure any form of abuse.

4.4   Abuse may take the form of physical violence, threats of violence, verbal abuse, sexual harassment, prolonged or unpleasant assault.

4.5   It is recognised that too often members of staff persevere with diffi-cult clients beyond the point of reasonableness. This is because of their sense of responsibility and because they are concerned about what will happen to the client if they complain.

4.6   Sometimes it is not easy to discuss how you are feeling about the abuse you may be suffering. However, if you feel that you have suf-fered abuse from either a client or his/her family member, then you must notify your manager as soon as possible.

4.7   Your manager's role is to assist you in feeling safe in your work and to support you if issues of abuse arise. It is reasonable for you to expect to be informed of the circumstances of any client that you are attending.

4.8   It is important that full recording of incidents takes place and you will be asked by your manager to complete an Abuse at Work form. This will enable your manager to keep client records up to date and, if necessary, keep colleagues informed.

4.9   *Your rights*

4.9.1   You can insist on a second member of staff accompanying you when visiting a client if you feel concerned or threatened.

4.9.2   You can ask for an urgent review/assessment of your client if you feel at risk/unsure.

4.9.3   Should you find yourself in a difficult/threatening situation you have the right to withdraw immediately from the client's home.

4.9.4   Where assistance is required urgently, you can call the police. Advise your manager if you do so.

5 Confidentiality

5.1   All Home-Care staff are in a position of trust. This is particularly important where they have access to personal information relating to clients. Home-Care staff spend most of their time in clients' homes and see a great many different people in the course of their duties.

5.2   It is particularly important that you understand the following STATEMENT ON CONFIDENTIALITY and how this relates to the way that you do your work.

  5.2.1 Home-Care staff will, in the course of their duties, have access to a considerable amount of personal information relating to clients.

  5.2.2 It is expected that all staff understand the importance of treating information in a discreet and confidential manner.

  5.2.3 Written records and correspondence must be kept securely at all times when not being used by a member of staff.

  5.2.4 No information regarding clients may be disclosed either orally or in writing to unauthorised persons, especially to other clients.

  5.2.5 Sometimes people ring up to seek information about clients. If this happens, refer them to your manager.

  5.2.6 Conversations relating to confidential matters affecting clients should not take place in situations where they may be overheard by passers-by, ie in public places.

  5.2.7 Any breach of confidentiality may be regarded as misconduct and the subject of serious disciplinary action.

  5.2.8 This means that all information that you become aware of about your clients should not be discussed with anyone other than your manager.

5.3   The Department also has an Open Files policy, which means clients have a right to see what is written about them. If you are recording something on progress notes about a client or leaving a note, always be aware of what you are writing and try to be accurate and objective. If you are stating how you feel or what you think, make this clear.

   Never promise a client that you will not say anything to your manager. You have a duty to report all information relating to your client's condition.

5.4.   Any records in clients' homes should be returned to your manager at once should the client die or move away.

6 Dealing with Abnormal Situations

6.1   These procedure guidelines have been prepared in order to try to provide guidance for staff dealing with unusual situations. The following is a list of possible reasons why you may need to seek support/advice from your manager.

6.2   *No entry*

   If client normally opens the door and you cannot gain entry:

  6.2.1 Check neighbours to see if they have any information on client's whereabouts, eg gone to hospital.

  6.2.2 Check to see if client is visible, eg through windows, back doors, letter box, etc.

  6.2.3 If not, phone your manager. If it is decided to call Emergency Services you may be required to wait at the premises, in which case discuss completion of duties for other clients with your manager.

  6.2.4 Ensure that situation is reported to the next Home Carer who will visit the client.

6.3   *Death of client*
If you arrive and find your client has died:
6.3.1   Phone 999 and ask for an ambulance.
6.3.2   Phone manager to advise of situation.
6.3.3   If client is taken away before you leave the premises:
    (a)   Make house secure, windows, doors, etc.
    (b)   Put out any rubbish.
    (c)   Empty commode, if appropriate.
    (d)   Deal with perishable food and fridge.
    (e)   Make sure lights and fires are off.
    (f)   Do not remove any property or cash from the dwelling.
6.3.4   Report position to manager.
6.4   *Collapse of client*
6.4.1   Make client comfortable wherever he/she is.
6.4.2   *Do not attempt to lift.*
6.4.3   Call ambulance 999.
6.4.4   If taken to hospital, ensure client takes keys to house, money and pension book and any other personal belongings that may be required, eg toiletries. You must not take responsibility for any money or property.
6.4.5   Follow procedure as 6.3.3.
6.4.6   Advise manager.
6.5   *No supplies of services, eg, Gas, Electric, etc*
6.5.1   If the client is not requiring attention but circumstances dictate that client cannot remain at home, eg no heating, flooded, burst pipes, house not safe, etc., report situation to your manager (out of hours). If the client cannot stay in the premises, ask your manager to assess for admission to emergency bed.
6.5.2   Discuss with your manager who should remain with client.
6.6   *Need assistance with client*
6.6.1   *Medical* Bleep District Nursing Sister on duty via [name of hospital and telephone number] or call GP.
6.6.2   *Non-medical* eg, difficulty with mobility requiring additional assistance, contact your manager.
6.6.3   Report action taken to your manager.
6.6.4   Report to next shift.

7 Other General Conditions of Service
7.1   *Parking fines/tickets*
These cannot be paid by the Council or the agency employing you.
7.2   *Identity cards*
All Home-Care workers must have a photo identity card. You should always present it to your clients for inspection or draw their attention to it at the beginning of every visit. This is especially important for forgetful clients or when you are visiting new clients or covering a client on a temporary basis. If you lose your card, tell your manager immediately.
7.3   *Smoking*
You must not smoke on duty unless you have the client's permission.
    The Council has a no-smoking policy for staff working in its offices and establishments. Therefore, if you attend a meeting/supervision session, you must not smoke.

7.4   *Taking others with you to clients' homes*
You must not take anyone on duty with you, including animals or children.

7.5   *Your possessions*
Always keep your possessions secure and separate from those of your clients while working.

7.6   *Financial matters*
When handling clients' money, this places you in an important position of trust. You need to account for all dealings involving clients' cash to avoid any misunderstandings and to protect the interests of both you and your client.

7.6.1   Do not handle large sums of money at any one time. Try to pay large bills in stages. If in doubt, consult your manager. Obtain receipts.

7.6.2   When collecting pensions and/or shopping, always write the amount collected and spent on the back of your time-sheet. Always obtain receipts.

7.6.3   *Never remove clients' money, pension books, bills, etc. and take them home with you.*

7.6.4   You must not collect more than two weeks' pension at any one time.

7.6.5   Under no circumstances should money be borrowed from or lent to clients.

7.7   *Wills/gifts to staff*
NEVER BECOME INVOLVED WITH MAKING WILLS FOR CLIENTS. ALWAYS TELL YOUR MANAGER IF ANY REQUESTS TO DO SO ARE MADE. YOU MUST NEVER ACCEPT MONEY OR GIFTS DURING OR AFTER THE LIFETIME OF CLIENTS FOR WHATEVER REASON. YOU MUST ADHERE TO THIS STRICT POLICY IF YOU WISH TO REMAIN EMPLOYED IN THE PROVISION OF SERVICES FOR THE COUNCIL.

7.8   *Client's absence from home*
You must never enter a client's home when he/she is not there. If a client has to leave, then so must you. In exceptional cases and only with the permission of your manager and the client will you be allowed to undertake essential tasks within the home in the client's absence. The client will also have to nominate someone to be present if this needs to happen.

7.9   *Accusations of theft*
Unfortunately, there are times when clients accuse Home-Care staff of stealing money, possessions, etc. This is obviously distressing and unpleasant. If you are accused by your client, inform your manager immediately. Clients are always advised to contact the police. If you are interviewed by a police officer, you should notify your manager immediately. Remember your rights as a citizen must be observed.

7.10   *Clients' laundry*
This must not be done in your own home.

7.11   *Cleaning common areas*
Where clients share amenities, eg hallways, bathrooms, etc, Home-Care staff can take the client's turn in cleaning these areas.

7.12   *Cleaning unused/spare rooms*
Do not spend time cleaning areas that are not lived in or are infrequently used by the client.

7.13 *Cleaning rooms inhabited by other people*
Home-Care staff will not clean the rooms of other adults living in the household.

7.14 *Tasks outside the home*
You must not undertake gardening duties for clients. However, as part of an agreed care plan you may escort a client to a day centre, club, etc.

8 Charges for Home-Care Service

8.1 *Home-Care service*
The Council provides its Home-Care service on the understanding that clients are charged for services received according to their financial circumstances. When assessing clients, Home-Care Officers will ask clients to complete a Financial Assessment Form (or a nominated person if the client is unable to do so).

8.2 *Minimum charge/stamp card clients*
After an initial assessment, clients will be asked to pay a set amount each week—the cost of the Home-Carer stamp—regardless of how much help they have.

8.2.1 Clients will be issued with a stamp card by the Council.

8.2.2 After the Home-Care Service has been provided, the stamp should be affixed to the appropriate week-ending square shown on the stamp card and signed over by the client. If a stamp is not available, the client should still be asked to sign the appropriate week-ending square to confirm the service was provided. When the stamp is subsequently purchased, it should be affixed to this square and signed over by the client to confirm payment has been made.

8.2.3 The client should be encouraged to purchase the stamps regularly. However, in the event of non-payment on more than three occasions, the card should be withdrawn and handed to your manager, who will contact the client with a view to resolving the matter. If you feel your client has a problem with payment, contact your manager straight away. Some clients cancel the service when they are in financial difficulty even though they badly need the help.

8.2.4 At the end of the accounting period shown on the last week-ending square, the card should be returned to your manager, who will issue a new stamp card for each stamp-paying client. If at this time any of your clients are in arrears, please ensure that this card is handed in to your manager so that the arrears can be entered on the new card in the payments-outstanding panel.

8.2.5 When clients purchase stamp(s) in payment of any arrears shown in the payments-outstanding panel, they should be affixed to the appropriate square in that panel and signed over as usual.

8.2.6 'Lost' cards must be reported as soon as possible so that a replacement can be issued. In the event of a 'lost' card being found at a later date, it must be returned to your manager.

8.2.7 Stamps must be purchased and fixed to stamp cards however long you spend with your client or whatever task is undertaken, eg just shopping.

8.2.8 If you have any concerns/difficulties, contact your manager straight away.

9 Hypothermia
9.1   *The main causes of hypothermia are:*
(a) exposure to cold;
(b) insufficient insulation against cold (eg inadequate clothing, malnutrition);
(c) lack of physical activity;
(d) Underlying disease, especially as in diseases of the brain, spine or skin which affect body-temperature control;
(e) drugs and poisons, eg alcohol.
9.2   *How to recognise hypothermia*
(a) The client is usually pale in appearance but can sometimes be pink.
(b) On touching the client's forehead you receive a cold sensation. If you touch the abdomen and this also feels cold, then this indicates a strong possibility of hypothermia.
(c) A mouth temperature of 96°F (35.6°C) or below.
(d) A rectal temperature of 96°F (35.6°C) or below.
(e) Speech may be slurred.
(f) Muscles may be rigid.
9.3   *How to prevent hypothermia*
9.3.1 Encourage adequate heating in one room at least (65–75°F 18–24°C).
9.3.2 Encourage elderly people to move around throughout the day as much as possible.
9.3.3 Encourage a good diet. At least one hot meal a day and frequent hot drinks.
9.3.4 Encourage the wearing of several layers of lightweight, comfortable clothing.
9.3.5 To ensure the maintenance of a reasonable temperature, see if any easy draughtproofing measures can be carried out (eg newspaper under carpet to prevent cold air coming up through the floorboards).
9.3.6 If only one room in the home is adequately heated, those at risk should be encouraged to sleep in that room. Otherwise the bedroom should be heated before going to bed and before getting dressed in the morning.
9.3.7 The bed itself should be heated, ideally with an electric overblanket *or* by a covered hot-water bottle (but not both).
9.3.8 Encourage the wearing of extra clothes in bed. (One third of body heat is lost through the head and so a night-cap, though comical, is an excellent aid to warmth, as are bedsocks and gloves.)
9.3.9 If heating appliances appear dangerous, they should be checked by an expert and, if necessary, replaced or repaired. People on Income Support are entitled to financial help to meet the cost of the repair or replacement of essential appliances.
9.4   *What to do in an emergency*
9.4.1 Call GP or 999.

9.4.2 The temperature of the client should only be raised gradually—do not give alcohol or very hot drink or very hot water bottle.

9.4.3 If available, wrap client in hypothermia or space blanket. Aluminium cooking foil is a good substitute.

9.4.4 Wrap client with blankets not forgetting to cover head and hands.

9.4.5 Try to avoid touching the client too much.

9.4.6 Try to get the client in a horizontal position.

10 Elsans/Commodes

10.1 When setting up the Elsan, follow instructions on Elsan bottle. These must be adhered to in all cases.

10.2 Always ensure there is an adequate supply of Elsan fluid. Replace the container before it becomes empty.

10.2.1 The Council does not supply Elsan fluid to all clients.

10.3 Elsans should be emptied twice a week or as often as is needed depending on the needs of the client.

10.3.1 Always empty the Elsan into a toilet—never into an outside drain (as stated above, this should be done twice a week).

10.3.2 Elsans and commodes should be cleaned thoroughly after emptying. This also applies to the housing container.

10.3.3 If clients have supports to enable them to use the Elsan, these also must be cleaned.

10.4 Remember
   (a) Keep fluid out of the way of children and animals.
   (b) The blue dye will stain linoleum, carpet, etc. Stand container on newspaper.
   (c) Always follow instructions on container.
   (d) If the Elsan is too heavy to lift alone, contact your Home-Care Officer.
   (e) Always wear protective clothing when dealing with Elsans.

Schedule I: Appendix Two

Person Specification for Home-Carer

	Essential	Desirable
1 Physical make-up	Good physical health and fitness	
2 Attainments		
(i) Educational	Fair standards as could be required to undertake future strategy or report in assessment writing	Pre-entry Social Services course
(ii) Occupational	Vehicle owner and driver	
(iii) Experience	Voluntary work or family care of elderly relative. Able to participate in the initiation of care plans. Must feel confident in budgeting and be financially aware	
3 General intelligence	Be able to benefit from training	

	Essential	Desirable
4 Special aptitudes	Good interpersonal skills	Communication skills, good verbal and behavioural communication
		Craft skills to undertake or teach
5 Disposition	Strong motivation to work in the community	Motivation for personal development
	Must be committed to independent living for clients	Concerned but practical
	Able to work as part of a team	Able to take initiatives on behalf of clients
	Able to work without immediate supervision of colleague support	Caring of human issues
		Has positive attitudes to ageing and independence of clients • risk taking • sexuality • incontinence • death • rights of individuals • residential/day/home rehabilitative care
6 Other factors	Understanding and commitment to Council's equal opportunities policy	Potential for future development

Schedule I: Appendix Three

Council Policy on Home-Care

CONTENTS

1 Aims of the Home-Care Service
2 Philosophy of the Home-Care Service
3 Criteria for Service
4 Operational Principles of the Home-Care Service
5 Operational Standards

1 Aims of the Home-Care Service

1.1   To provide service for people who have lost, either temporarily or permanently, the ability to carry out, or the means whereby others carry out on their behalf, key tasks and responsibilities necessary for independent living. Such people must have a home to live in or the promise of one. This service should be available for all client groups.

1.2   To encourage and assist clients to achieve an optimum level of independence.

1.3   To enable people who wish to remain in their own homes to do so.

1.4   To enable people living in institutions to move into more appropriate accommodation.

1.5   To respond to the service users' (clients') personal needs as well as their practical ones.

1.6   To provide a service which is sensitive to the service users' (clients')
       culture, disability, race or religion.

2 Philosophy of the Home-Care Service

2.1   The philosophy of the service is based upon six major values:

2.1.1   *Equity* People with similar needs should get the same stan-
         dard of care, regardless of where they live in the borough.

2.1.2   *Accessibility* Everyone should have ready access to the ser-
         vices they need, when they need them. People with differ-
         ent needs (eg those from a different race, culture or who
         speak a different language) should not be put at any disad-
         vantage.

2.1.3   *Effectiveness* From the perspective of the service users
         throughout, the service should meet their needs in the best
         possible way.

2.1.4   *Efficiency* The service should be organised and delivered in a
         way that gives the best value for money.

2.1.5   *Appropriateness* The service should meet local needs, and be
         flexible enough to cope with any need for change.

2.1.6   *Responsiveness* Within the framework of the criteria, the
         service should reflect what the service users want and
         expect.

3 Criteria for Service

3.1   Those who are eligible for the service are:

3.1.1   Service users who wish to remain at home and who might
         otherwise be admitted to residential/hospital care or would
         be at risk in the community and who need personal, practi-
         cal and emotional support and care.

3.1.2   Service users will need help in a number of areas:
         (a) personal care tasks
         (b) shopping and ancillary tasks
         (c) household tasks

3.1.3   The service will aim to ensure that those service users who
         are most at risk of residential care will be those service
         users/clients whose allocation of help most closely matches
         their assessed need. Provision will depend on the available
         resources and on other support available.

3.2   The service cannot provide:

3.2.1   Nursing care; this is the responsibility of the Health Author-
         ity.

3.2.2   Assistance for people who are lonely or isolated but who do
         not need help with tasks on the list. In such cases the Depart-
         ment will refer to the voluntary sector.

3.2.3   Care for people who only need assistance with domestic
         cleaning unless they would be deemed to be vulnerable of
         falling into the above categories without it. Where people are
         not deemed to be vulnerable, the Department will advise
         them of private domestic agencies available.

3.2.4   A night service (ie before 7.00am and after 10.00pm) except
         in extra care sheltered housing blocks and the departmental
         Crisis Intervention Team.

4 Operational Principles of the Home-Care Service
4.1　The service will operate within the Authority and Departmental poli-
　　　cies relating to:
　　　(a)　relationships with other Local Authority Services,
　　　(b)　relationships with health services,
　　　(c)　equal opportunities,
　　　(d)　relief/rotas,
　　　(e)　race and other minority ethnic issues,
　　　(f)　access to records,
　　　(g)　training/development,
　　　(h)　record-keeping and care planning.
4.2　The service will operate according to 20 major operational princi-
　　　ples:
　　　4.2.1　*Choice* The opportunity for service users to select indepen-
　　　　　　dently from a range of options offered to them.
　　　4.2.2　*Rights* The maintenance of all entitlements associated with
　　　　　　citizenship.
　　　4.2.3　*Fulfilment* The realisation of personal aspirations and abili-
　　　　　　ties in all aspects of daily life.
　　　4.2.4　*Independence* Opportunities to think and act without refer-
　　　　　　ence to another person, including a willingness to incur a
　　　　　　degree of calculated risk.
　　　4.2.5　*Privacy* The service user's right to be alone or undisturbed
　　　　　　and to be free from intrusion or public attention in relation
　　　　　　to his/her affairs.
　　　4.2.6　*Dignity* A recognition of the intrinsic value of people regard-
　　　　　　less of circumstances by respecting their uniqueness and their
　　　　　　personal needs.
　　　4.2.7　*Confidentiality* The maintenance of appropriate discretion
　　　　　　about all aspects of service users' personal affairs.
　　　4.2.8　*Equity* The meeting of identical needs with the same stan-
　　　　　　dard of care, regardless of where service users live or their
　　　　　　circumstances.
　　　4.2.9　*Accessibility* The ease of gaining information regarding pro-
　　　　　　vision of, and the absence of physical or administrative bar-
　　　　　　riers to, the service.
　　　4.2.10　*User involvement* The right for service users to be involved in
　　　　　　all decisions affecting their lives.
　　　4.2.11　*Responsiveness* Reflecting what the service users want and
　　　　　　expect within the framework of criteria for service.
　　　4.2.12　*Continuity and consistency* The maintenance of consistency
　　　　　　of service regardless of changes in workers and the minimum
　　　　　　number of changes in workers allocated to service users.
　　　4.2.13　*Reliability* A commitment to providing the service as speci-
　　　　　　fied.
　　　4.2.14　*Redress* Providing opportunities for service users to give
　　　　　　feedback about the service they receive.
　　　4.2.15　*Staff support* Ensuring that staff are suitably prepared for the
　　　　　　tasks they are asked to perform.
　　　4.2.16　*Integration* Uniting with other agencies to ensure the widest
　　　　　　possible choice with the greatest ease of access to other ser-
　　　　　　vices.

4.2.17 *Efficiency* The organisation of delivery of service to give the best value for money.

4.2.18 *Intensiveness* The direction of the service is towards the provision of intensive care for service users with high dependency needs.

4.2.19 *Prioritisation* The first priority for the service should be those service users who, for reason of physical and/or mental frailty, need services for life preservation and/or who without these services would require residential care and also their carers.

5 Operational Standards

5.1 *Choice*

The service should actively seek to enable service users to exercise as much choice as possible about the content of their lives.

5.1.1 The service will recognise the inherent value to service users' well-being of being able to exercise choice about the content of their daily lives.

5.1.2 The service will assess service users' physical and mental capacities, and knowledge of the extent to which each person wishes and is able to make choices.

5.1.3 The service will ensure that service users have adequate information on which to base decisions.

5.1.4 The service will facilitate and encourage service users to exercise choice regarding personal affairs, care and lifestyle in the context of an agreed notion of acceptable risk and constraints of community life.

5.1.5 The service's aim is to create a physical environment in which service users can be safe from hazards and can be referred for aids for their disabilities, so that inaccessibility or fear of accidents should not limit scope for exercising choice.

5.1.6 The service will provide safeguards to ensure that any limitations placed on the users' right to exercise choice are explained, justified and reviewed regularly.

5.1.7 The service provided will be selected from a range of options as an informed choice by the service user, with involvement of relatives and other advisers as appropriate to his or her ability to exercise choice.

5.1.8 The service will provide mechanisms for monitoring its performance in safeguarding service users' rights to make choices.

5.2 *Rights*

The service should seek to safeguard human rights, defined as 'the maintenance of all entitlements associated with citizenship'.

5.2.1 The service will ensure that safeguards exist to guarantee that service users are not subjected to inhuman or degrading treatment, whether physical or mental.

5.2.2 The service will ensure that freedom of expression is encouraged.

5.2.3 The service will ensure that service users' rights to liberty are safeguarded.

5.2.4 The service will respect the service users' private and family life, their individuality, confidentiality of personal affairs and personal space.

5.2.5   The service will ensure that information to service users is supplied and apply appropriate types and levels of support to encourage and enable them to exercise their rights.

5.2.6   The service will safeguard individual rights without discrimination on any grounds, whether gender, age, race, sexuality, colour, language, status or political or other opinion.

5.2.7   The service will ensure that where it is deemed necessary to interfere with or restrict an individual's rights (for the protection of that person or the rights and freedom of others, or for any other reasons) such actions are recorded, explained to the individual and other interested parties and reviewed regularly according to an agreed procedure.

5.2.8   The service will have mechanisms for monitoring its performance in safeguarding service users' rights.

5.3   *Fulfilment*

The service should seek to assist service users in the 'realisation of personal aspirations and abilities in all aspects of daily life'.

5.3.1   The service will endeavour to learn the background of service users and the skills and interests that they retain.

5.3.2   The service will help service users to continue to use such skills and follow such interests, if they so wish, and to aspire to new ones.

5.3.3   The service will foster the maintenance of established personal relationships and help to facilitate new ones, where so desired.

5.3.4   The service should build on service users' positive features, such as experience and knowledge, rather than merely 'manage' negative features such as confusion or physical incapacity.

5.3.5   The service will help service users to use their physical and mental faculties, within the limit of their abilities and wishes, but recognise and cater for those who have no wish to be active or sociable.

5.3.6   The service should endeavour to understand and cater for the emotional needs of service users.

5.3.7   The service will encourage and enable service users to participate in making decisions about their own lifestyle in so far as they are willing and able to do so.

5.3.8   The service will help to create a stimulating environment according to service users' wishes and assist with referrals to appropriate supporting services.

5.3.9   The service will ensure that it is flexible and able to adapt and develop as service users' needs change.

5.3.10 The service will have mechanisms for monitoring its performance in safeguarding service users' rights to fulfilment.

5.4   *Independence*

The service should provide service users 'with opportunities to think and act without reference to another person, including a willingness to incur a degree of calculated risk'. The service should aim to actively help service users to achieve a level of independence compatible with their wishes and abilities.

5.4.1 The service will endeavour to have some knowledge of service users' previous lifestyles and consult with them and their relatives/advisers so as to understand their expectations and wishes regarding independence.

5.4.2 The service will help and encourage service users to think and act independently as far as this is compatible with their own abilities, their impact on other people, the constraints of community life and the risks involved.

5.4.3 The service will encourage and enable users to participate in making decisions about their lifestyle and the running of their home in so far as they wish and are able to do so.

5.4.4 The service will ascertain the views of service users about any proposed action that would affect their lifestyle in their home.

5.4.5 The service will advise and assist in providing a physical environment that enables service users to do as much as possible for themselves without having to rely on staff assistance or having things done for them.

5.4.6 The service will monitor each service user's condition and behaviour so as to ensure that a reasonable balance is achieved between independence and risk-taking.

5.4.7 The service should create safeguards to ensure that any limitations placed on service users' scope to act independently are explained, justified, recorded and reviewed regularly.

5.4.8 The service will have mechanisms for monitoring its performance in safeguarding service users' rights to independence.

5.5 *Privacy*
The service should seek to safeguard the service users' 'right to be alone or undisturbed and to be free from intrusion or public attention in relation to his/her affairs'.

5.5.1 The service will have some knowledge of service users' previous lifestyles so as to understand their expectations regarding personal privacy.

5.5.2 The service will enable service users to have conversation, make or receive telephone calls, correspond and receive visitors without being overlooked or overheard and without having to account to anyone for their actions.

5.5.3 The service will ensure that where staff assistance is required to enable service users to dress, bathe, wash or use the toilet, this is kept to the minimum commensurate with service users' abilities and is performed with due regard to the need for safe guarding the privacy of the individual.

5.5.4 The service will ensure that staff deal discreetly with the affairs of service users and safeguard the confidentiality of information held about them.

5.5.5 The service will create safeguards to ensure that any erosion of privacy that is considered by management to be necessary in order to provide essential care for individuals is explained, justified, recorded and reviewed regularly.

5.5.6 The service will have mechanisms for monitoring its performance in safeguarding the service users' right to privacy.

5.6   *Dignity*

The service should pay due regard to the 'recognition of the intrinsic value of people regardless of circumstances by respecting their uniqueness and their personal needs'.

5.6.1   The service will establish a clear policy that will ensure the maintenance of dignity, in both life and death.

5.6.2   The service will involve people in making decisions for themselves, including those where risk is involved, and involving relatives and other agencies as appropriate.

5.6.3   The service will recognise the whole person as he/she is now in the context of his/her previous life experiences.

5.6.4   The service will recognise and cater for cultural needs and norms in both life and death.

5.6.5   The service will take the view of those receiving the service in establishing practices related to their needs rather than those of staff.

5.6.6   The service will respect and safeguard privacy and confidentiality.

5.6.7   The service will receive and act on views of service users.

5.6.8   The service will respond sensitively and promptly to any complaints from service users, their relatives or carers.

5.6.9   The service will approach the ownership and maintenance of necessary documentation with openness and availability to the person concerned. Where limitations are necessary, they will be explained, justified, recorded and reviewed regularly.

5.6.10 The service will have mechanisms for monitoring its performance in safeguarding the service users' rights to dignity.

5.7   *Confidentiality*

The service should maintain 'appropriate discretion about all aspects of service users' personal affairs'.

5.7.1   The service should protect and reflect the confidentiality of the personal affairs of service users.

5.7.2   The service will ensure that staff are aware of the policy on confidentiality.

5.7.3   The service will ensure that service users are informed of the policy.

5.7.4   The service will have mechanisms for monitoring its performance in safeguarding confidentiality.

5.8   *Equity*

The service should ensure that people with similar needs should get the same standard of care, regardless of where they live in the borough.

5.8.1   The service will ensure that resources are evenly distributed.

5.8.2   The service should ensure that resources are allocated in similar ways across the borough.

5.8.3   The service will ensure that staff are trained, supported and instructed in similar ways across the borough.

5.8.4   The service will ensure that service users are not discriminated against on any grounds.

5.8.5   The service will ensure that policies are interpreted in similar ways across that borough.

5.8.6 The service will have mechanisms for monitoring its performance in safeguarding equity.

5.9 *Accessibility*

The service should ensure that information regarding provision is readily available in whatever form service users require, and that there are no physical or administrative barriers to gaining the service.

5.9.1 The service will ensure that service users have access to adequate information regarding the provision of services.

5.9.2 The service will ensure that this information is adequately communicated to other agencies.

5.9.3 The service will ensure that all relevant material is available in a full range of languages.

5.9.4 The service will ensure that all material is offered in a manner that is acceptable to all cultures.

5.9.5 The service will have mechanisms for monitoring its performance in safeguarding accessibility.

5.10 *User involvement*

The service should ensure that there is opportunity for service users to be involved in all decisions affecting their lives unless there are demonstrable reasons why this is not possible or appropriate.

5.10.1 The service will ensure that service users are involved in their assessment for service.

5.10.2 The service will ensure that written care plans are developed in consultation with service users and other members of their caring network to facilitate clarity of understanding, expectations and individuality.

5.10.3 The service will ensure that service users are involved in the arrangements regarding provision of specific services.

5.10.4 The service will ensure that service users are responded to appropriately when complaining.

5.10.5 The service will ensure that service users are included in quality assurance processes.

5.10.6 The service will have mechanisms for monitoring its performance in safeguarding the appropriate use of care plans and the service users' involvement.

5.11 *Responsiveness*

The service should, within the framework of the criteria for service, reflect what the service users want and expect.

5.11.1 The service will ensure that arrangements are made for keeping service users informed of changes in their service.

5.11.2 The service will ensure that service users are assessed as quickly as possible after the referral is made.

5.11.3 The service will ensure that commencement of service delivery is made as quickly as possible after assessment.

5.11.4 The service will ensure that services can be delivered across the full range of day-time hours (ie between 7.00am and 10.00pm).

5.11.5 The service will ensure that it can make arrangements to meet special needs where appropriate.

5.11.6 The service will specify clearly which tasks cannot be undertaken with recorded explanation and justification.

5.11.7 The service will have mechanisms for monitoring its performance in responsiveness.

5.12 *Continuity and Consistency*
The service should provide maximum continuity and consistency in
terms of staff and service supplied.

5.12.1 The service will ensure that allocation of staff processes
maximise continuity and consistency of staff.

5.12.2 The service will ensure that all staff attending are aware of
the assessed needs and requirements of the service users.

5.12.3 The service will ensure that staff are trained and supported
consistently.

5.12.4 The service will have mechanisms for monitoring its performance in continuity and consistency.

5.13 *Reliability*
The service should ensure that there is commitment to providing the
service as specified to the service users.

5.13.1 The service should communicate clearly to service users what
they should expect from the service.

5.13.2 The service will ensure that service users receive the level of
cover they are expecting/needing.

5.13.3 The service will ensure that cover is provided as frequently as
expected/needed.

5.13.4 The service will have mechanisms for monitoring its performance in reliability.

5.14 *Redress*
The service should ensure that service users, carers, relatives and
other agencies are able to give feedback about the service they
receive and be sure that they will be listened to.

5.14.1 The service will ensure that it consults service users about significant aspects of their daily life.

5.14.2 The service will ensure that service users feel able to raise
matters of concern in relating to the service.

5.14.3 The service will ensure that service users know how to make
a complaint.

5.14.4 The service will ensure that it responds in a proper manner
when a service user complains.

5.14.5 The service will ensure that complaints procedures are
known, accessible and responsive.

5.14.6 The service will ensure that staff are suitably trained to
engage in redress processes.

5.14.7 The service will have clear procedures for addressing complaints by service users and carers about any aspect of the
service or the provision of the service.

5.14.8 The service will have mechanisms in place for monitoring
complaints and its performance in providing redress.

5.15 *Staff Support*
The service should take appropriate steps to ensure that staff are
suitably prepared for the tasks they are asked to perform.

5.15.1 The service will ensure that its recruitment processes
appoint appropriate staff to maintain high levels of service
delivery within an equal opportunities framework.

5.15.2 The service will have a written induction and training strategy for staff (including managers and frontline staff) and defined training objectives.

5.15.3 The strategy will reflect the job specifications.

5.15.4 The service will ensure that staff are encouraged to participate in appropriate training activities.

5.15.5 The service will ensure that new staff are provided with basic information on their role in the community and home environment, eg confidentiality, health and safety, professional responsibilities, etc.

5.15.6 The service will ensure that all staff are given equal access to induction and training opportunities regardless of the hours or times that they work, their gender, age, race, sexuality, colour, language, religion, status or political or other opinion.

5.15.7 The service will ensure that staff have guidance notes on good practice that identify the expected standards.

5.15.8 The service will provide for all staff support, development and involvement in decision-making.

5.15.9 The service will ensure that staff receive appropriate level of support and supervision.

5.15.10 The service will ensure that training is integrated with that of other agencies.

5.15.11 The service will ensure that staff are able to demonstrate awareness of the philosophy, values and expectations of the department.

5.15.12 The service will ensure that managers and staff keep abreast of current developments and legislation in the field of social care.

5.15.13 The service should have a method of evaluating the competence of staff.

5.15.14 The service will ensure that management value the contribution of all staff to the running of the service, taking account of their views about future development and design.

5.15.15 The service will have a mechanism for monitoring its performances in recruiting, training and developing staff.

5.16 *Integration with Other Agencies*

The service should be integrated with other agencies to ensure the widest possible choice with the greatest ease of access to other services.

5.16.1 The service should ensure that appropriate personnel from health service, private and voluntary sector agencies contribute to assessments and reviews.

5.16.2 The service will receive and send referrals to the full range of services, paying due regard to confidentiality, in consultation with the service users and other members of their caring network.

5.16.3 The service should ensure that other agencies understand the role and function of the service.

5.16.4 The service should ensure that it keeps itself informed about the role and function of other services.

5.16.5 The service will have mechanisms for monitoring its performance in safeguarding integration with other agencies.

5.17 *Efficiency*
The service should be organised and delivered in a way that, in addition to being appropriate and sensitive, gives the best value for money.

    5.17.1 The service will ensure that it is delivered in the most economical way that is compatible with high quality standards of service delivery.

    5.17.2 The service will ensure that the highest number of client contact hours are produced to the standards specified within the budget provided.

    5.17.3 The service will ensure that staff are not engaged in undertaking tasks that can be delegated in a cost-effective and reasonable way.

    5.17.4 The service will have mechanisms for monitoring its efficiency.

5.18 *Intensiveness*
The service should ensure that resources are directed towards the provision of intensive care for service users with high dependency needs.

    5.18.1 The service will ensure that resources are prioritised towards the provision of intensive care.

    5.18.2 The service will ensure that resources are prioritised towards service users with high dependency needs.

    5.18.3 The service will have mechanisms for monitoring its provision of intensive care for service users with high dependency needs.

5.19 *Prioritisation*
The service should ensure that the first priority for the service should be those service users who, for reason of physical and/or mental frailty, need services for life preservation and/or who without these services would require residential care.

    5.19.1 The service should ensure that shortfall of service is directed towards low-priority tasks.

    5.19.2 The service should ensure that shortfall of service is directed towards service users with low dependency needs.

    5.19.3 The service will have mechanisms for monitoring its prioritisation of services.

LEGAL SERVICES SPECIFICATION EXAMPLE

CONTENTS

A Introduction

(a) General Description of Services Required
  (i) The Employer requires legal services in the following subject areas:
- Child Care
- Civil Litigation
- Conveyancing
- Criminal Litigation
- Planning

 (ii) These subject areas carry individual requirements detailed in section D below.
(iii) Requirements common to all subject areas are set out in Section C below.

(iv) Location
  1. Whilst the delivery of the services does not always require a local office, the capacity of the Contractor to be in attendance will be important for certain areas of work set out in Section D below.
  2. The Contractor's attendance at Council Offices will be required, at meetings; for access to the Council's Title Deeds and Documents; and for document collection and delivery.
  3. The Contractor will be required to indicate the location(s) from which services will be provided and other arrangements which it has made to comply with this part of the Specification.

(v) Accessibility of Fee Earners
  1. The Employer will require access to relevant partners and employees of the Contractor and detailed requirements are set out in section D below.
  2. The Instructions to Tenderer will require the Contractor to indicate in a Statement of Operation the arrangements which it has made to enable it to comply with this part of this Specification.

B. Preliminaries

(a) Client Arrangements and Monitoring

(i) Contract Supervisor
The Council's Contract Supervisor will:
  1. have overall responsibility for management and co-ordination of the Contract;
  2. liaise with the Contractor in respect of matters of overall performance and quality and will call and chair regular review meetings;
  3. be the first point of contact in the event of any problems arising as a consequence of the overall performance of the Contract;
  4. maintain the list of Client Officers for the Contract and other officers authorised on the council's behalf;
  5. analyse all complaints and performance reports;
  6. be responsible for reporting to the council on the performance of the contractor.

(ii) Client Officers
Unless other arrangements are notified in writing to the Contractor, day to day instructions under the Contract will be given by Client Officers who will deal with problems arising in individual cases. Any problem which cannot be resolved between Client Officers and the Contractor shall be referred to the Contract Supervisor.

(iii) Monitoring
  1. Performance of the Contract will be monitored by the Contract Supervisor to whom Client Officers will report on a regular basis.
  2. The Contractor will provide reports as required on progress and performance to the Contract Supervisor and appropriate Client

Officers for evaluation and such reports will be used at review meetings between the Contract Supervisor, Client Officers and the Contractor.

3. The Contract Supervisor and Client Officers may require additional meetings with the Contractor on matters of concern as necessary.

4. The Contract Supervisor will have unrestricted access to case files, which shall include any necessary supporting information in respect of the recoverable disbursements and where relevant, chargeable hours incurred by the Contractor in accordance with the Conditions of Contract.

5. The Contractor will supply the Contract Supervisor with copies of all instructions it receives from Client Officers within four working days of receipt.

6. The Contractor will provide details of its financial and management information systems in its Statement of Operation and general Method Statements.

(b) Conflicts of Interest

(i) The Contractors shall at all times in the provision of the Services act so as to avoid any conflict of interest arising between its duties and obligations as a Solicitor to the Employer and any other client for whom the Contractor is acting as a Solicitor. The Contractor shall, have particular regard to and comply at all times with such rules of professional conduct or guidance issued from time to time by the Law Society with regard to the avoidance of conflicts of interest.

(ii) The Contractor shall be required to accept any and all instructions issued by the council with regard to any of the subject areas within this Specification. The Contractor shall accordingly not accept any instructions from any other client which may cause the Contractor to be placed in a position where he would be unable to accept instructions from the council due to a conflict of interest with any such other client from whom instructions have previously been accepted. In the event that the Contractor is acting for any existing client with regard to any of the subject areas of the Specification, prior to the commencement of the Contract, he shall be required to cease to act for such existing other client forthwith.

(iii) The Contract Supervisor may at any time direct the Contractor to cease to act for any other client if in his view any conflict of interest exists or has arisen between the duties of the Contractor as a Solicitor to the council and to any such other client.

(iv) The Employer attaches particular importance to its Solicitor/Client relationship with the Contractor, given the nature and scale of the Contract for the provision of legal services to a major Local Authority. Accordingly, the Contractor shall also not act for any other client in the circumstances set out in Section D of the Specification, whether or not so to act would give rise to any conflict of interest.

(c) Work Volumes

The anticipated volumes of instructions based on historic data are indicated in the Pricing Schedule to be supplied with the tender documents but should be treated as indicative only. Actual volumes are not known and will depend on the level of support required by front line services, legislative changes, internal organisation changes and other factors.

(d) Pricing

(i)   The Contractor shall be paid the rates and prices contained in the Pricing Schedule in accordance with the Conditions of Contract.

(ii) Section D of the Specification indicates whether work is to be charged by reference to a unit price, an hourly rate, or a combination of both. Where any job type which comprises a contested matter is to be priced with reference to an hourly rate the Contractor shall only be entitled to receive an amount equivalent to the unit price, where applicable, payable in respect of that job type if uncontested, together with such amount charged with reference to the appropriate hourly rate as shall reflect the work reasonably incurred by the Contractor in addition to that arising in respect of such job type if uncontested.

(iii) The rates and prices shall form the entire and exclusive payments to which the Contractor shall be entitled in respect of any and all work required to deal properly and effectively with the particular matter in accordance with the requirements of the Specification including any advice which may be required to be given during the course of or in relation to the particular matter save where the Section D of the Specification provides for the payment to the Contractor of specified recoverable disbursements and the Contractor shall accordingly include in its rates and prices for all overheads, costs, travel time and any other expenditure incurred. No mark up will be allowed for care and conduct, nor any additional payment made for attendance at meetings, provision of management and financial information or for compliance with any instruction of the Contract Supervisor.

(iv) Where a particular matter is chargeable to the council on the basis of a unit rate and it for any reason fails to proceed to its ultimate conclusion through no fault of the Contractor (which shall include where the Contractor has issued advice that any such matter should not proceed any further), it shall receive such proportion of the relevant unit price as shall reflect the work reasonably incurred by it in respect of such matter and in those cases where the Contractor is to be paid by reference to an hourly rate it shall be entitled to receive the amount equal to the chargeable hours reasonably incurred by the Contractor for the relevant item of work multiplied by the appropriate hourly rate contained in the Pricing Schedule.

(e) Recoverable Disbursements

Recoverable disbursements are specifically identified in two categories in Section D of the Specification. The first can be incurred without prior approval. The second requires the prior approval of the Client Officer.

(f) Use of Counsel

(i)   The rates and prices to which the Contractor shall be entitled to payment in accordance with the Conditions of Contract shall be inclusive of the cost of any advocacy or other services of Counsel. The Contractor shall not be entitled to additional reimbursement in respect of the cost of instructing Counsel, save in the following circumstances:

1. Where the Contractor does not enjoy a right of audience before the Court or Tribunal before which the relevant matter is to be heard.
2. With the consent of the Contract Supervisor, such consent not to be unreasonably withheld, where the particular matter is of such complexity that it is expedient in the interests of the Employer that Counsel be instructed.
3. With the consent of the Contract Supervisor, such consent not to be unreasonably withheld, where the particular matter is likely to be of such duration that not to instruct Counsel would adversely affect the provision by the Contractor of the Service.
4. Where in his absolute discretion, the Contract Supervisor so approves or requires:

(ii) It will be reasonable for the Contract Supervisor to decline approval under paragraphs (g)(i)2 and 3 where complex issues of law arise which nevertheless should be capable of being dealt with by a Contractor with experience of local authority law, which would have traditionally been dealt with by in-house lawyers of the Employer and the use of Counsel would add to the cost of the case.

(iii) The Contract Supervisor may require the Contractor to instruct Counsel on any matter and the Contract Supervisor shall always have the right to specify the use of particular counsel or to identify counsel who shall not be used.

(iv) Where the use of Counsel is approved or required as aforesaid the Contractor shall seek the approval of the Client Officer before agreeing any Counsel's brief fee or fee for advice in excess of £500.00, and with the Contract Supervisor before agreeing any such fee in excess of £1000.00.

(v) In any case where Counsel is instructed by the Contractor, the name of counsel shall be immediately notified in writing to the Contract Supervisor and relevant Client Officer. This requirement shall also apply where there is a change of Counsel.

(vi) The Contractor shall withdraw any instructions/brief issued to Counsel to appear on behalf of the council upon receipt of any directions from the Contract Supervisor to that effect.

(vii) It shall be the duty of the Contractor to ensure that a person of sufficient experience in the relevant area of work, having regard to the complexity and subject matter of the particular case, shall attend upon Counsel. The Contract Supervisor may require somebody of a particular level of experience to attend upon Counsel or may stipulate the attendance of the particular fee earner to whom any matter has been allocated.

(viii) The Contractor may, with the leave of the council in such cases as may be permissible having regard to any rules or guidance with regard to professional conduct, brief Counsel to appear without any representative of the Contractor being in attendance, save that the Contractor shall be required to attend upon Counsel in accordance with the requirements of the above paragraph in any case where he is so directed by the Contract Supervisor, notwithstanding the provisions of this clause.

C. General Specification Requirements

(a) **Working Relationships**
 (i) The Contractor will be expected to develop close working partner-
      ships with Client Departments.
 (ii) The Contractor must demonstrate an understanding of the political
      complexion of the council; its policy objectives and become familiar
      with local circumstances which may be relevant to future decisions.

 1.   Positive Approach
 1.1   The Contractor must demonstrate a positive approach to all the
       council's activities. Legal advice and action must therefore pro-
       vide effective and constructive solutions rather than barriers to
       action whilst ensuring that the council remains firmly within the
       law.
 1.2   Advice and action must be tailored to the best interests of the
       council.
 1.3   The Contractor is to be familiar with the internal organisation
       of the council's departments, particularly those who are the
       direct client for the types of work included the Contract.
 1.4   In working for a local authority the contractor will have to
       respond to considerable fluctuations in demand and to changes
       arising from legislation and other local and national policy ini-
       tiatives. In particular the contractor will have a duty to advise
       Client Officers of changes in the law and prepare any necessary
       consequential amendments to standard documentation for
       approval by the Contract Supervisor.
 1.5   The Contractor will be expected to minimise any risks to the
       council. Any situation which may have implications for the lia-
       bility of the council shall be drawn immediately to its attention,
       and appropriate and timely advice given as to how such risk
       may be avoided or minimised.

 2.   General Local Authority Law and Specialist Knowledge
       In order to perform the Service required by the Employer, the
       Contractor will need to demonstrate that it has and can main-
       tain throughout the life of the contract, legal specialist skills,
       knowledge of local government law and practice, general prin-
       ciples of administrative law, and experience in all the Subject
       Area Specifications.

 3.   Client Care and Development of Service
 3.1   The Employer seeks a service provider which will work closely
       with the Client Officers to enable them to provide the most
       effective service to the public and other users.
 3.2   The Contractor will need to demonstrate a positive commit-
       ment to this type of approach and to the development of the ser-
       vices over the Contract period.

 4.   Corporate Responsibility
 4.1   The Contractor is reminded that the Contract provides for a
       solicitor/client relationship between itself and the council. The

individual Client Officers have delegated authority to issue instructions but they do so on behalf of the council and it is to the council that the duty of the Contractor ultimately lies.

4.2 The Contractor will be familiar with the statutory duties placed upon the Council's Monitoring Officer and shall have regard to such duties in the provision of the Service and the need to consider whether the attention of the Contract Supervisor should be drawn to any particular course of action which may be in contemplation by the council of which the Contractor becomes aware. The Contractor shall likewise have regard at all times in the provision of the Service to the corporate impact of the legal implications of any course of action taken or which may be in contemplation by the council. In such cases the matter shall be drawn to the attention of the Contract Supervisor. In the event of the council becoming the subject of any public law proceedings the Contractor shall identify the relevant Client Officer and advise immediately upon the effect of such proceedings upon any course of action proposed or being undertaken by the council.

4.3 The Contractor shall have regard to any advice given or action taken on behalf of the council by any other legal adviser. If in the exercise of its judgement it is concerned as to the implications of any such advice or action it shall refer the matter to the Contract Supervisor.

4.4 In any such case where the Contractor is required to draw any matter to the attention of the Contract Supervisor it shall notwithstanding the provisions of the Specification take no action with regard to any instructions issued by any Client Officer save for such interim action as may be necessary to protect the interests of the council until it has obtained appropriate instructions from the Contract Supervisor.

(b) Quality

 (i) The council is seeking a high quality, responsive legal service to enable it to deliver to its customers the policy objectives to which it is committed.

 (ii) The council will require the Contractor to demonstrate in its Statement of Operation and throughout the life of the Contract, that it operates quality control procedures acceptable to the council.

(iii) The Contractor will as a minimum be required to demonstrate compliance with the Law Society's Practice Management Standards as may be prescribed from time to time and shall satisfy the council that it is in all respects adequately resourced to meet the demands of the Contract.

(iv) In pursuance of the Contractor's obligations under this part of this Specification the Contract Supervisor may at any time require the Contractor to produce such information or afford access to its operations as will enable the council to be satisfied that it is adequately performing the Contract.

 (v) The Contractor shall ensure, throughout the duration of the Contract, that each job type is dealt with by a person suitably qualified and experienced to perform services of that nature, value and complexity.

(c) Requirements common to all worktypes

(i) The tasks and standards given below apply to all job types covered by Section D.

(ii) As indicated in the introduction, this Specification is not wholly prescriptive. In addition to the Contractor showing how it proposes to meet the prescribed standards, it shall where necessary propose more detailed or additional standards to meet the requirements of this Specification. The tasks relating to the Subject Areas and individual Job Types in particular are given in outline only and the Contractor shall provide Method Statements detailing the processes and stages it will follow to comply with the requirements of this Specification.

1.   Instructions

1.1   Instructions will be in an agreed standard form acceptable to the council. The Contractor shall produce a standard form of Instructions sheet for each Individual Method Statement.

1.2   Except where the Subject Area Specifications provide otherwise or the urgency of the situation requires, Instructions shall be in writing. Where verbal Instructions are permitted they will be confirmed in writing by the Contractor within one working day of receipt.

1.3   Instructions will be received either from a Client Officer or from such other designated person referred to in Section D below or as notified from time to time to the Contractor. A copy of the Instructions shall be sent by the Contractor to the Contract Supervisor within four working days of receipt.

1.4   The Contractor shall act expeditiously in dealing with Instructions. The Contractor shall be satisfied it is in receipt of all relevant information to enable it to achieve the council's objective and in the event that its Instructions are in any way inadequate it shall offer appropriate advice and obtain such additional Instructions as may be necessary from the Client Officer.

2.   Allocation of Work and Acknowledgment

2.1   Upon receipt of Instructions the matter shall be allocated to the appropriate partner or employee of the contractor and a new file opened with a unique reference number.

2.2   All instructions shall be acknowledged in writing and the Client Officer shall be notified of the appropriate partner or employee of the contractor responsible for that particular matter, together with the said partner or employee's reference.

2.3   Any partner or employee of the contractor to whom a matter is allocated shall be suitably experienced with regard to the nature of the particular matter, shall be responsible for the conduct of that matter and all communications with regard to such matter shall be addressed through that partner or employee.

2.4   The Contractor will be required to provide a system for receiving and allocating cases, identifying key staff and responsibilities. This is likely to vary from area to area and should be covered in the Contractor's General Method Statements.

2.5   The Contractor shall notify the Client Officer of any change of identity of the partner or employee of the contractor to whom the case has been allocated. The Contract Supervisor may where, in his judgement, the continued involvement of the original partner or employee is essential to the proper conduct of the matter require such partner or employee to continue to be responsible for that matter.

2.6 The Contractor shall have suitable arrangements to ensure that some other partner or employee suitably experienced in the work in question shall be responsible for those matters allocated to a particular partner or employee in the prolonged absence of such fee earner. (A prolonged absence shall be any period of absence in excess of 28 days or such other period as the Contract Supervisor shall prescribe).

2.7 The Contractor shall ensure that suitable arrangements exist for another appropriately experienced partner or employee to take immediate responsibility for the conduct of any urgent matter, in the short term absence of the partner or employee to whom a matter has been originally allocated.

3. Supervision Arrangements
The Contractor shall have in place effective arrangements for the supervision of all work performed.

4. Documentation of Progress
4.1 The Contractor shall undertake all steps necessary to ensure the matter is concluded and documented to the council's satisfaction.

4.2 The various steps required and undertaken should be clearly documented on the file on a summary sheet which shows sufficient details of work done in relation to each step. Evidence of each step shall also be maintained via other documentation such as correspondence, pleadings etc. Files should be kept in a tidy fashion with all documentation properly recorded in date order.

4.3 The Contractor must provide and agree with the council all the standard documentation to be used under the Contract.

4.4 Further details of the council's requirements are contained in Section D below.

5. Authorisation
5.1 The Contractor must always act in the best interests of the council and, accordingly, any instructions received which appear to be contrary to the council's interests either in their own right or in the light of information received from other sources must be referred to the Contract Supervisor and where there is a disagreement between the Contractor and the Client Officer, the Contract Supervisor's decision shall be final.

5.2 The Contractor must be familiar with the council's authorisation procedures and before completing any matter it must ensure that proper authority exists. The authority will consist either of the relevant Committee minute and report or an appropriate delegated authority to the relevant Client Officer or Contract Supervisor.

6.   **Enquiries from Council Members and Members of Parliament**

6.1   Verbal or written enquiries from a **Council Member** or Member of Parliament as to progress on a specific matter shall be dealt with as a matter of priority but the Client Officer and Contract Supervisor shall always be consulted before any response is given. The Contractor must familiarise itself with and apply the law relating to disclosure of information to Council Members. .

6.2   At no time shall the Contractor take instructions from a Council Member. If a Council Member attempts to give directions to the Contractor, the Contractor shall report immediately to the Client Officer and Contract Supervisor for further instructions.

7.   **Public Statements**

The Contractor shall not make any public statement or make any communication to the media with regard to anything within the subject matter of the contract without the express authorisation of the Contract Supervisor who may require any such statement or communication to be in such form as shall be prescribed.

8.   **Data Protection**

8.1   The Contractor shall be aware of and apply:
(a)   the law relating to data protection in all dealings on behalf of the council; and
(b)   the law relating to the rights of members of the public and press to have access to the council's information.

8.2   In the event of the council being required to afford access pursuant to the above rights any actual disclosure shall be effected only by the Contract Supervisor.

9.   **Safekeeping of Documents**

The Contractor shall provide in its Statement of Operations its procedure for the safe and confidential custody of the files, documents, and photocopies whilst in its possession and for the return of the entire file (which shall include all relevant correspondence and documentation) to the council immediately on completion of each matter.

10.   **Disclosure of Documents**

The Contractor shall not disclose any documents or any other item in the ownership of the council without the consent of the Client Officer save in those cases where the council is required by Court Order. The Contractor shall issue advice to the Client Officer as to whether or not it is appropriate in any particular case to seek to resist any disclosure which the council would in normal circumstances be required to make on the grounds of public interest immunity.

11.   **Receipt of Money**

The Contractor shall at all times comply with the council's procedures for receiving, handling and accounting for money.

D Subject Area Specification

Note: for each subject area (see A(a)(i) before) it will be necessary to specify nominated client officers, work tasks and standards, how instructions are to be delivered, how work is to be allocated and conducted, the basis of pricing, the qualifications of the partner as employee performing the tasks, the reports required by the client officer, provision and safekeeping of documents, decisions to be referred to the client officer, any special accounting or monetary arrangements, attendance at meetings, disbursements and costs. Finally it will be necessary to detail the tasks falling within the Subject Area.

SAMPLE TENDERING DOCUMENTATION

Reproduced by kind permission of the London Borough of Enfield

Conditions of Tendering

2 Contracts

1 The Tender shall be made on the Tender Form supplied herein, and shall be sent by registered post or recorded delivery, or delivered by hand, in a plain sealed envelope bearing no indication of the Tenderer's name marked on the envelope, addressed to the Borough Secretary and Solicitor   so as to arrive not later than NOON on   199 .

2 The Tender shall have attached to it the completed Certificate of Bona Fide Tender, the Declaration, the Conditions of Contract and schedules comprising the Specification, the priced Tender and these Instructions.

3 Unless stated otherwise, the Tender shall remain open for acceptance for a period of twenty-six weeks from the date of the Tender and the Tenderer shall make due allowance for this in the rates and prices inserted in the Tender.

4 If any unauthorised alterations, additions or omissions are made to any of the Contract Documents or if the Tender and Schedule of Rates are not properly complete or if these instructions are not followed, the tender may be rejected.

5 If the Tenderer fails to complete the Certificate of Bona Fide Tender, the Tender shall be rejected.

6 Tenders must be submitted strictly in accordance with the Contract Document, ie without qualifications. Any point of doubt or difficulty should be cleared with the Director of   as early as possible in the tender period.

7 Should any alterations, additions or omissions to the Contract Documents as issued to Tenderers be deemed necessary prior to the date of submission of Tenders, these shall be issued to Tenderers in the form of Supplementary Documents and shall form part of the Contract Documents.

8 Except insofar as may be directed in writing by the Director of   or the Deputy Director of   no agent

or servant in the Council's employ has any authority to make any representation or explanation to persons or corporations tendering or desirous of tendering as to the meaning of the Conditions of Contract, Specification, Tender or other documents, or as to anything to be done or not to be done by the accepted Tenderer, or as to these Instructions, or as to any other matter or thing, so as to bind the Employer or bind or fetter the judgement or discretion of the Director of under the Contract in the exercise of the powers and duties under the Contract.

9   **Tenderers should note that the Annual Sum required is a fixed annual price to be varied on the anniversary of the commencement date of the contract in line with the General Index of Retail Prices (All Items).**

10   Tenderers should note that tenders and supporting documents must be written in English.

11   Unit rates and prices shall be quoted in pounds and decimals of a pound.

12   On receiving notification in writing from the Director of that the Tender has been accepted, the Contractor shall whenever required by notice in writing under the hand of the Borough Secretary & Solicitor execute a contract having the Form of Tender, Form of Contract, the Certificate of Bona Fide Tender, the Declaration, the Conditions of Contract, the Specification, these Instructions, and the Tender included.

13   (i)   The Contractor shall be required to submit to the Director of insurance policy documents or copies thereof to enable the Council to check the insurance cover for its adequacy and appropriateness to the Contract.

(ii)   No work shall commence until the Council has been satisfied in respect of the aforementioned insurance documents.

14   Tenderers shall treat the details of the Contract Documents as private and confidential.

15   The successful contractor shall be supplied with three additional copies of the full Conditions of Contract and specification.

16   The Council is not bound to accept the lowest or any Tender.

The tenderer will be required to state agreement or otherwise with the Councils view as to the applicability or non-applicability of the Transfer of Undertakings (Protection of Employment) Regulations 1981 as set out in the advertisement for interested parties and/or the letter inviting tenders.

NAME OF TENDERER: . . . .

TENDER FOR . . . .

CONTRACT REFERENCE . . . .

Form of Tender

Dear Sirs,

You are hereby invited to tender for the above quoted contract in accordance with the documents contained herein and subject to the following:

(1)   The Council does not bind itself to accept the lowest or any tender.

(2) A Tender will be considered only if made out on the Tender Form and accompanied by the Schedule of Prices, duly signed in the spaces provided and returned in a plain sealed envelope, bearing the enclosed label but not bearing any name or mark indicating the sender, so as to be received no later than the date stipulated above.

(3) All communications regarding this tender **must** be directed through the above office.

Yours faithfully,

*

CERTIFICATE OF BONA FIDE TENDER

The essence of tendering is that the Council shall receive bona fide competitive tenders from all firms tendering. In recognition of this principle, we certify that this is a bona fide tender, intended to be competitive, and that we have not fixed or adjusted the amount of the tender by or under or in accordance with any agreement or arrangement with any other person. We also certify that we have not done and we undertake that we will not do at any time before the returnable date for this tender any of the following acts:

(a) communicating to a person other than the person calling for these tenders the amount or approximate amount of the proposed tender;

(b) entering into any arrangement or agreement with any other person that he shall refrain from tendering or as to the amount of any tender to be submitted.

(c) offering or paying or giving or agreeing to pay or give any sum of money or valuable consideration directly or indirectly to any person for doing or having done or causing or having caused to be done in relation to any other tender or proposed tender for the said work any act or thing of the sort described above.

In this Certificate, the word 'person' includes any persons and any body or association, corporate or unincorporate, and 'any agreement or arrangement' includes any such transaction, formal or informal, and whether legally binding or not, and the plural includes the singular.

SIGNED . . . .

ON BEHALF OF . . . .

DATE . . . .

DECLARATION

TO:

I/We the Undersigned:

(1) Hereby undertake to supply and deliver all, or any of the goods, materials or services, or to carry out the work/s enumerated on the Specifications and Schedules, annexed hereto, in such quantities, in such manner and at such time as the Council may direct and to its entire satisfaction at the price(s) or sum(s) in the said Schedule during the above-mentioned period.

(2) Hereby undertake to observe the Conditions of Contract annexed hereto.

(3) Hereby agree that if my/our Tender is accepted by the Council within twenty-six weeks after the date hereof, that this Tender shall be considered a binding contract between us.

(4) Hereby agree that if the Council so desires on the acceptance of this Tender, will enter into and execute a contract incorporating this Tender and the said Specification, Schedule and Conditions of Contract.

SIGNED .... DATE ....

DESIGNATION ....

FOR AND ON BEHALF OF ....

ADDRESS ....

....

....

....

TELEPHONE NO ....

Appendix VII

EXTERNALISATION EXAMPLES

HOST TRANSACTIONS AND TRADE SALES

Authority	Service	Date	Company
Barrow	Multi Manual	1994	Sita
Berkshire	Highways/Planning	1993	Babtie
Berkshire	Multi Manual	—	BET
Bexley	Pensions Advice	—	Hartshead Ltd
Bexley	Multi Manual/Client Services	—	Facilities Management Contracting Services Ltd
Bexley	Revenue Services	1995	Capita
Brent	Business rate collection	—	P-Sec
Brent	Revenue/Benefits	1995	EDS
Brighton	Multi Manual/Leisure	1995	Ecovert (South)
Bristol	Multi Manual	1994	Sita (GB) Ltd
Bromley	Highways Engineering	—	Buller and Partners
Bromley	Multi Manual	—	Sita
Bromley	Exchequer	—	Capita Managed Services Ltd
Cambridgeshire	Highway Maintenance	1995	Ringway Highway Services
Cambridgeshire	Payroll	—	Data Services
Cheshire	Architectural	1994	MRM Partnership
Cheshire	Residential Homes	—	County Lifestyle Services
Croydon	Legal	1994	Stoneham Langton & Passmore
Ealing	Property/Technical	1994	Brown & Root
Elmbridge	Multi Manual	—	—
Essex	Highways Consultancy	1994	—
Essex	Property	—	W S Atkins
Essex	Residential Homes	—	Runwood Properties
Gloucestershire	Highway Maintenance	1993	Ringway Highway services
Gloucestershire	Multi Manual	—	BET
Oxfordshire	Financial	—	P-Sec
Portsmouth	Multi Manual	—	—

Authority	Service	Date	Company
Rushmoor	Multi Manual/Leisure	1994	Quadron (Rushmoor) Ltd
Rutland	Housing Management	1993	CSL Managed Services
Shropshire	Multi Manual	1995	Shropshire County Contracting (John Doyle Group)
Shropshire	Highways Consultancy	1995	Babtie
South Oxfordshire	Engineering	1994	Babtie
South Oxfordshire	Financial	—	P-Sec
South Wight	Multi Manual	1995	Ecovert
Surrey Heath	Multi Manual	—	Ecovert
Tamesside	Residential Homes	—	Tamesside Enterprises Ltd
Teignbridge	Multi Manual	1995	Onyx UK
Teignbridge	Street Cleansing and Building Maintenance	1995	Onyx UK
Thanet	Multi Manual/Leisure	1994	Serco
Warwick	Multi Manual	—	AAH Environmental Services
Waverley	Multi Manual	1993	Arkeco (MRS)
Winchester	Multi Manual	1995	Serco
Wokingham	Multi Manual	1992	OCS Cleanmaster
Woodspring	Revenue/Benefits	1995	CSL
Woodspring	Multi Manual	—	Quadron Services Ltd
Wychavon	Architectural	—	Various

MANAGEMENT BUY-OUTS

Authority	Service	Date	Company
Bath	Multi Manual	1989	Contractor Services Group (Bath)
Berkshire	Grounds Maintenance	1990	Land Technology Ltd
Berkshire	Purchasing Supplies	1990	County Supplies and Services Ltd
Berkshire	Cleaning	1990	County Schools and Offices Ltd
Berkshire	Financial	1993	Total Resource Management
Bromley	Architectural	1990	Architects Joint Partnership
Cambridgeshire	Information Technology	1986	Cambridgeshire Information Technology Services Ltd
Cambridgeshire	Printing	1990	Victoire Press
Chesterfield	Bus Operation	—	Chesterfield Transport
Croydon	Financial	1994	Croydon Services Ltd
Dartford	Multi Manual	—	Direct Force (formerly Dart Force)

Authority	Service	Date	Company
Derby	Vehicle Maintenance	1989	Derby City Transport
Eastbourne	Multi Manual	1990	Sercoserve
Hastings	Architectural	—	Adams Johns Kennard
Hertfordshire	Residential Homes	1993	Quantum Care Ltd
Hinckley & Bosworth	Leisure	1988	Sport and Leisure Management (Hinckley) Ltd
Isle of Wight	Architectural	1990	Rainey Petrie Designs
Lancashire	Project Development	1989	Lancashire Enterprises PLC
Mid-Sussex	Multi Manual	1989	Prime Contractors Ltd
Milton Keynes	Management Services	1989	Performance Management Services
Northampton shire	Multi Manual	1990	Serco (Northants)
North Avon	Grounds Maintenance	1989	Parkfield Landscapes
Rochford	Leisure	1988	Serco Leisure (now City Grove)
St Albans	Leisure		Relaxion Ltd
South Oxfordshire	Computer	1990	McClintock Ltd
Southampton & South West Hampshire D.H.A	Management Services	1989	Salter Baker Associates
South West Thames R.H.A.	Estates and Valuation	1990	Estate Design and Management Ltd
Stratford Upon Avon	Multi Manual/Leisure	1989	Fosse Group
Trent R.H.A.	Architectural	1990	Trent Architecture and Design
West Midlands R.H.A.	Management Services	1989	Quality Assured (QA) Business Service
Westminster	Refuse Collection/ Street Cleansing	1988	MRS Environmental Services Ltd
Westminster	Leisure	1988	City Leisure Ltd
West Wiltshire	Computing	1988	West Wiltshire Information Systems (now defunct)
West Wiltshire	Legal	1989	Wilkie-Maslen

COMPUTER FACILITIES MANAGEMENT ARRANGEMENTS

Authority	Date	Company
Berkshire	1993	CFM
Bexley	1994	ACT
Birmingham	1989	IT Net
Bolton	1994	CFM

Authority	Date	Company
Boston	1991	CFM
Breckland	1989	ACT
Brighton	—	Data Services/Bull
Broadland	1992	CFM
Bromley	—	Capita
Cambridge	1993	CMS
Cambridgeshire	1990	Data Services
Cherwell	1990	CFM
Croydon	1994	IT Net
Daventry	1991	CFM
Delyn	1993	MDIS
Derby	1989	CFM
Eastbourne	1988	CFM
East Cambridgeshire	1991	CFM
Forest of Dean	—	CFM
Gloucestershire	1990	CFM
Greenwich	1994	CFM
Hackney	1993	LOLA/CFM
Haringey	1993	LOLA/CFM
Hertfordshire	1991	IT Net
Hillingdon	1993	LOLA/CFM
Hinckley & Bosworth	1993	Capita
Kent	—	Capita
Mendip	1993	Capita
Milton Keynes	—	Midsummer
Motherwell	—	MDIS
North Kesteven	1989	CFM
North Warwickshire	1990	CFM
Oxfordshire	1991	Capita
Rochester Upon Medway	1994	MDIS
Rochford	—	VIS Perthcrest
Rutland	1993	Capita
South Buckinghamshire	1992	Hoskyns
Southwark	1995	Integris
Spelthorne	1989	ACT
Suffolk Coastal	1991	CFM
Tendring	1993	Capita
Thamesdown	1993	CFM
Three Rivers	—	BIS Perthcrest
Torfaen	1991	Capita
Tower Hamlets	1993	LOLA/CFM
Tynedale	1992	Capita
Wandsworth	1991	CFM
Warwickshire	1989	CFM
Welwyn & Hatfield	1993	Capita
West Lindsey	1989	CFM
Westminster	1992	IT Net
Wiltshire	1992	Capita
Windsor & Maidenhead	1994	PCL
Woodspring	1991	ACT

STATUTORY INSTRUMENTS, CIRCULARS AND EUROPEAN DIRECTIVES

ORDERS AND REGULATIONS

Local Government (Direct Labour Organisations) (Accounts) Regulations 1981 (SI 1981 No 339)

Local Government, Planning and Land Act 1980 (Commencement No 5) Order 1981 (SI 1981 No 341)

Local Government (Direct Labour Organisations) (Amendment of Local Acts) Order 1982 (SI 1982 No 229)

Local Government (Direct Labour Organisations) (Competition) Regulations 1983 (SI 1983 No 685) [revoked by SI 1989 No 1588]

Local Government Act 1988 (Commencement No 1) Order 1988 (SI 1988 No 979)

Local Government Act 1988 (Defined Activities) (Competition) (England) Regulations 1988 (SI 1988 No 1371)

Local Government Act 1988 (Defined Activities) (Exemptions) (England) Order 1988 (SI 1988 No 1372)

Local Government Act 1988 (Defined Activities) (Specified Periods) (England) Regulations 1988 (SI 1988 No 1373)

Local Government Act 1988 (Defined Activities) (Competition) (Wales) Regulations 1988 (SI 1988 No 1468)

Local Government Act 1988 (Defined Activities) (Exemptions) (Wales) Order 1988 (SI 1988 No 1469)

Local Government Act 1988 (Defined Activities) (Specified Periods) (Wales) Regulations 1988 (SI 1988 No 1470)

Local Government (Direct Labour Organisations) (Competition) Regulations 1989 (SI 1989 No 1588)

Local Government (Direct Labour Organisations) (Specified Number of Employed Persons) Order 1989 (SI 1989 No 1589)

Local Government Act 1988 (Competition in Sports and Leisure Facilities) Order 1989 (SI 1989 No 2488)

Local Government Act 1988 (Defined Activities) (Competition) (England) Regulations 1990 (SI 1990 No 1564)

Local Government Act 1988 (Defined Activities) (Competition) (Wales) Regulations 1990 (SI 1990 No 1498) [revoked by SI 1991 No 232]

Local Government Act 1988 (Defined Activities) (Competition) (Wales) (No 2) Regulations 1990 (SI 1990 No 2280)

Local Government Act 1988 (Defined Activities) (Specified Periods) (Inner London) Regulations 1990 (SI 1990 No 2468)

Local Government Act 1988 (Defined Activities) (Competition) (Wales) Regulations 1991 (SI 1991 No 232)

Local Government Act 1988 (Defined Activities) (Exemption) (Wales) Order 1991 (SI 1991 No 262)

Local Government Act 1988 (Defined Activities) (Exemption) (England) Order 1991 (SI 1991 No 312)

Public Works Contracts Regulations 1991 (SI 1991 No 2680)

Local Government (Direct Labour Organisations) (Competition) (Exemption) (England) Regulations 1992 (SI 1992 No 582)

Local Government Act 1988 (Defined Activities) (Exemption) (England) Order 1992 (SI 1992 No 583)

Local Government Act 1988 (Defined Activities) (Exemption) (Small Schools) Order 1992 (SI 1992 No 1626)

Local Government Act 1992 (Commencement No 2) Order 1992 (SI 1992 No 3241)

Local Government (Direct Service Organisation) (Competition) Regulations 1993 (SI 1993 No 848)

Public Services Contracts Regulations 1993 (SI 1993 No 3228)

Local Government (Direct Labour Organisations) (Competition) (Amendment) (England) Regulations 1994 (SI 1994 No 1439)

Local Government Act 1988 (Competition) (Defined Activities) (Housing Management) Order 1994 (SI 1994 No 1671)

Local Government Act 1988 (Competition) (Housing Management) (England) Regulations 1994 (SI 1994 No 2297)

Local Government Act 1988 (Competition) (Defined Activities) Order 1994 (SI 1994 No 2884)

Local Government Act 1988 (Competition) (Defined Activities) (construction and property Services) Order 1994 (SI 1994 No 2888)

Local Government Act 1988 (Competition) (Legal Services) (England) Regulations 1994 (SI 1994 No 3164)

Local Government Act 1988 (Construction and Property Services) (England) Regulations 1994 (SI 1994 No 3166)

Local Government Changes for England (Direct Labour and Service Organisations) Regulations 1994 (SI 1994 No 3167)

Public Supply Contract Regulations 1995 (SI 1995 No 201)

Local Government Changes for England and Local Government Act 1988 (Competition) (Miscellaneous Amendments) Regulations 1994 (SI 1995 No 1326)

Local Government (Direct Service Organisations) (Competition) (Amendment) Regulations 1995 (SI 1995 No 1336)

Local Government Act 1988 (Competition) (Defined Activities) Order 1995 (SI 1995 No 1915)

Local Government Act 1988 (Security Work) (Exemption) (England) Order 1995 (SI 1995 No 2074)

Local Government Act 1988 (Competition) (Financial Services) (England) Regulations 1995 (SI 1995 No 2916)

Local Government Act 1988 (Competition) (Personnel Services) (England) Regulations 1995 (SI 1995 No 2101)

Local Government Act 1988 (Competition) (Information Technology (England) Regulations 1995 (SI 1995 No 2813)

CIRCULARS

DoE circular 19/88 (LGA 1988: Part I and Schedule I)
DoE circular 1/91 (LGA 1988 Part I)
Joint circular DoE 10/81 and Welsh Office 12/82 (LGPLA 1980: DLOs)
Joint circular DoE 6/82 and Welsh Office 12/82 (LGPLA 1980: DLOs)
Joint circular DoE 19/83 and Welsh Office 26/83 (LGPLA 1980: DLOs: year 3– 1983/4)
Joint circular DoE 8/88 and Welsh Office 12/88 (public supply and works contracts: non-commercial matters)
Joint circular 9/91 and DES 8/91 (Statutory Instrument 1989 No 2488: competition in sports and leisure facilities)
DOE Circular 10/93 (LGA 1992: section 9)
DOE Circular 12/94 (LGPLA 1980: DLOs)

CIRCULAR LETTERS

DOE 21 January 1994 (Handling of TUPE matters in relation to CCT Statement by Secretary of State for the Environment 11 March 1993 Local Authority CCT and TUPE)
DOE 10 June 1994 (Guidance on the avoidance of anti-competitive behaviour)
DOE 12 December 1994 (Guidance on the avoidance of anti-competitive behaviour)
DOE 19 December 1994 (Guidance on the arrangements for handling compulsory competitive tendering and local government re-organisation)

SCOTTISH STATUTORY INSTRUMENTS

Local Government (Direct Labour Organisations) (Competition) (Scotland) Regulations 1982 (SI 1982 No 318)
Local Government (Direct Labour Organisations) (Accounts) (Scotland) Regulations 1982 (SI 1982 No 319)
Local Government (Direct Labour Organisations) (Competition) (Scotland) Amendment Regulations 1988 (SI 1988 No 956)
Local Government Act 1988 (Defined Activities) (Competition) (Scotland) Regulations 1988 (SI 1988 No 1413)
Local Government Act 1988 (Defined Activities) (Specified Periods) (Scotland) Regulations 1988 (SI 1988 No 1414)
Local Government Act 1988 (Defined Activities) (Exemptions) (Scotland) Order 1988 (SI 1988 No 1415)
Local Government Act 1988 (Defined Activities) (Competition and Specified Periods) (Scotland) Regulations 1990 (SI 1990 No 1484)
Local Government Act 1988 (Defined Activities) (Exemptions) (Scotland) Amendment Order 1990 (SI 1990 No 1485)

Local Government (Direct Labour Organisations) (Competition)
(Scotland) Regulations 1990 (SI 1990 No 1782)
Local Government (Direct Labour Organisations) (Specified Number of
Employed Persons) (Scotland) Order 1990 (SI 1990 No 1783)
Local Government Act 1988 (Defined Activities) (Competition) (Scotland)
Amendment Regulations 1990 (SI 1990 No 2286)
Local Government Act 1988 (Defined Activities) (Competition) (Scotland)
Amendment (No 2) Regulations 1990 (SI 1990 No 2498)
Local Government (Direct Labour Organisations) (Competition)
(Scotland) Amendment Regulations 1991 (SI 1991 No 243)
Local Government Act 1988 (Defined Activities) (Competition and
Specified Periods) (Scotland) Amendment Regulations 1991 (SI 1991
No 2548)
The Local Government Act 1988 (Defined Activities) (Specified Periods)
(Scotland) Amendment Regulations 1993 (SI 1993 No 178)
The Local Government Act 1988 (Defined Activities (Exemption)
(Livingston Development Corporation) Order 1994 (SI 1994 No
3084)
The Local Government Act 1988 (Supervision of Parking) (Exemption)
(Scotland) Order 1994 (SI 1994 No 3107)
The Local Government Act 1988 (Defined Activities) (Exemption of
Development Corporations) (Scotland) Order 1995 (SI 1995 No 517)
The Local Government, Planning and Land Act 1980 (Competition)
(Scotland) Regulations 1995 (SI 1995 No 677)
The Local Government (Exemption from Competition) (Scotland) Order
1995 (SI 1995 No 678)
The Local Government Act 1988 (Defined Activities) (Competition)
(Scotland) Amendment Regulations 1995 (SI 1995 No 1972)

SCOTTISH OFFICE CIRCULARS AND LETTERS

Letter dated 16 December 1992 (LGA 1992)
Letter dated 29 March 1993 (SI 1993 No 848)
Circular 13/93 (LGA 1992: section 9)
Letter dated 31 December 1993 (LGA 1992)
Issues paper dated 21 January 1993 (Handling of TUPE matters in
relation to CCT)
Circular 11/94 (LGPLA 1980 DLO Rates of Return)
Circular 22/94 (LGPLA 1980 Financial Objectives)
Letter dated 27 January 1995 (CCT and Local Government
Reorganisation in Scotland)
Letter dated 16 March 1995 (Handling of Pensions Matters in Relation
to CCT)
Circular 10/95 (Extension of CCT)
Letter dated 19 May 1995 (Extension of CCT: Information Technology,
Finance and Personnel Services)
Letter dated 1 June 1995 (SI 1995 No 1336)
Circular 13/95 (SI 1995 No 678 and SI 1995 No 677)
Letter dated 27 July 1995 (CCT and the Local Government
Ombudsman)
Letter dated 14 August 1995 (SI 1995 No 1915 and SI 1995 No 1972)

TABLE OF EUROPEAN DIRECTIVES

The Acquired Rights Directive 1977 EEC/77/187
Public Procurement Works Directive 1971 EEC/71/305
Public Procurement Works Directive 1989 EEC/89/440
Public Procurement Services Directive 1992 EEC/92/50
Public Procurement Utilities Directive 1992 EEC/92/13
Public Supply Contracts Directive 77/62
Public Supply Contracts Directive 80/767
Public Supply Contracts Directive 88/295
Compliance Directive 89/665
Public Procurement Utilities Directives 90/531 and 93/38
Remedies For Public Utilities Directive 92/13
Co-ordination of Procedures for the Award of Public Services Contracts
   Directives 92/50 and 93/97
Consolidated Supplies Directive 93/36
Consolidated Works Directive 93/37
Consolidated Utilities Directive 93/38
Unfair Contract Terms Directive 93/13

SELECT BIBLIOGRAPHY

General

Ascher, Kate, *The Politics of Privatisation* (1987) Macmillan

Barker, Lymion, *Competing for Quality: A Manager's Guide to Market Testing* (1994) Longman

Cirell, S.D. and Bennett, J., *Compulsory Competitive Tendering Law and Practice* (1990) Longman

Davis-Coleman, Cliff (ed), *The Contracts Handbook* (1992) CDC

Department of the Environment, *Competing for Quality: Competition in the Provision of Local Services* (1991) HMSO

Department of the Environment, *CCT and Local Government in England: Annual Report for 1993* (1994)

Department of the Environment, *CCT and Local Government in England: Annual Report for 1994* (1995)

Local Government Information Unit, *CCT on the Record* (1994) LGIU 1–5 Bath Street, London, EC1V 9QQ

McCarthy, Austin and Shaw, Dr Keith, *Compulsory Competitive Tendering in Local Government: An annotated Bibliography* (1993) Earlsgate Press

Office of Public Service and Science, *The Government's Guide to Market Testing* (1994) HMSO

Walsh, Kieron, *Tendering for Local Authority Service: Initial Experiences* (1990) HMSO

Chapter 3: The Tendering Process

Centre for Public Service, *A detailed Handbook of Tender Evaluation* (1994)

LGMB, *Guidance on the Assessment of Quality in the Application of CCT to Blue Collar Front Line Services* (1995) Local Government Management Board

LGMB, *Guidance on the Assessment of Quality in the Application of CCT to White Collar and Professional Servies* (1994) Local Government Management Board

Lyons, M.T. and Johnson, A., *Preparing the winning Bid* (1992) Charles Knight Publishing

Chapter 4: Contract Technology

Allwright, A.D. and Oliver, R.W., *Contracting for Goods and Services* (1986) Institute of Purchasing and Supply

Association of Metropolitan Authorities, *A Guide for Local Authorities to Pre-contract Practice* (1991)

Standard Core Conditions and Documentation (1991)

Boyce, Tim, *Successful Contract Administration* (1992) Hawksmere/-Bookprint Ltd

Deventer, Van, *The Law of Construction Contracts* (1993) Construction Law Library

Chapter 5: Contract Compliance

Commission for Racial Equality, *Local Authority and Contracts and Racial Equality: Implications of the Local Government Act 1988* (1988)

Chapter 6: Contractors' Rights and Challenges

Adam Smith Institute, *Working with Contractors* (1982)

Chapter 7: Client and Contractor Separation and Organisation

Audit Commission, *Realising the benefits of Competition: The Client Role for contracted Services* (1993) HMSO

Walsh, K. and Davis, H., *Competition and Services: The Impact of the Local Government Act 1988* (1993) HMSO

Chapter 8: Internal Council Considerations in the Implementation of CCT

Association of Direct Labour Organisations, *Managing to Survive: Running Local Authority Services Under Competition* (1986)

Association of Metropolitan Authorities, *Service Level Agreements: Agreeing on Quality?* (1991)

CIPFA, *Business Plans: A Move in the Right Direction* (1992)

Flynn, Norman and Walsh, Keiron, *Managing Direct Labour Organisations* (1982) Institute of Local Government Studies

GMB and TGWU, *New Model DSOs: Strategies for Survival and Success* (1995)

Rogers, Phillip and Chaytor, Steven, *Managing a Leisure Management Contract* (1994) Longman

Chapter 9: Staffing Matters

Elias, Patrick, QC and Bowers, John, *Transfer of Undertakings: The Legal Pitfalls* (1994) Longman

LGMB, *Pensions and Transfers: An Information Guide for Local Authorities* (1995) Local Government Management Board

Mead, Malcolm, *Unfair Dismissal* (1991) Longman
Upex, Robert, *Termination of Employment* (1991) Sweet and Maxwell
Wallington, Peter (ed), *Employment Law Handbook, 6th Edition* (1993) Butterworths

Chapter 10: Local Authority Service Provision to Other Bodies

Bennett, John and Cirrell, Stephen, *Municipal Trading* (1992) Longman

Chapter 11: The Extension of Competition to Professional Services

Cirrell, Stephen and Bennett, John, *Competitive Tendering for Professional Services* (1994) Longman

Chapter 12: Tendering Construction and Property Services

Hughes, Michael, *CCT: The Environmental Agenda* (1995) Local Government Management Board

Chapter 13: Tendering Legal Services

Robinson, Christopher (ed), *Handbook of Local Authority Legal Practice* (1994) Sweet and Maxwell
Law Society, *Competition Tendering for Legal Services: Guidance on Tendering and Contracts* (1995) Law Society

Chapter 17: Tendering Housing Management

AMA, *Specifying Housing Management* (1994) AMA
DoE: *Compulsory Competitive Tendering of Housing Management – Reports from the Pilot Programme Numbers 1–9* (1994) DoE
Garland, D. and Parker, J., *Managing Houses in a Competitive Environment* (1993) Longman
Institute of Housing, *The Housing Standards Manual* (1993) Institute of Housing
Rabot, J., *CCT and Housing Manual* (1993) Longman

Chapter 19: Tendering in Social Services

Adirondack, Sandy and Macfarlane, Richard, *Getting Ready for Contracts: A Guide for Voluntary Organisations* (1993) Directory of Social Change, Radius Works, Back Lane, London NW3
Allen, Isobel (ed), *Purchasing and Contracting* (1990) Policy Studies Institute
Department of Health, *Implementing Community Care: Purchaser, Commissioner and Provider Roles* (1991) HMSO

Chapter 20: Ensuring Service Quality

Association of Metropolitan Authorities, *Quality Services; An Introduction to Quality Assurance for Local Authorities* (1991)

Bone, Clive, *Modern Quality Management Manual* (1991) Longmans

Institute of Management, *Achieving Quality Standards* (1994) Pitman Publishing

Jackson, Peter, and Ashton, David, *Implementing Quality Through BS5750 (1509000)* (1994) Kogan-Price

Lockley, Andrew (ed), *The Pursuit of Quality: A Guide for Lawyers* (1993) Tolley

Reed, Richard C. (ed), *Applying Total Quality Management to the Law Office* (1993) Altman Weil Pensa Publications Inc USA

Waller, Jenny, Allen, Derek and Burns, Andrew, *The Quality Management Manual* (1994) Kogan-Price

Chapter 21: European Law

Arrowsmith, Professor Sue, *Public Procurement in the European Community, Volume 2: A Guide to the Procurement Cases of the Court of Justice* (1993) Earlsgate Press

Arrowsmith, Professor Sue (ed), *Public Procurement in the European Community Volume 4: Remedies for Enforcing the Public Procurement Rules* (1993) Earlsgate Press

Arrowsmith, Professor Sue (ed), *Public Procurement in the European Community Volume 5: Remedies for Enforcing the Utilities Procurement Rules* (1993) Earlsgate Press

Bennett, John and Digings, Lee, *EC Public Procurement: Law and Practice* (1992) Longman

Cox, Professor Andrew, *Public Procurement in the European Community, Volume 1: The Single Market Rules and Enforcement Regime After 1992* (1993) Earlsgate Press

Cox, Professor Andrew and Lamont, Frances, (eds), *Public Procurement in the European Community, Volume 3: The Texts of the Community Directives, Recommendations, Proposals, Decisions, Resolutions and Communications in Force* (1993) Earlsgate Press

Digings, Lee, *Competitive Tendering and the European Communities* (1991) Association of Metropolitan Authorities

Trepte, Peter-Armin, *Public Procurement in the European Community* (1993) CCH Editions Ltd, Telford Road, Bicester

Watson, Dr Philippa and O'Reilly, James, *EC Public Procurement* (1992) Chancery Law Publishing Ltd

Chapter 22: Externalisation

Cooke, Darryl J., *Management Buy-Outs* (1993) Longman

Lacity, Mary C. and Hirschheim, Rudy, *Information Systems Outsourcing: Myths Metaphors and Realities* (1993) John Wiley & Sons Ltd

Randall, Simon, Birch, Frank and Heath, Philip, *The Future for Local Authority Direct Service Organisations (2nd Edition)* (1995) Lawrence Graham Solicitors

Randall, Simon, Birch, Frank and Pugh, Richard, *Duties and Liabilities of Directors of Local Authority Companies* (1992) Lawrence Graham Solicitors

Randall, Simon, Heath, Philip and Smith, Andrew, *Companies for Local Authorities and Social Housing* (1995) Lawrence Graham Solicitors

Sparke, Andrew, *A Practical Guide to Externalising Local Authority Services* (1994) Longman

INDEX

Accounts
DSO, requirements for, 73
rate of return–
   failure to achieve, 52
   target, as, 73
surpluses, use of, 71
trading, 79, 80
Administrative services
proposed extension of CCT to,
   abandonment, 11
Advertising
tenders, inviting, 13, 14
Annual report
defined activities, for, 74
Anti-competitive behaviour
housing, in relation to, 156–158
non-commercial considerations taken into
   account, 44
provisions on, 3, 4
provisions preventing, 1
self-policing, 4
written explanation of conduct, Secretary
   of State requiring, 52
Apprentices
cost of employing, evaluation of, 23
Arts facilities
management, proposed extension of CCT
   to, 11
Audit Commission
CCT for legal services, introduction of,
   128, 129
cross-boundary tendering, views on, 100,
   105, 106

Buildings
cleaning, 6
   small schools, in, 163–165

Cartels
price fixing, 56
Catering
civic or municipal, 7
non-food, 7
schools and welfare, 7
staff, 7

Citizen's Charter
client responsibilities in relation to,
   77
proposals of, 177
Cleaning
buildings, of, 6
   small schools, in, 163–165
streets, of, 7
Client
assets, use of, 75
Citizen's Charter, responsibilities in
   relation to, 77
competition, preparing for, 58
contingency planning, 76
contract supervision, 76
contractor functions, disentangling from,
   58
contractor, separation from, 60
contractual relationship, creation and
   management of, 59
DSO, post-tender relationship with, 76,
   77
functions–
   contracting staff, using, 60
   in-house, 59
   interest, focus of, 75
   strategic planning, 58
organisation, 64
responsibility of, 59
Colleges
services provided for, 104, 105
Competition-free allowance
meaning, 3
Compulsory competitive tendering
functional implications of, 57,
   58
future of, 199, 200
future regulation of, 65
meaning, 1
process. *See* TENDERING PROCESS
services to which applied, 1, 5–11
statutory instruments, 289–290
Computer services *See* INFORMATION
   TECHNOLOGY SERVICES
Construction and property services
activities included, 118

299